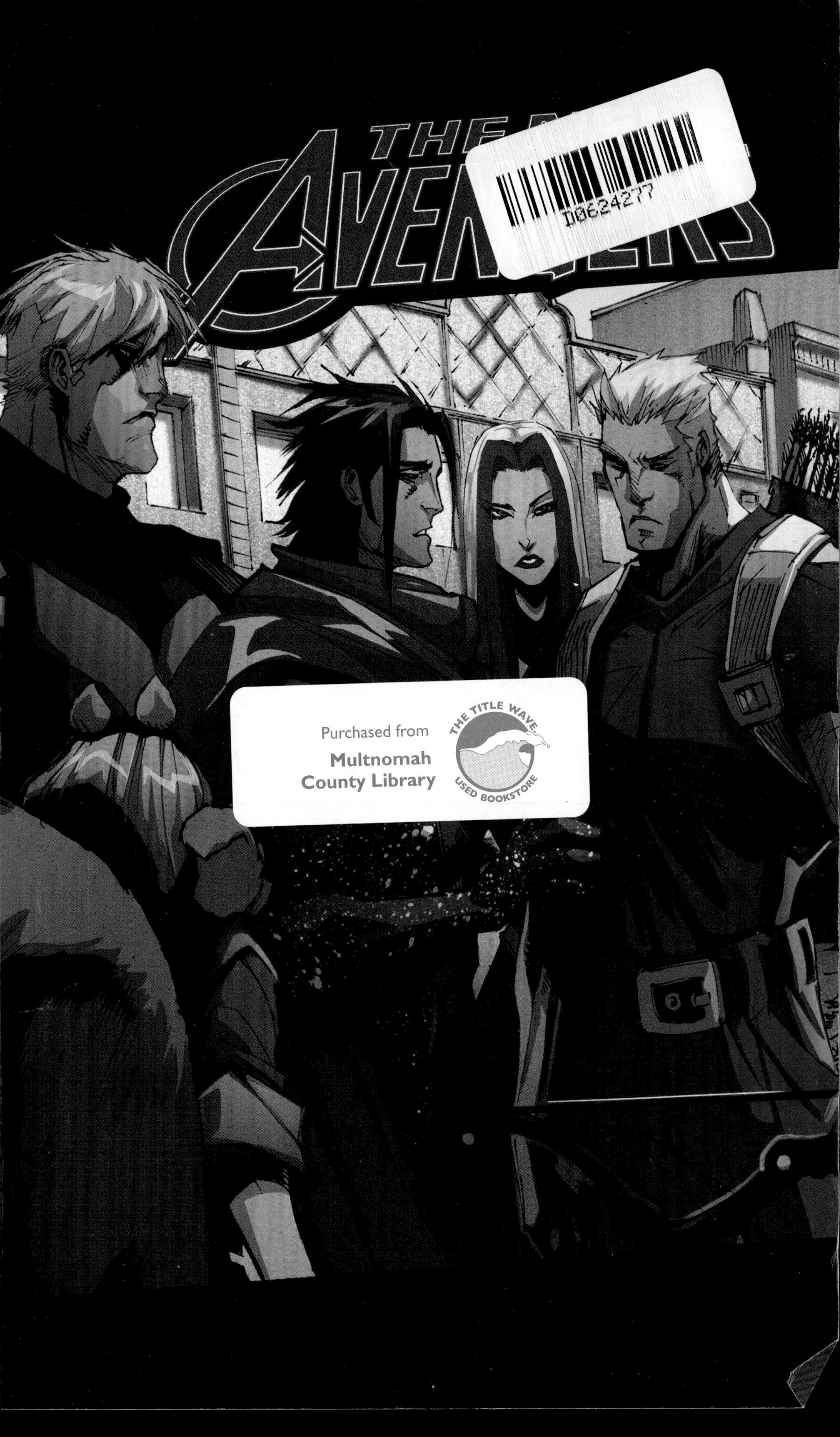

NEW AVENGERS: A.I.M. VOL. 2 — STANDOFF. Contains material originally published in magazine form as NEW AVENGERS #7-11. First printing 2016. ISBN# 978-0-7851-9649-5. Published by MARVEL WORLDWIDE, INC., a subsid MARVEL ENTERTAINMENT, LLC. OFFICE OF PUBLICATION: 135 West 50th Street, New York, NY 10020. Copyright © 2016 MARVEL No similarity between any of the names, characters, persons, and/or institutions in this magazine with th any living or dead person or institution is intended, and any such similarity which may exist is purely coincidental. **Printed in Canada.** ALAN FINE, President, Marvel Entertainment; DAN BUCKLEY, President, TV, Publishing & Brand Manage JOE QUESADA, Chief Creative Officer; TOM BREVOORT, SVP of Publishing; DAVID BOGART, SVP of Business Affairs & Operations, Publishing & Partnership; C.B. CEBULSKI, VP of Brand Management & Development, Asia; DAVID GABRIE of Sales & Marketing, Publishing; JEFF YOUNGQUIST, VP of Production & Special Projects; DAN CARR, Executive Director of Publishing Technology; ALEX MORALES, Director of Publishing Operations; SUSAN CRESPI, Production Manager LEE, Chairman Emeritus. For information regarding advertising in Marvel Comics or on Marvel.com, please contact Vit DeBellis, Integrated Sales Manager, at vdebellis@marvel.com. For Marvel subscription inquiries, please call 888-511 **Manufactured between 6/10/2016 and 7/18/2016 by SOLISCO PRINTERS, SCOTT, QC, CANADA.**

10 9 8 7 6 5 4 3 2 1

NEW TECH.
NEW IDEAS.
NEW MISSION.
THEY ARE...

NEW AVENGERS

STANDOFF

ROBERTO DA COSTA BOUGHT THE VILLAINOUS ORGANIZATION A.I.M. AND TRANSFORMED IT INTO
AVENGERS IDEA MECHANICS, A GROUP DEDICATED TO INTERNATIONAL RESCUE OPERATIONS.
BACKED BY AN ARMY OF THE BEST SCIENTISTS AND ENGINEERS IN THE WORLD, THE NEW
AVENGERS WORK TO PROTECT EARTH FROM ANYTHING THAT THREATENS THE PEACE.

ONE OF THOSE THREATS IS THE MAKER, AN ALTERNATE-REALITY VERSION OF REED RICHARDS
WHOM THE NEW AVENGERS HAVE INADVERTENTLY FOILED SEVERAL TIMES.

AND HE'S GETTING A LITTLE TIRED OF IT...

WRITER: AL EWING

NEW AVENGERS #7

ARTIST: J. CASSARA

COLOR ARTIST: RACHELLE ROSENBERG

COVER ARTIST: YASMINE PUTRI

NEW AVENGERS #8-10

ARTIST: MARCUS TO WITH JUANAN RAMÍREZ

COLOR ARTIST: DONO SÁNCHEZ ALMARA

COVER ART: JEFF DEKAL (#8),
LEINIL FRANCIS YU & SUNNY GHO (#9) AND
DECLAN SHALVEY & JORDIE BELLAIRE (#10)

NEW AVENGERS #11

ARTIST: GERARDO SANDOVAL

COLOR ARTIST: DONO SÁNCHEZ ALAMARA

COVER ART: DECLAN SHALVEY
& JORDIE BELLAIRE

LETTERER: VC'S JOE CARAMAGNA

ASSISTANT EDITOR: ALANNA SMITH

EDITORS: TOM BREVOORT WITH WIL MOSS

AVENGERS CREATED BY STAN LEE & JACK KIRBY

COLLECTION EDITOR:
JENNIFER GRÜNWALD

ASSOCIATE EDITOR:
SARAH BRUNSTAD

ASSOCIATE MANAGING EDITOR:
ALEX STARBUCK

EDITOR, SPECIAL PROJECTS:
MARK D. BEAZLEY

VP, PRODUCTION & SPECIAL PROJECTS:
JEFF YOUNGQUIST

SVP PRINT, SALES & MARKETING:
DAVID GABRIEL

BOOK DESIGN:
JAY BOWEN

EDITOR IN CHIEF:
AXEL ALONSO

CHIEF CREATIVE OFFICER:
JOE QUESADA

PUBLISHER:
DAN BUCKLEY

EXECUTIVE PRODUCER:
ALAN FINE

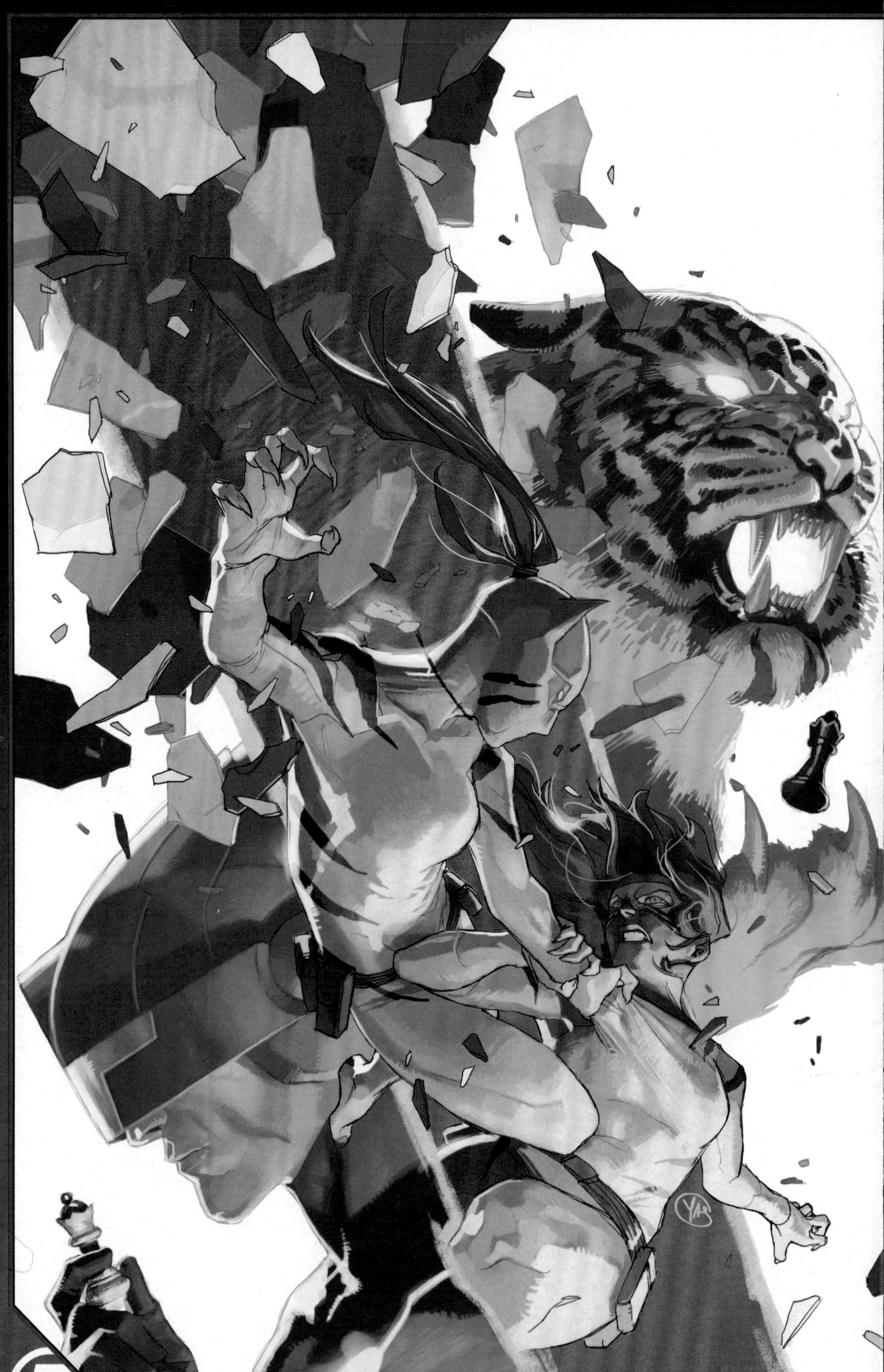

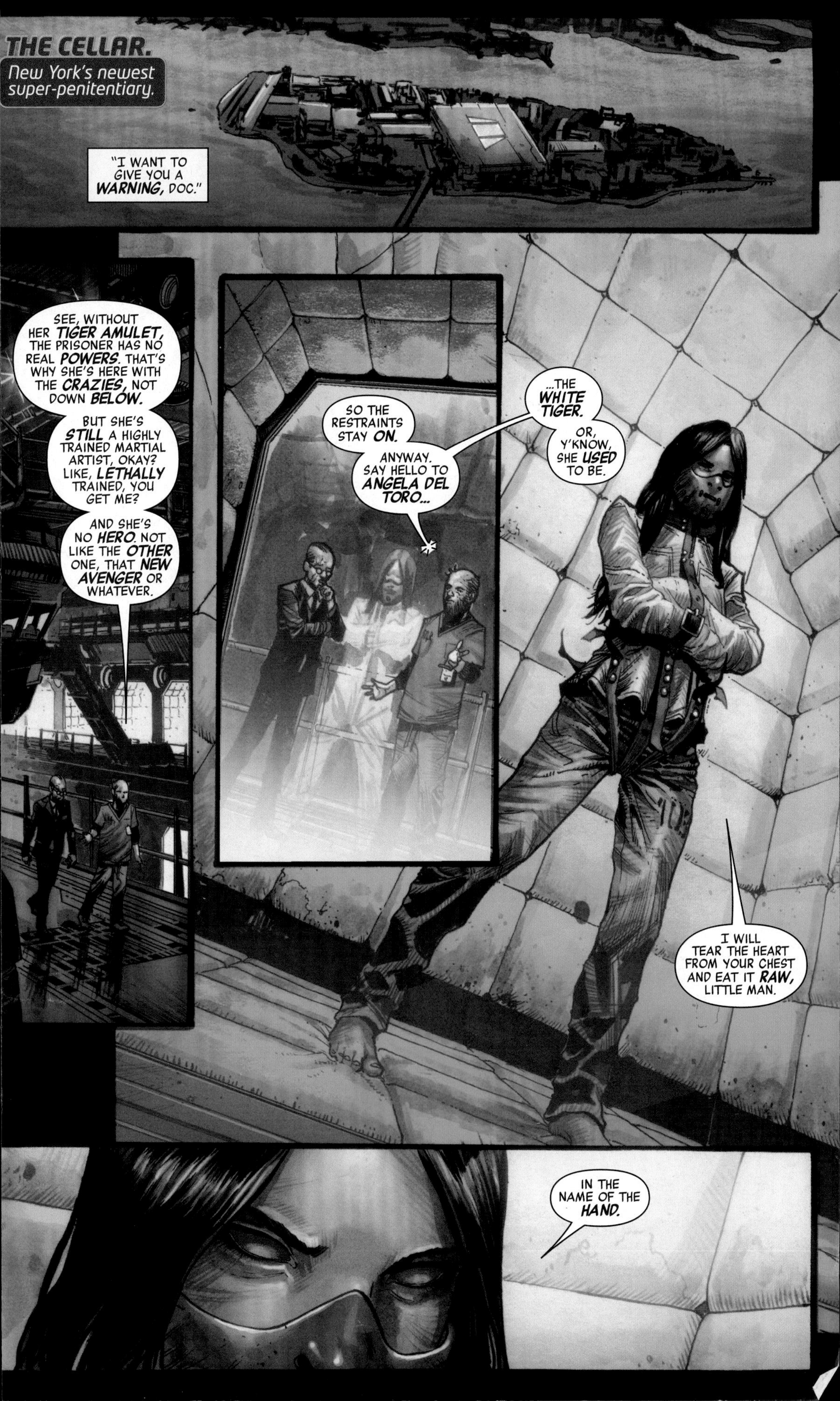
THE CELLAR.
New York's newest super-penitentiary.
"I WANT TO GIVE YOU A WARNING, DOC."
SEE, WITHOUT HER TIGER AMULET, THE PRISONER HAS NO REAL POWERS. THAT'S WHY SHE'S HERE WITH THE CRAZIES, NOT DOWN BELOW.
BUT SHE'S STILL A HIGHLY TRAINED MARTIAL ARTIST, OKAY? LIKE, LETHALLY TRAINED, YOU GET ME?
AND SHE'S NO HERO. NOT LIKE THE OTHER ONE, THAT NEW AVENGER OR WHATEVER.
SO THE RESTRAINTS STAY ON.
ANYWAY. SAY HELLO TO ANGELA DEL TORO...
...THE WHITE TIGER.
OR, Y'KNOW, SHE USED TO BE.
I WILL TEAR THE HEART FROM YOUR CHEST AND EAT IT RAW, LITTLE MAN.
IN THE NAME OF THE HAND.

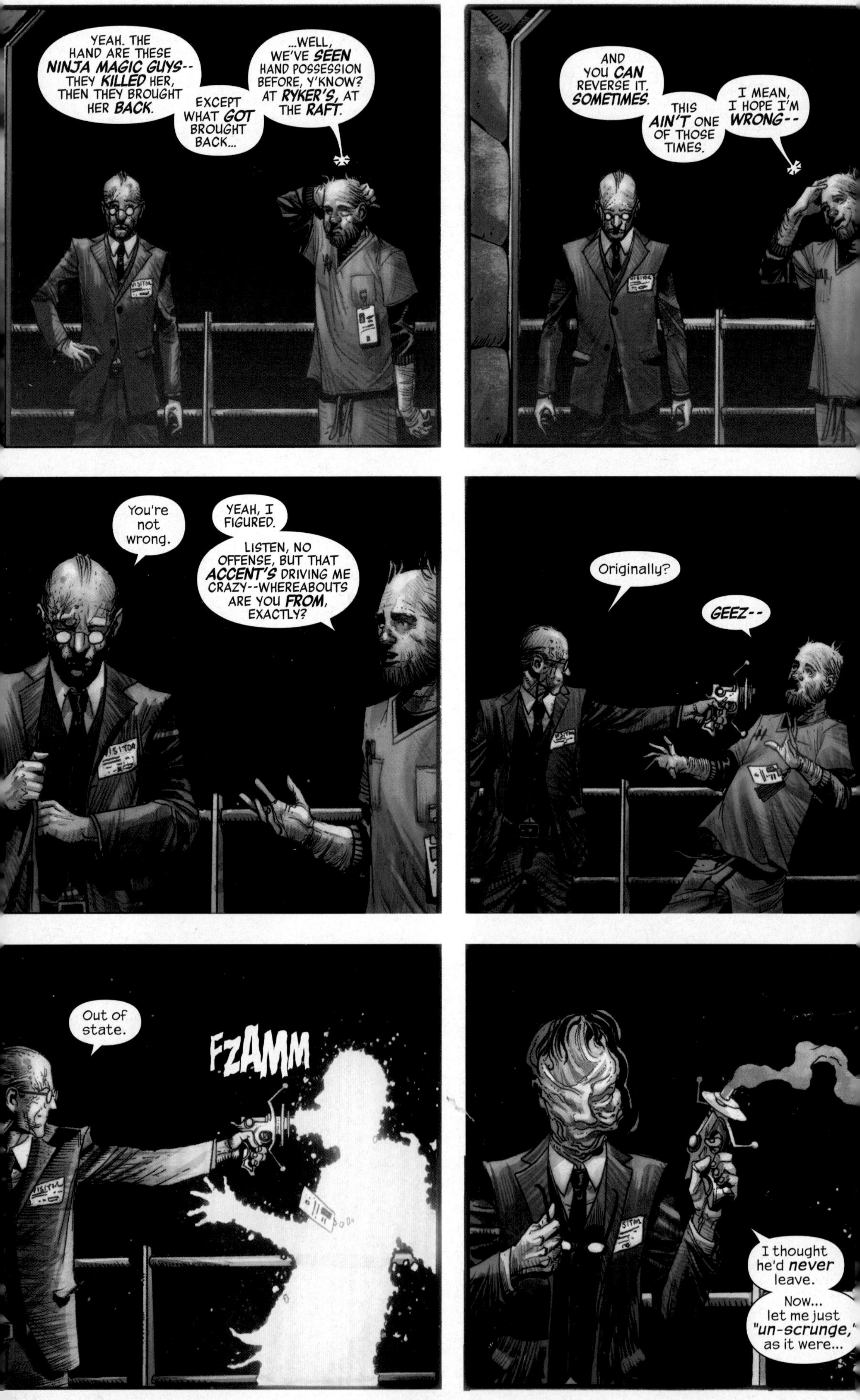
YEAH. THE HAND ARE THESE NINJA MAGIC GUYS-- THEY KILLED HER, THEN THEY BROUGHT HER BACK.
EXCEPT WHAT GOT BROUGHT BACK...
...WELL, WE'VE SEEN HAND POSSESSION BEFORE, Y'KNOW? AT RYKER'S, AT THE RAFT.
AND YOU CAN REVERSE IT. SOMETIMES.
THIS AIN'T ONE OF THOSE TIMES.
I MEAN, I HOPE I'M WRONG--
You're not wrong.
YEAH, I FIGURED.
LISTEN, NO OFFENSE, BUT THAT ACCENT'S DRIVING ME CRAZY--WHEREABOUTS ARE YOU FROM, EXACTLY?
Originally?
GEEZ--
Out of state.
FZAMM
I thought he'd never leave.
Now... let me just "un-scrunge," as it were...

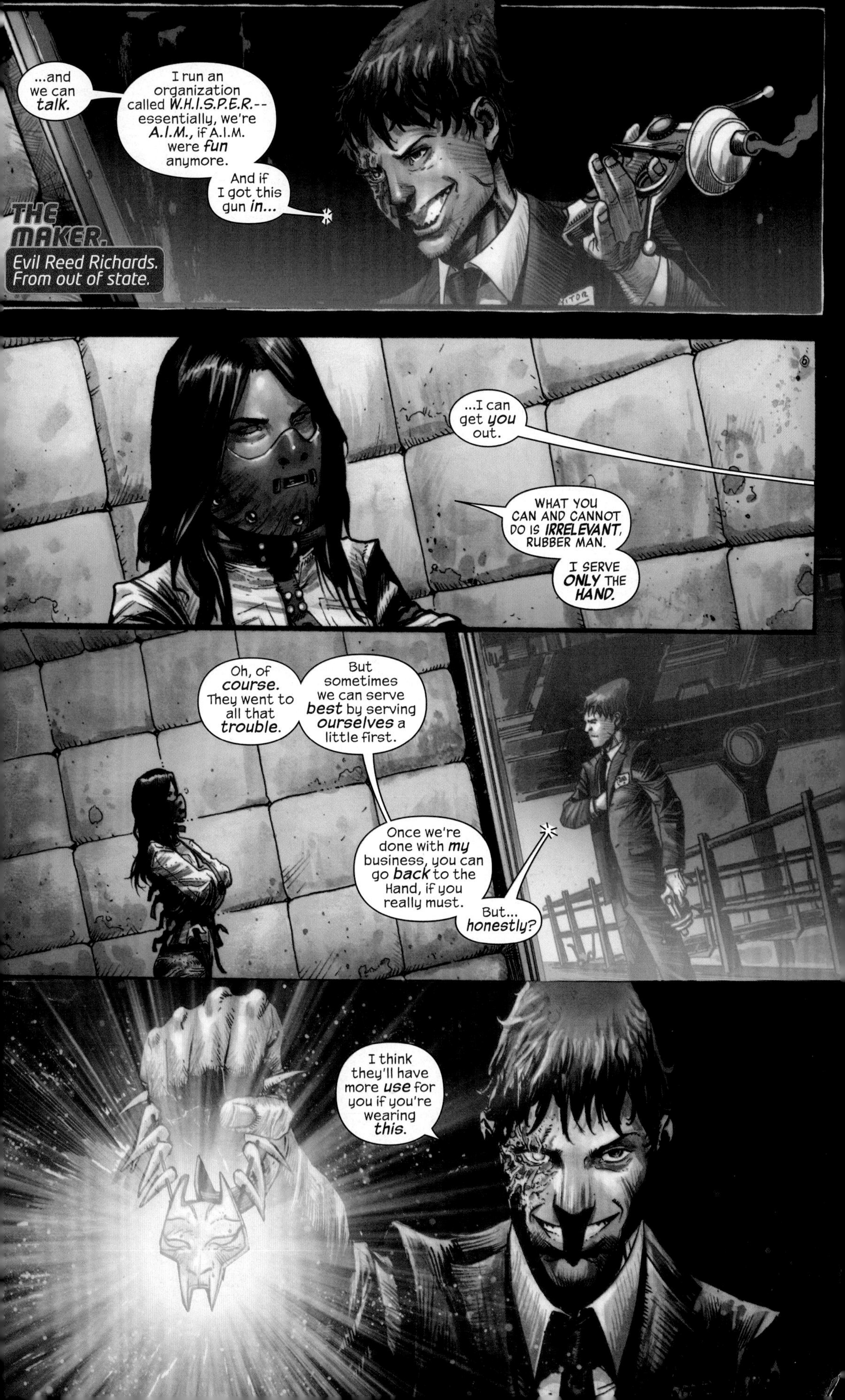

...and we can *talk.*
I run an organization called *W.H.I.S.P.E.R.*-- essentially, we're *A.I.M.,* if A.I.M. were *fun* anymore.
And if I got this gun *in...*
THE MAKER.
Evil Reed Richards. From out of state.
...I can get *you* out.
WHAT YOU CAN AND CANNOT DO IS *IRRELEVANT,* RUBBER MAN.
I SERVE *ONLY* THE *HAND.*
Oh, of *course.* They went to all that *trouble.*
But sometimes we can serve *best* by serving *ourselves* a little first.
Once we're done with *my* business, you can go *back* to the Hand, if you really must.
But... *honestly?*
I think they'll have more *use* for you if you're wearing *this.*

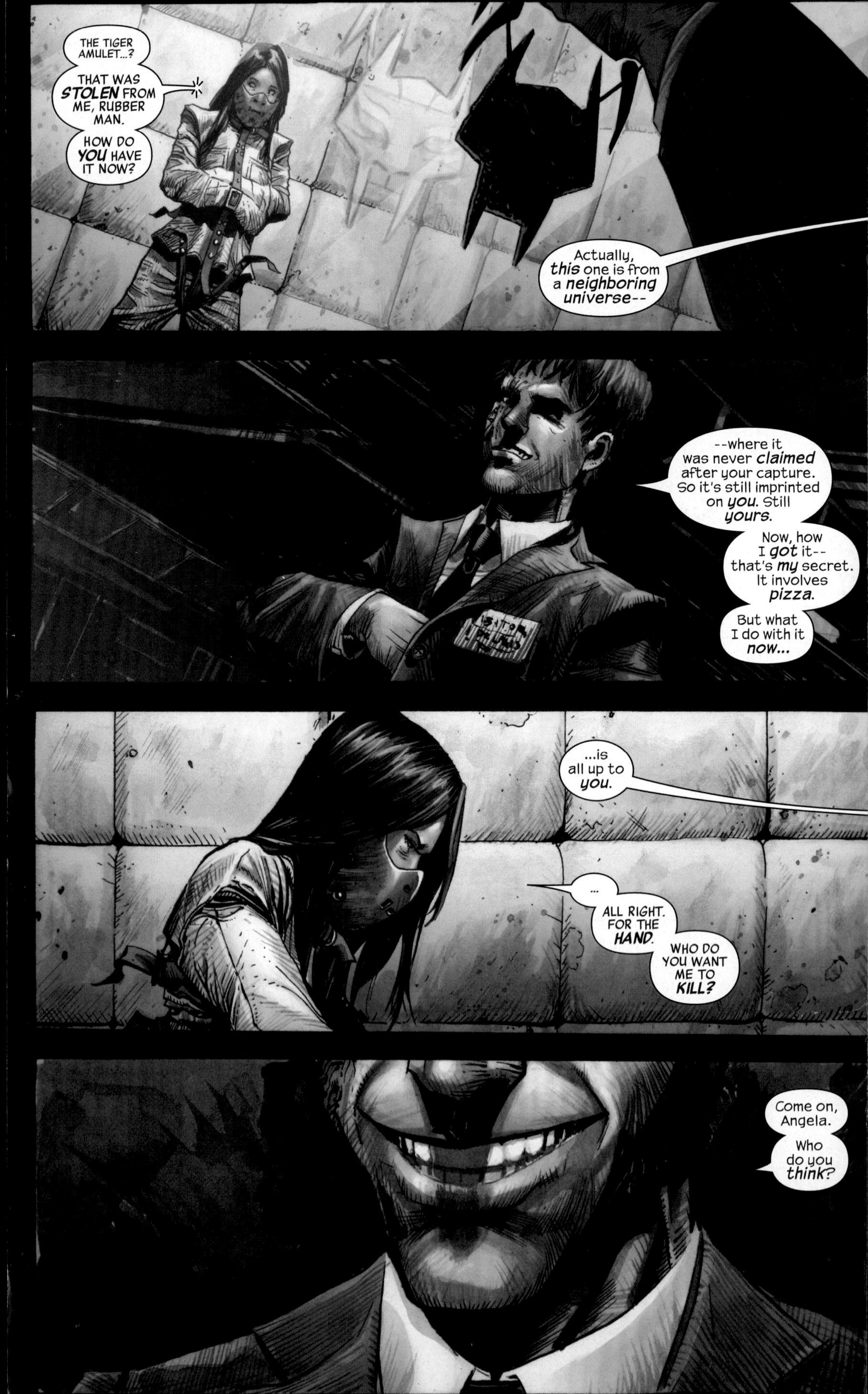
THE TIGER AMULET...?
THAT WAS STOLEN FROM ME, RUBBER MAN.
HOW DO YOU HAVE IT NOW?
Actually, this one is from a neighboring universe--
--where it was never claimed after your capture. So it's still imprinted on you. Still yours.
Now, how I got it-- that's my secret. It involves pizza.
But what I do with it now...
...is all up to you.
...
ALL RIGHT. FOR THE HAND.
WHO DO YOU WANT ME TO KILL?
Come on, Angela.
Who do you think?

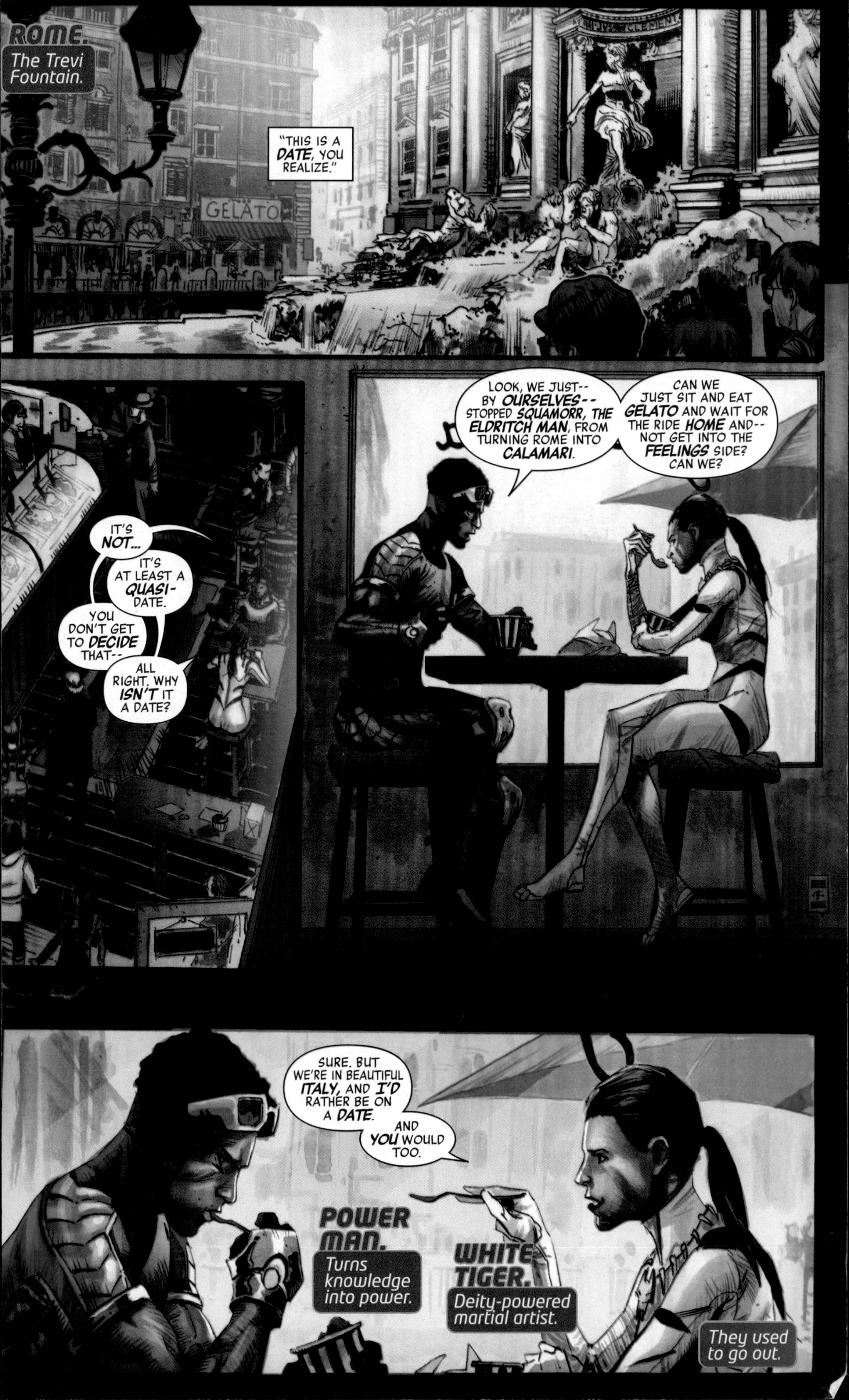

ROME.
The Trevi Fountain.
"THIS IS A DATE, YOU REALIZE."
GELATO
IT'S NOT...
IT'S AT LEAST A QUASI-DATE.
YOU DON'T GET TO DECIDE THAT--
ALL RIGHT. WHY ISN'T IT A DATE?
LOOK, WE JUST-- BY OURSELVES-- STOPPED SQUAMORR, THE ELDRITCH MAN, FROM TURNING ROME INTO CALAMARI.
CAN WE JUST SIT AND EAT GELATO AND WAIT FOR THE RIDE HOME AND-- NOT GET INTO THE FEELINGS SIDE? CAN WE?
SURE. BUT WE'RE IN BEAUTIFUL ITALY, AND I'D RATHER BE ON A DATE.
AND YOU WOULD TOO.
POWER MAN.
Turns knowledge into power.
WHITE TIGER.
Deity-powered martial artist.
They used to go out.

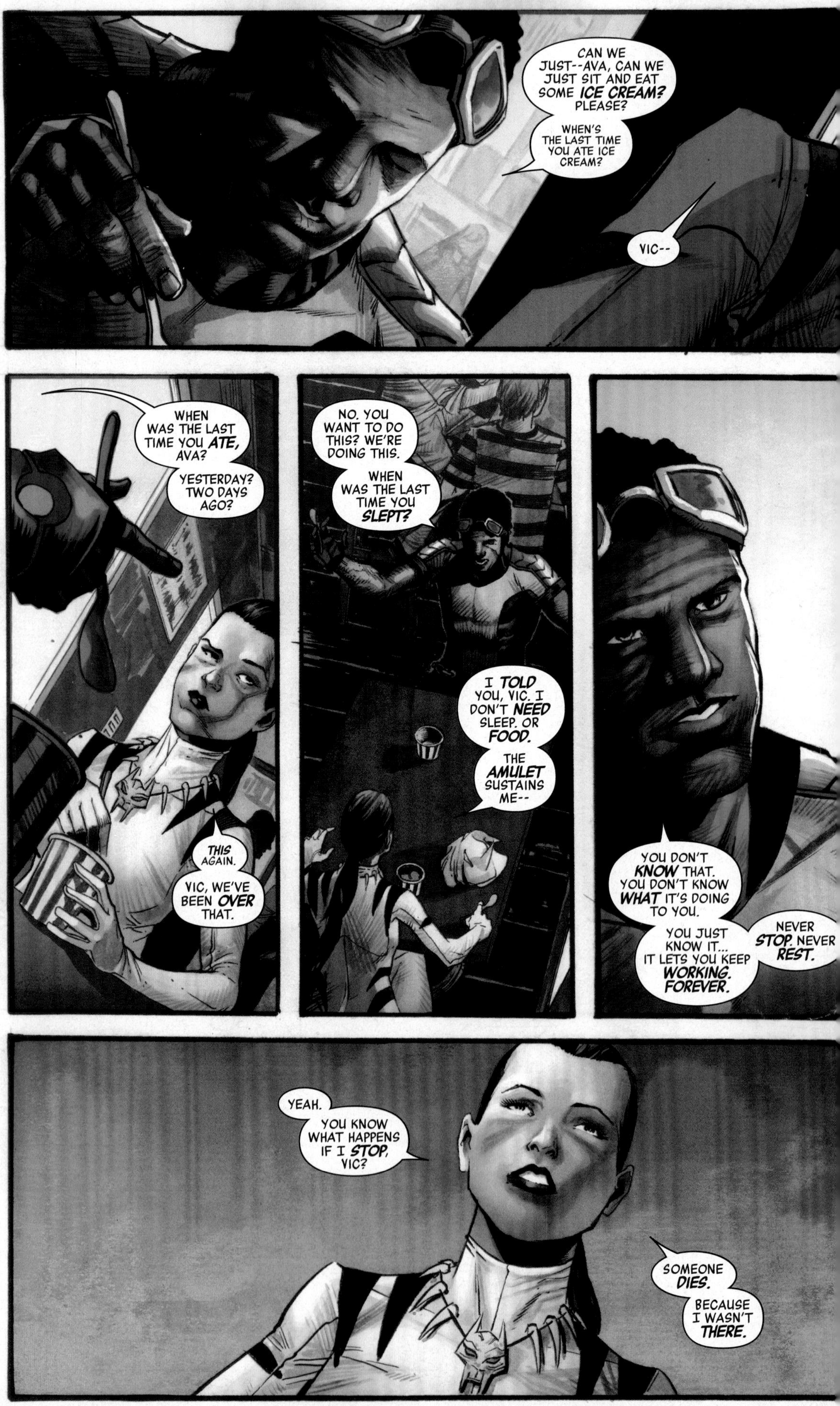
CAN WE JUST--AVA, CAN WE JUST SIT AND EAT SOME ICE CREAM? PLEASE?
WHEN'S THE LAST TIME YOU ATE ICE CREAM?
VIC--
WHEN WAS THE LAST TIME YOU ATE, AVA?
YESTERDAY? TWO DAYS AGO?
THIS AGAIN.
VIC, WE'VE BEEN OVER THAT.
NO. YOU WANT TO DO THIS? WE'RE DOING THIS.
WHEN WAS THE LAST TIME YOU SLEPT?
I TOLD YOU, VIC. I DON'T NEED SLEEP. OR FOOD.
THE AMULET SUSTAINS ME--
YOU DON'T KNOW THAT. YOU DON'T KNOW WHAT IT'S DOING TO YOU.
YOU JUST KNOW IT... IT LETS YOU KEEP WORKING. FOREVER.
NEVER STOP. NEVER REST.
YEAH.
YOU KNOW WHAT HAPPENS IF I STOP, VIC?
SOMEONE DIES.
BECAUSE I WASN'T THERE.

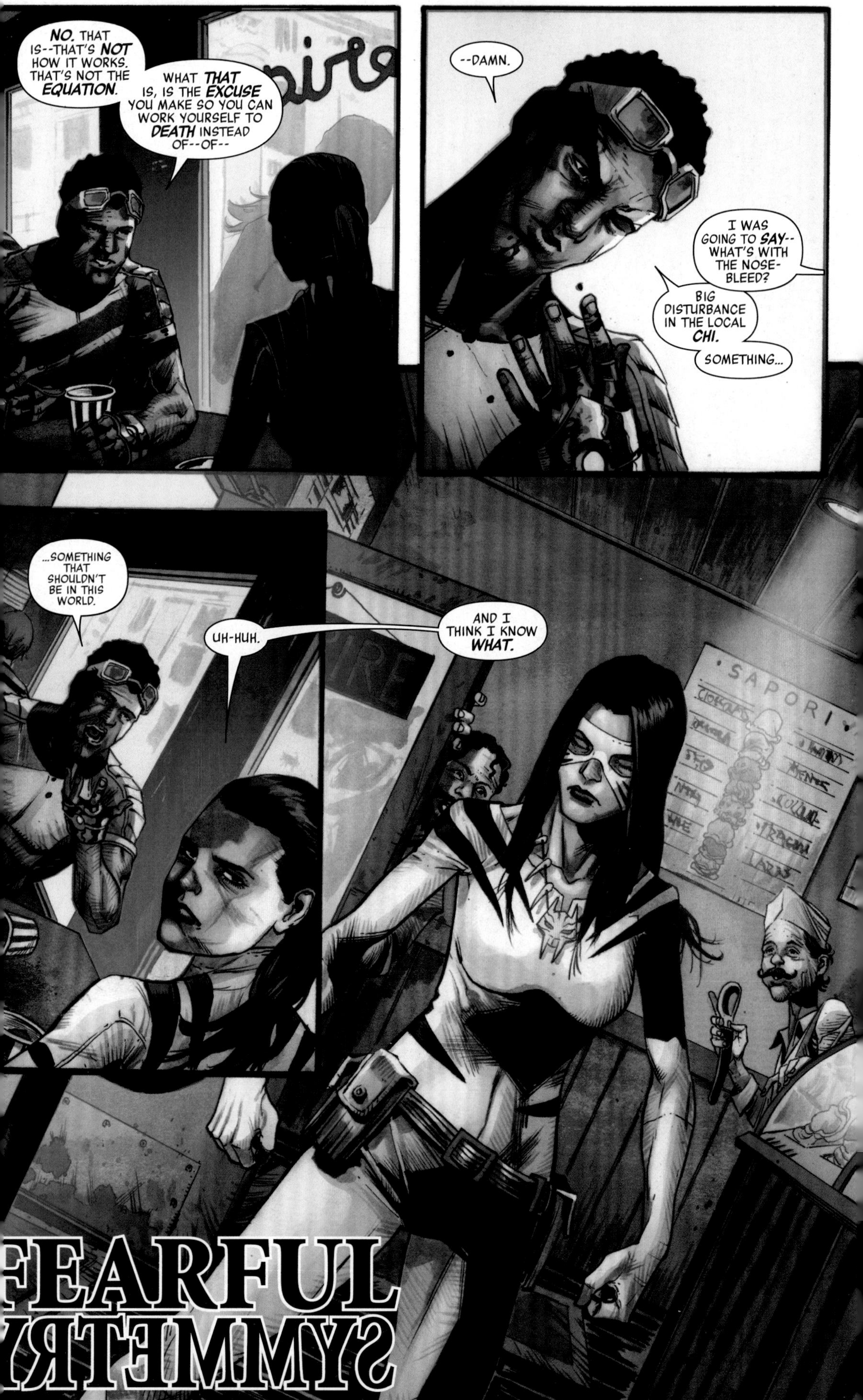

NO. THAT IS--THAT'S NOT HOW IT WORKS. THAT'S NOT THE EQUATION.
WHAT THAT IS, IS THE EXCUSE YOU MAKE SO YOU CAN WORK YOURSELF TO DEATH INSTEAD OF--OF--
--DAMN.
I WAS GOING TO SAY--WHAT'S WITH THE NOSE-BLEED?
BIG DISTURBANCE IN THE LOCAL CHI.
SOMETHING...
...SOMETHING THAT SHOULDN'T BE IN THIS WORLD.
UH-HUH.
AND I THINK I KNOW WHAT.
SAPORI
FEARFUL
SYMMETRY

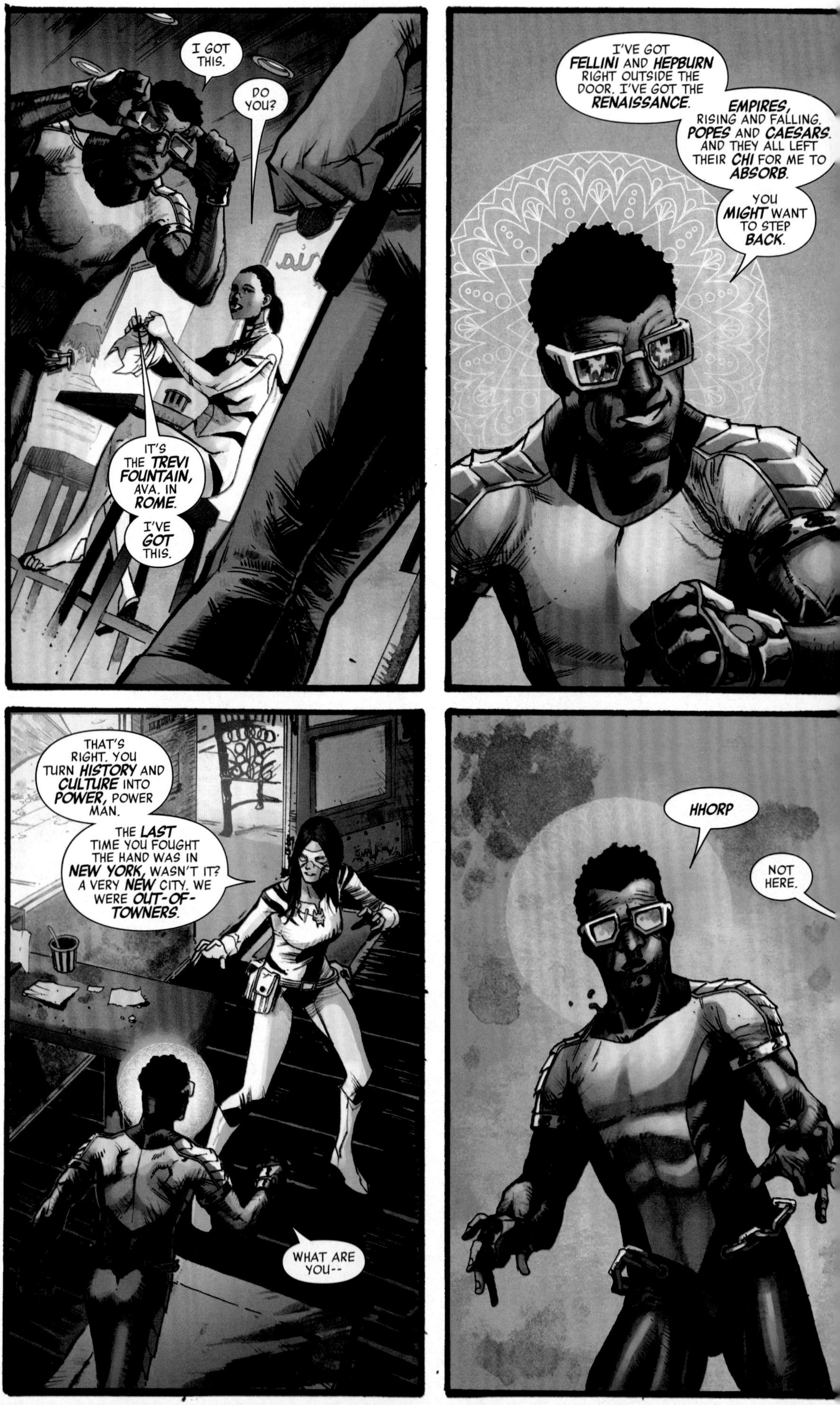
I GOT THIS.
DO YOU?
IT'S THE TREVI FOUNTAIN, AVA. IN ROME.
I'VE GOT THIS.
I'VE GOT FELLINI AND HEPBURN RIGHT OUTSIDE THE DOOR. I'VE GOT THE RENAISSANCE.
EMPIRES, RISING AND FALLING. POPES AND CAESARS. AND THEY ALL LEFT THEIR CHI FOR ME TO ABSORB.
YOU MIGHT WANT TO STEP BACK.
THAT'S RIGHT. YOU TURN HISTORY AND CULTURE INTO POWER, POWER MAN.
THE LAST TIME YOU FOUGHT THE HAND WAS IN NEW YORK, WASN'T IT? A VERY NEW CITY. WE WERE OUT-OF-TOWNERS.
WHAT ARE YOU--
HHORP
NOT HERE.

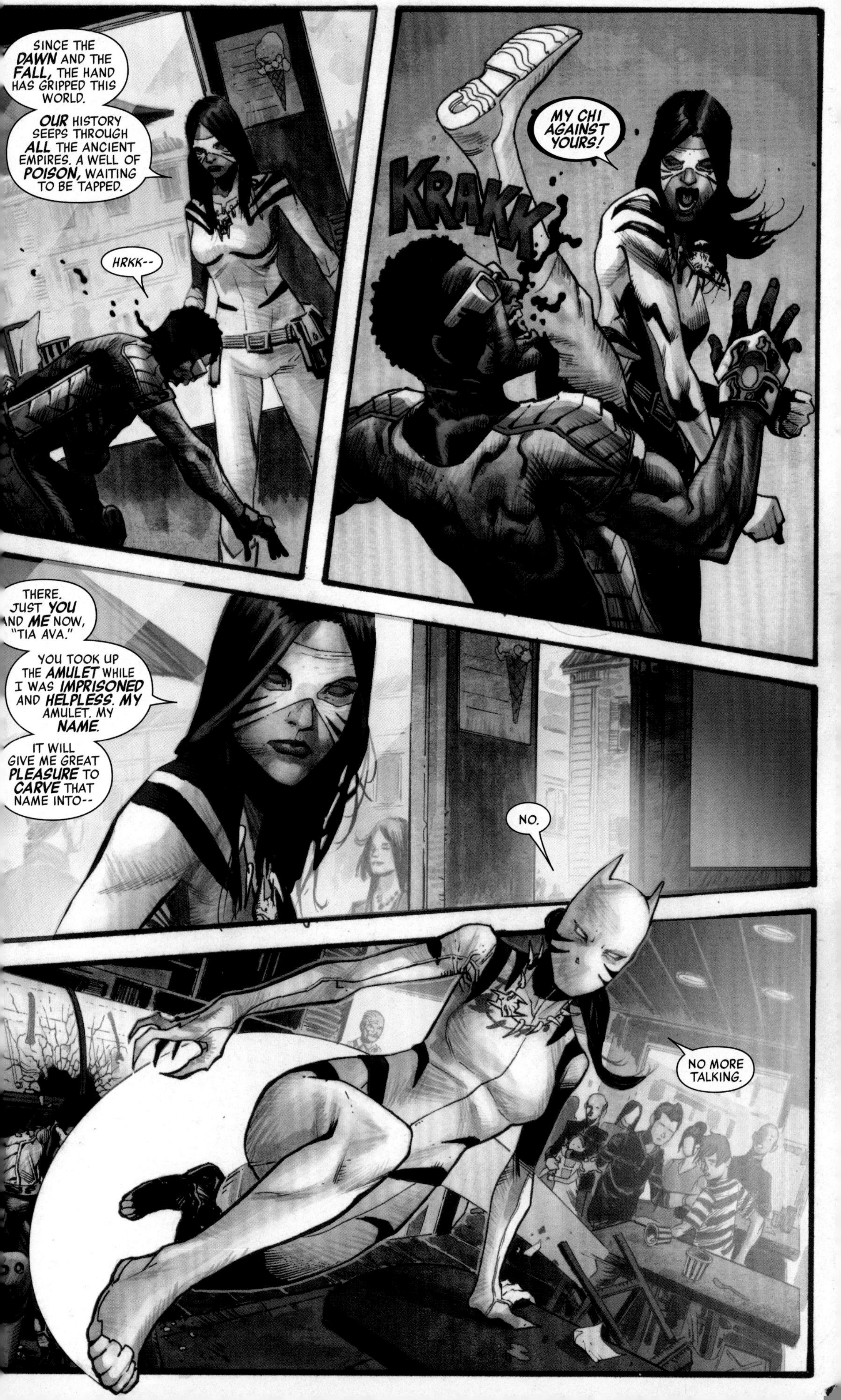
SINCE THE DAWN AND THE FALL, THE HAND HAS GRIPPED THIS WORLD.
OUR HISTORY SEEPS THROUGH ALL THE ANCIENT EMPIRES. A WELL OF POISON, WAITING TO BE TAPPED.
HRKK--
MY CHI AGAINST YOURS!
KRAKK
THERE. JUST YOU AND ME NOW, "TIA AVA."
YOU TOOK UP THE AMULET WHILE I WAS IMPRISONED AND HELPLESS. MY AMULET. MY NAME.
IT WILL GIVE ME GREAT PLEASURE TO CARVE THAT NAME INTO--
NO.
NO MORE TALKING.

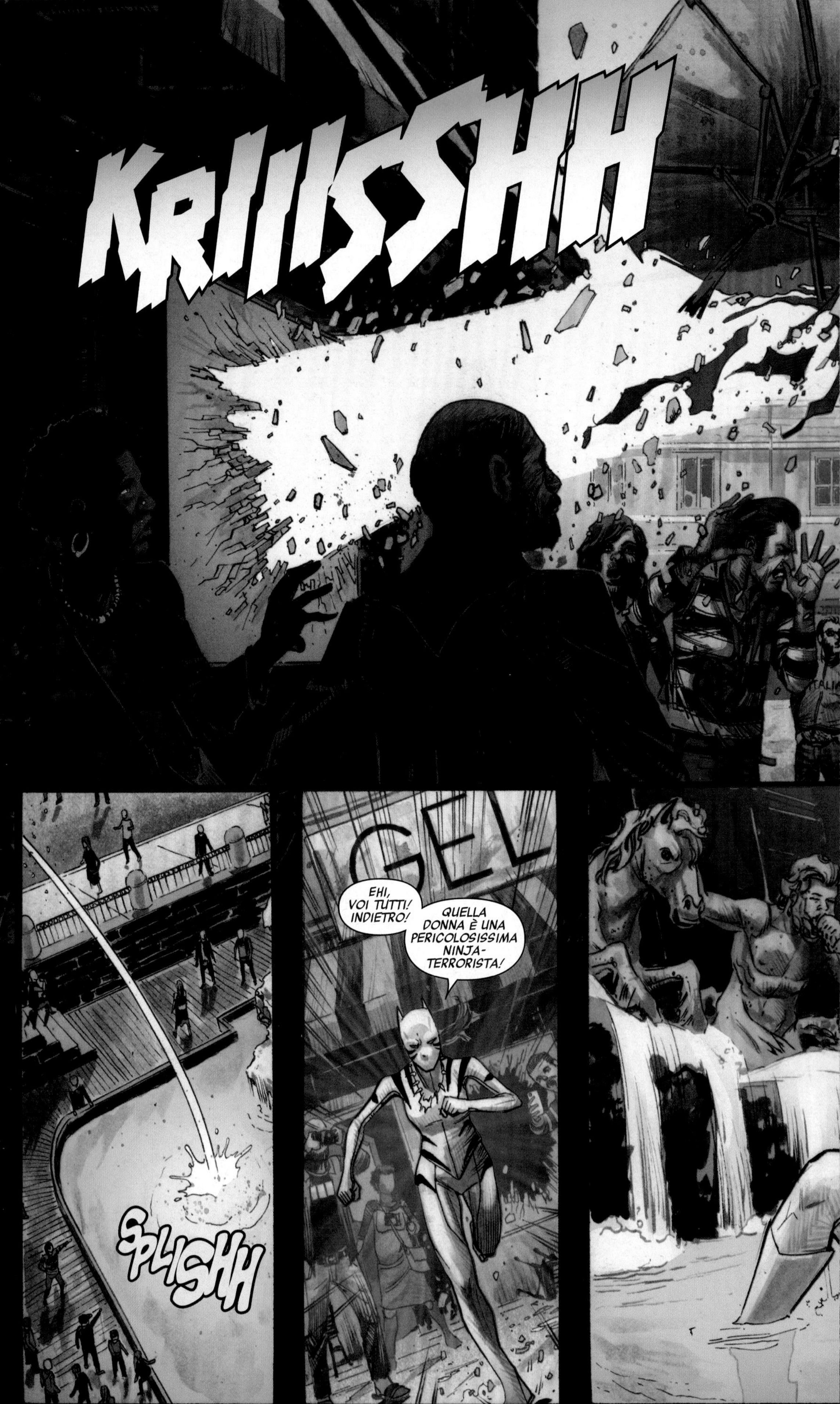
KRIIISHH
SPLISHH
EHI, VOI TUTTI! INDIETRO!
QUELLA DONNA È UNA PERICOLOSISSIMA NINJA-TERRORISTA!
GEL

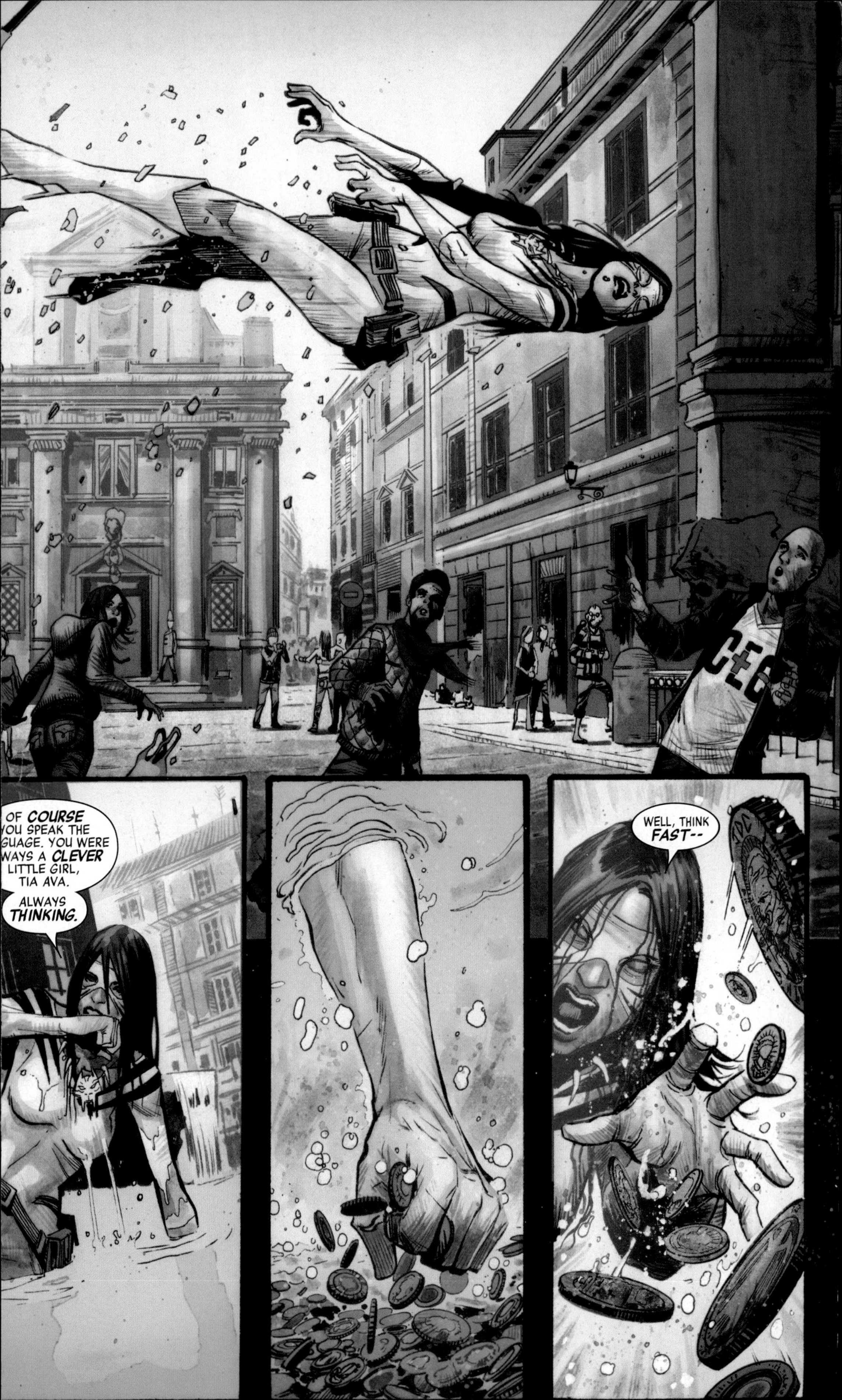
OF COURSE
OU SPEAK THE
GUAGE. YOU WERE
WAYS A CLEVER
LITTLE GIRL,
TIA AVA.
ALWAYS
THINKING.
WELL, THINK
FAST--

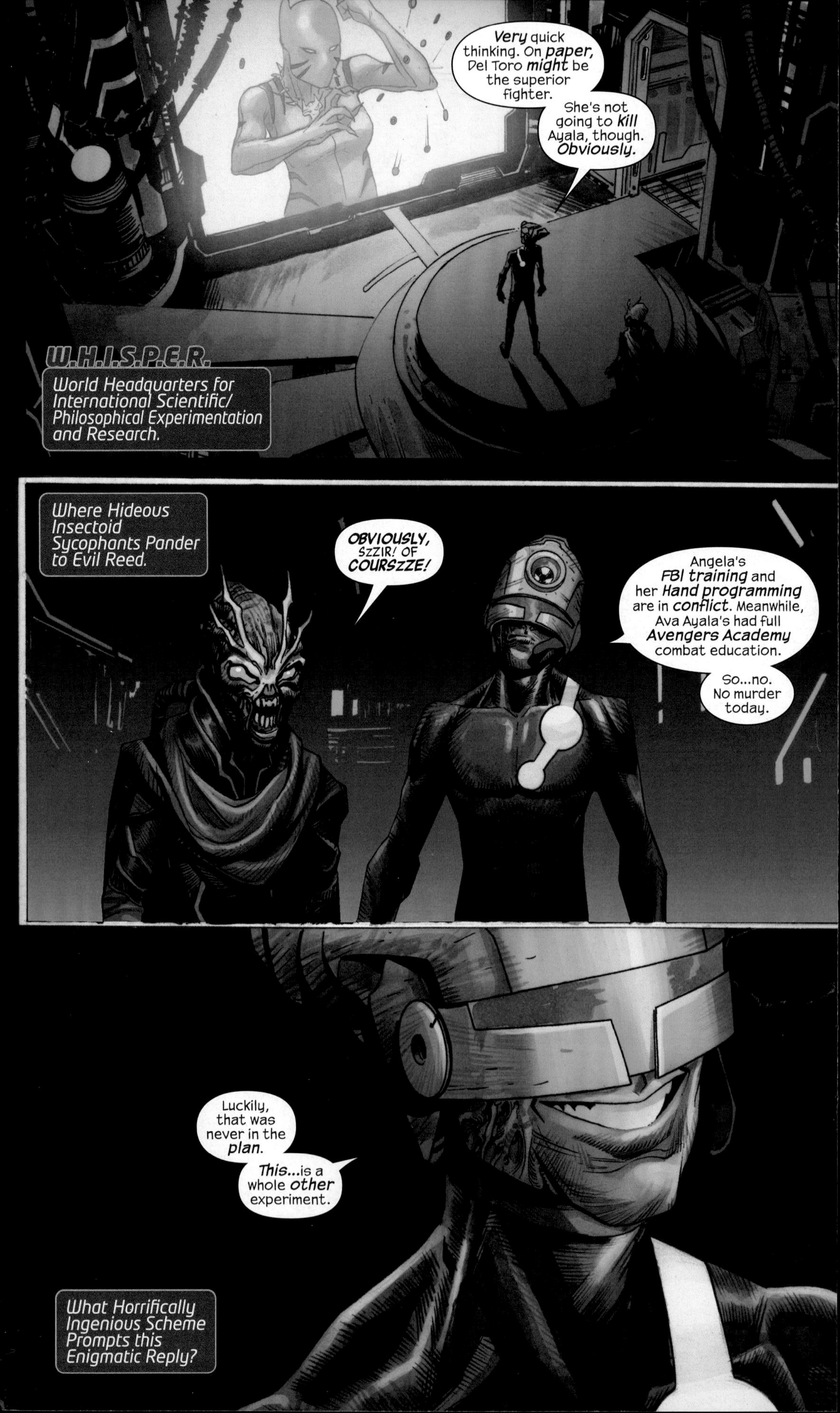
Very quick thinking. On paper, Del Toro might be the superior fighter.
She's not going to kill Ayala, though. Obviously.
W.H.I.S.P.E.R.
World Headquarters for International Scientific/ Philosophical Experimentation and Research.
Where Hideous Insectoid Sycophants Pander to Evil Reed.
OBVIOUSLY, SZZIR! OF COURSZZE!
Angela's FBI training and her Hand programming are in conflict. Meanwhile, Ava Ayala's had full Avengers Academy combat education.
So...no. No murder today.
Luckily, that was never in the plan.
This...is a whole other experiment.
What Horrifically Ingenious Scheme Prompts this Enigmatic Reply?

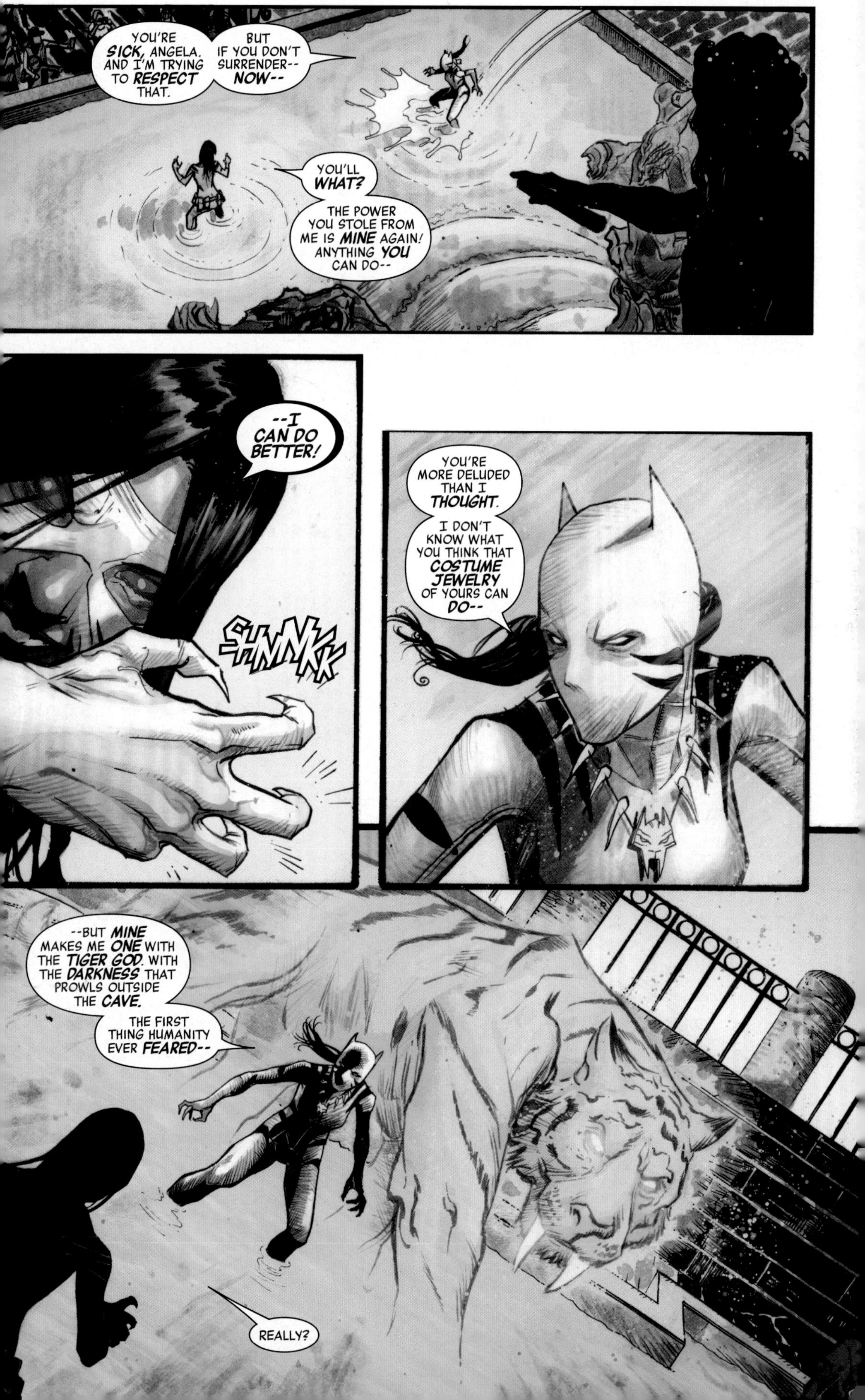
YOU'RE SICK, ANGELA. AND I'M TRYING TO RESPECT THAT.
BUT IF YOU DON'T SURRENDER-- NOW--
YOU'LL WHAT?
THE POWER YOU STOLE FROM ME IS MINE AGAIN! ANYTHING YOU CAN DO--
--I CAN DO BETTER!
SHNNKK
YOU'RE MORE DELUDED THAN I THOUGHT.
I DON'T KNOW WHAT YOU THINK THAT COSTUME JEWELRY OF YOURS CAN DO--
--BUT MINE MAKES ME ONE WITH THE TIGER GOD. WITH THE DARKNESS THAT PROWLS OUTSIDE THE CAVE.
THE FIRST THING HUMANITY EVER FEARED--
REALLY?

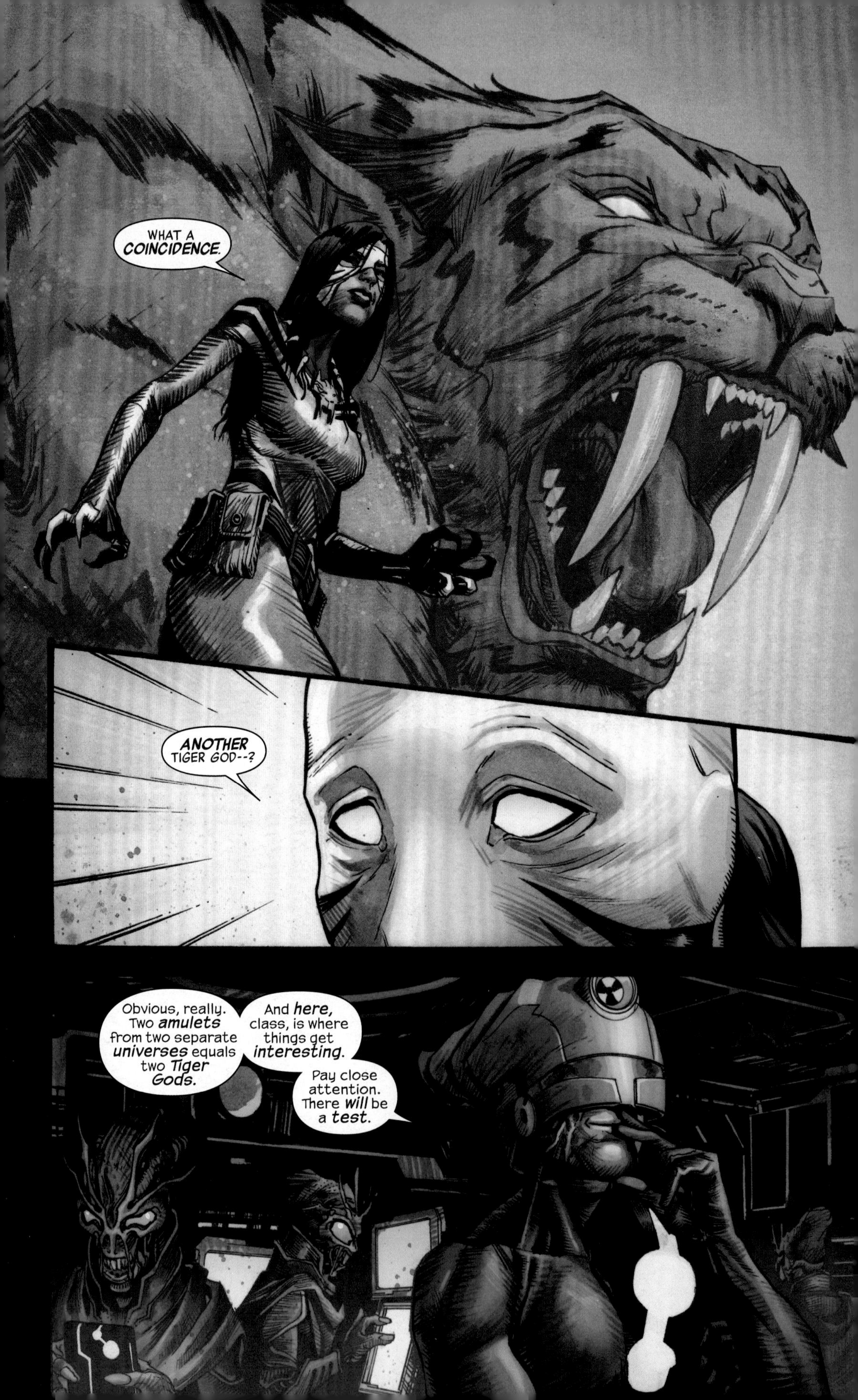
WHAT A COINCIDENCE.
ANOTHER TIGER GOD--?
Obvious, really. Two amulets from two separate universes equals two Tiger Gods.
And here, class, is where things get interesting.
Pay close attention. There will be a test.

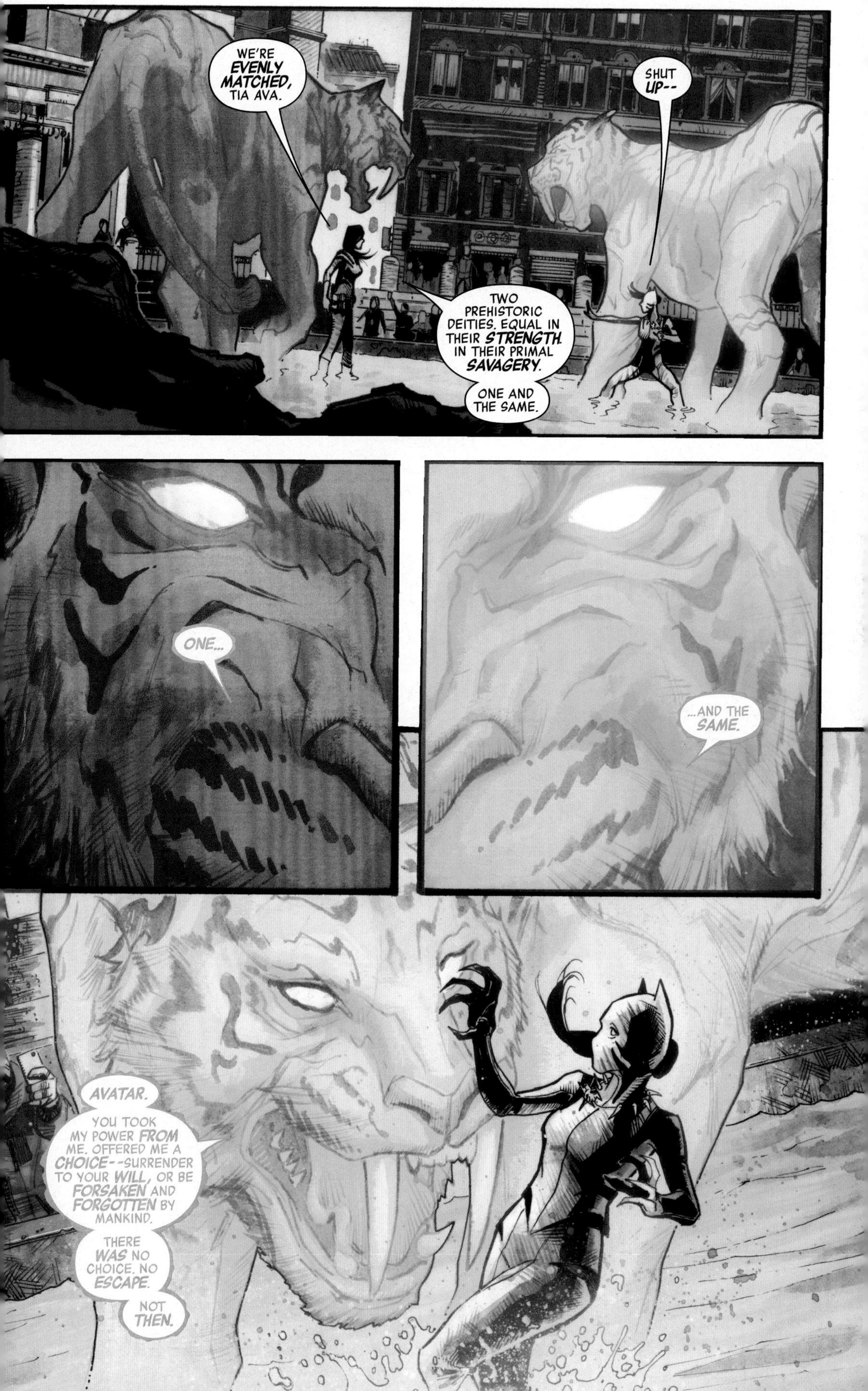
WE'RE EVENLY MATCHED, TIA AVA.
SHUT UP--
TWO PREHISTORIC DEITIES. EQUAL IN THEIR STRENGTH. IN THEIR PRIMAL SAVAGERY.
ONE AND THE SAME.
ONE...
...AND THE SAME.
AVATAR.
YOU TOOK MY POWER FROM ME. OFFERED ME A CHOICE--SURRENDER TO YOUR WILL, OR BE FORSAKEN AND FORGOTTEN BY MANKIND.
THERE WAS NO CHOICE. NO ESCAPE.
NOT THEN.

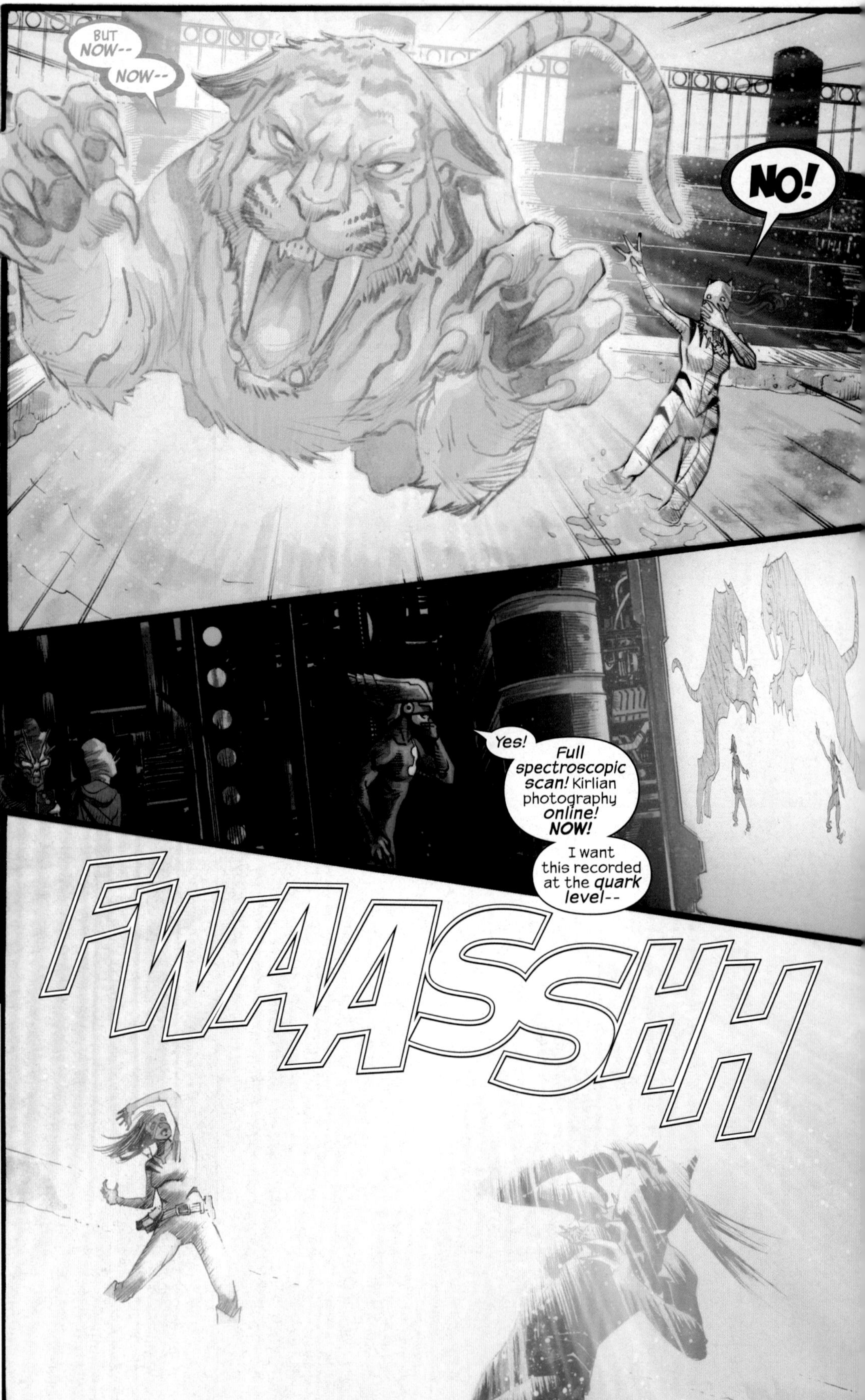
BUT NOW--
NOW--
NO!
Yes!
Full spectroscopic scan! Kirlian photography online! NOW!
I want this recorded at the quark level--
FWAASHH

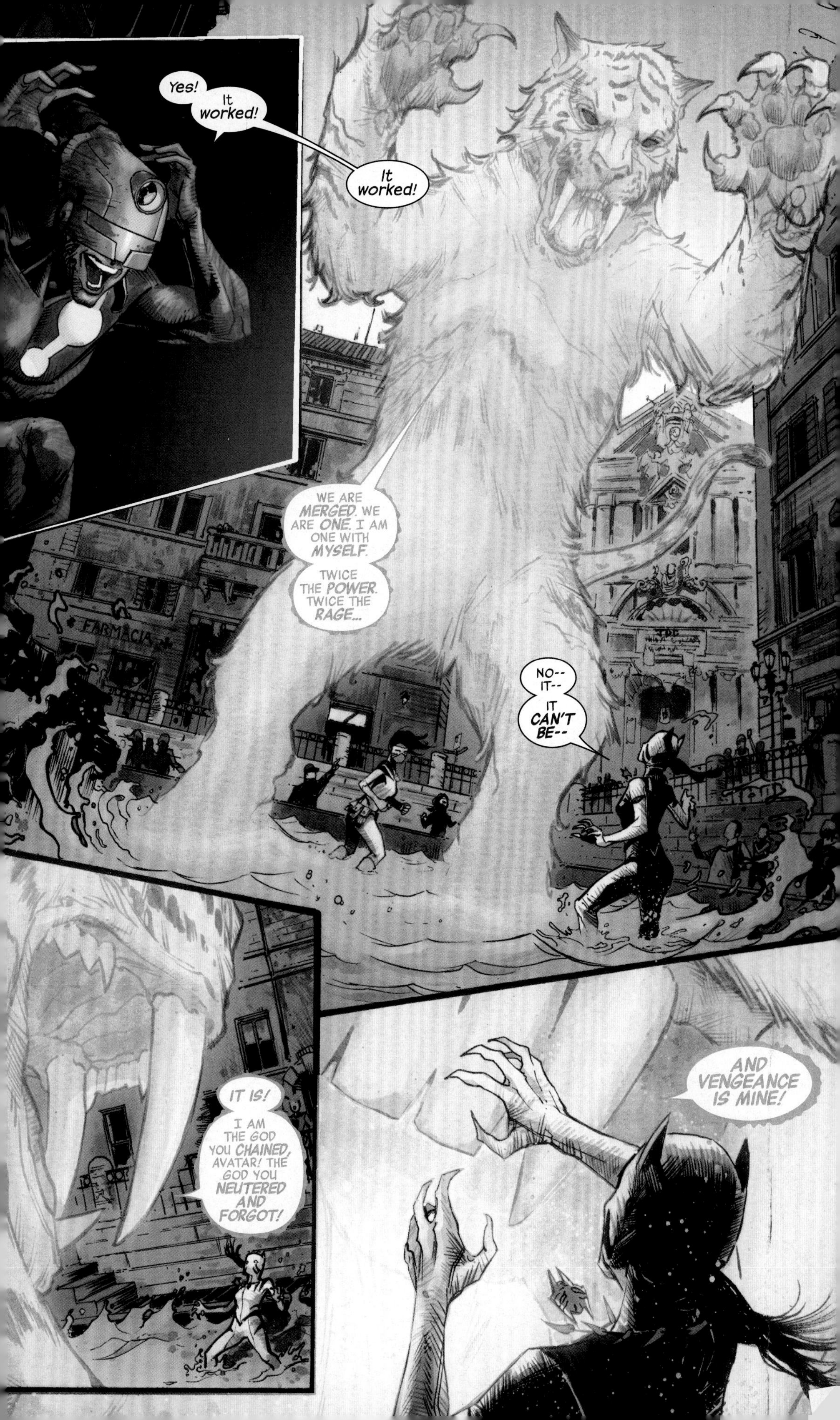
Yes!
It worked!
It worked!
WE ARE MERGED. WE ARE ONE. I AM ONE WITH MYSELF.
TWICE THE POWER. TWICE THE RAGE...
FARMACIA
NO-- IT--
IT CAN'T BE--
IT IS!
I AM THE GOD YOU CHAINED, AVATAR! THE GOD YOU NEUTERED AND FORGOT!
AND VENGEANCE IS MINE!

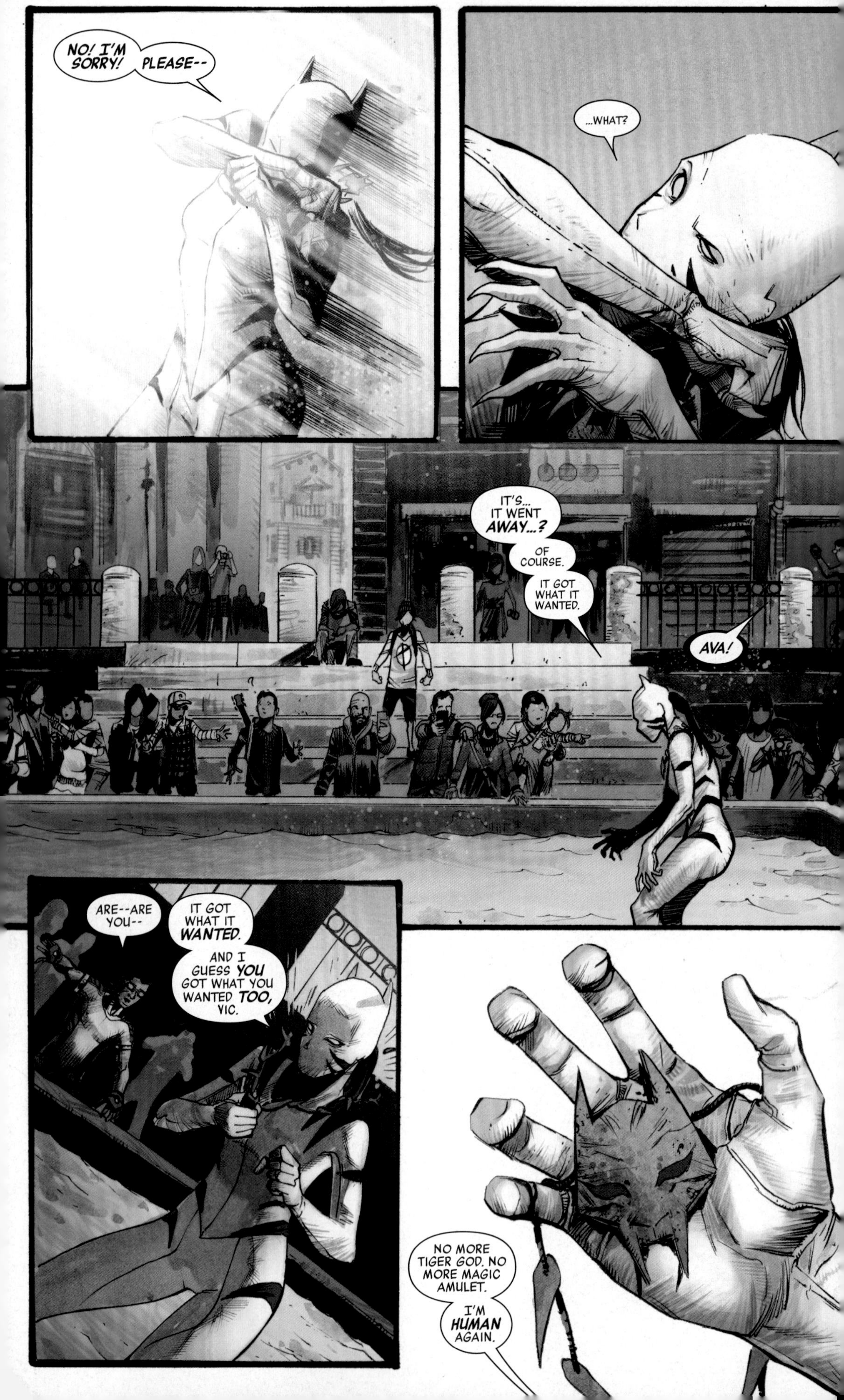
NO! I'M SORRY!
PLEASE--
...WHAT?
IT'S... IT WENT AWAY...?
OF COURSE.
IT GOT WHAT IT WANTED.
AVA!
ARE--ARE YOU--
IT GOT WHAT IT WANTED.
AND I GUESS YOU GOT WHAT YOU WANTED TOO, VIC.
NO MORE TIGER GOD. NO MORE MAGIC AMULET.
I'M HUMAN AGAIN.

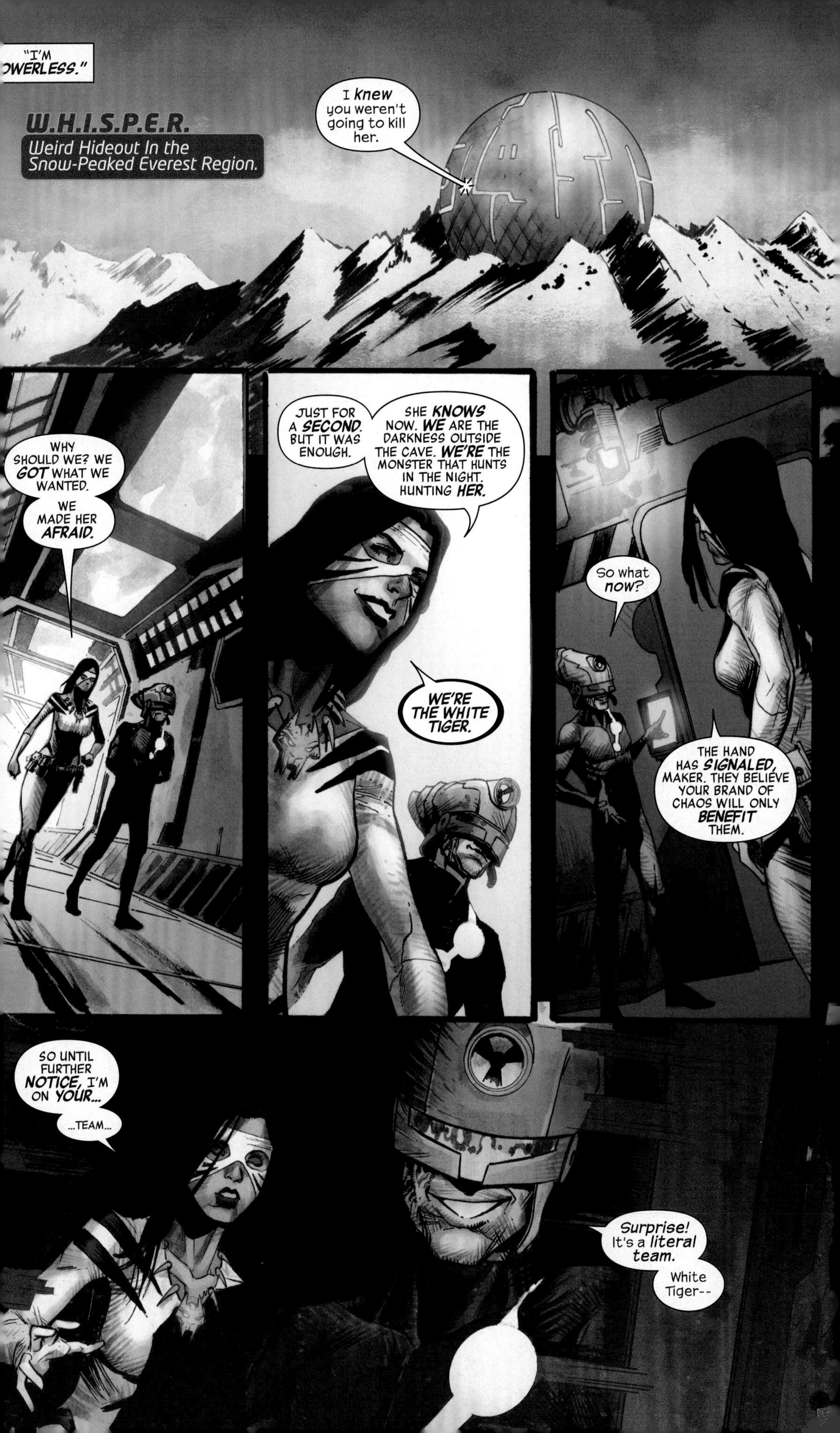
"I'M
OWERLESS."
W.H.I.S.P.E.R.
Weird Hideout In the Snow-Peaked Everest Region.
I knew you weren't going to kill her.
WHY SHOULD WE? WE GOT WHAT WE WANTED.
WE MADE HER AFRAID.
JUST FOR A SECOND. BUT IT WAS ENOUGH.
SHE KNOWS NOW. WE ARE THE DARKNESS OUTSIDE THE CAVE. WE'RE THE MONSTER THAT HUNTS IN THE NIGHT. HUNTING HER.
WE'RE THE WHITE TIGER.
So what now?
THE HAND HAS SIGNALED, MAKER. THEY BELIEVE YOUR BRAND OF CHAOS WILL ONLY BENEFIT THEM.
SO UNTIL FURTHER NOTICE, I'M ON YOUR...
...TEAM...
Surprise! It's a literal team.
White Tiger--

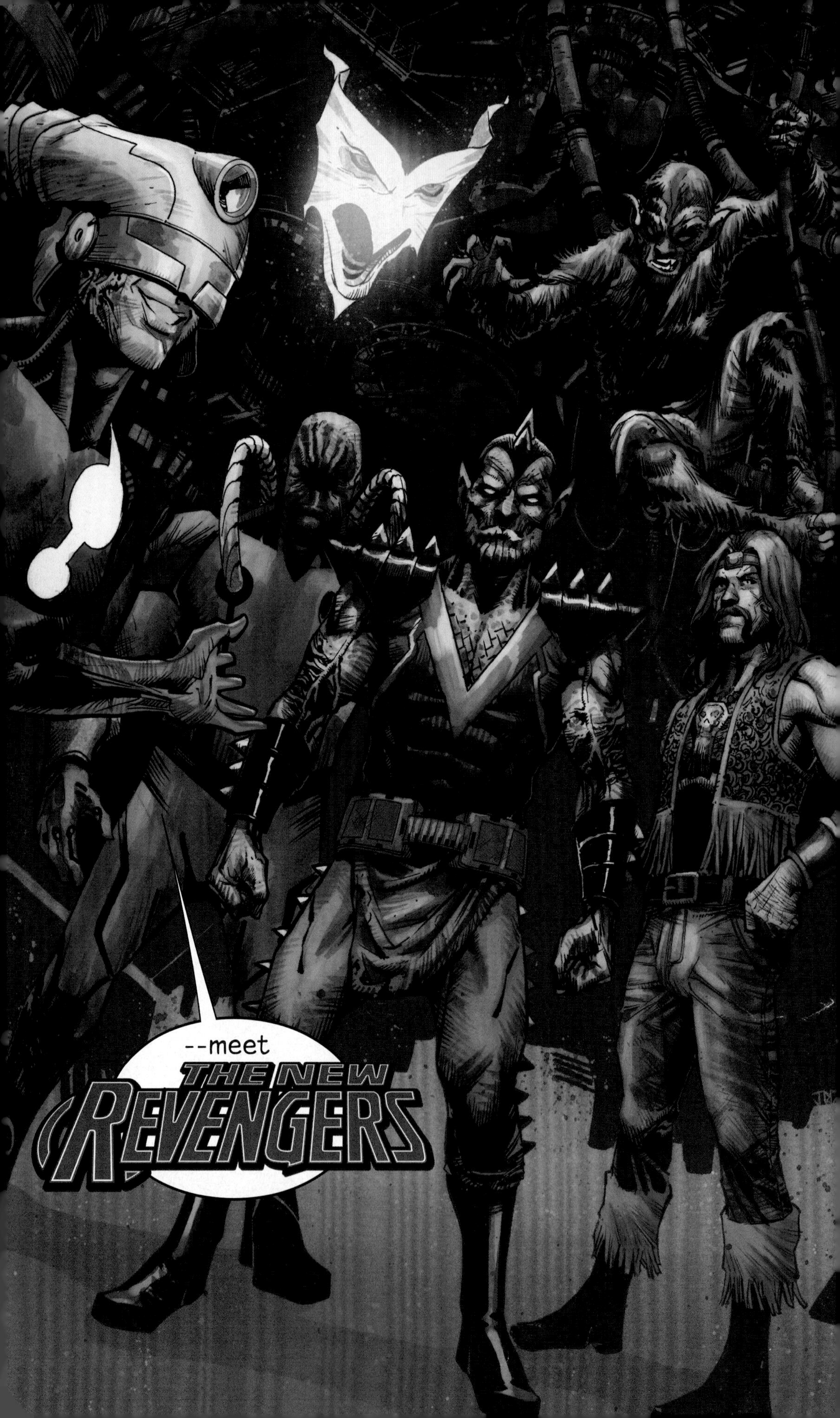
--meet
THE NEW REVENGERS

WANTED
FOR TREASON
ROBERTO DA COSTA
Alias: SUNSPOT
A.I.M. Supreme Leader
HIGHLY DANGEROUS -- DO NOT APPROACH
8

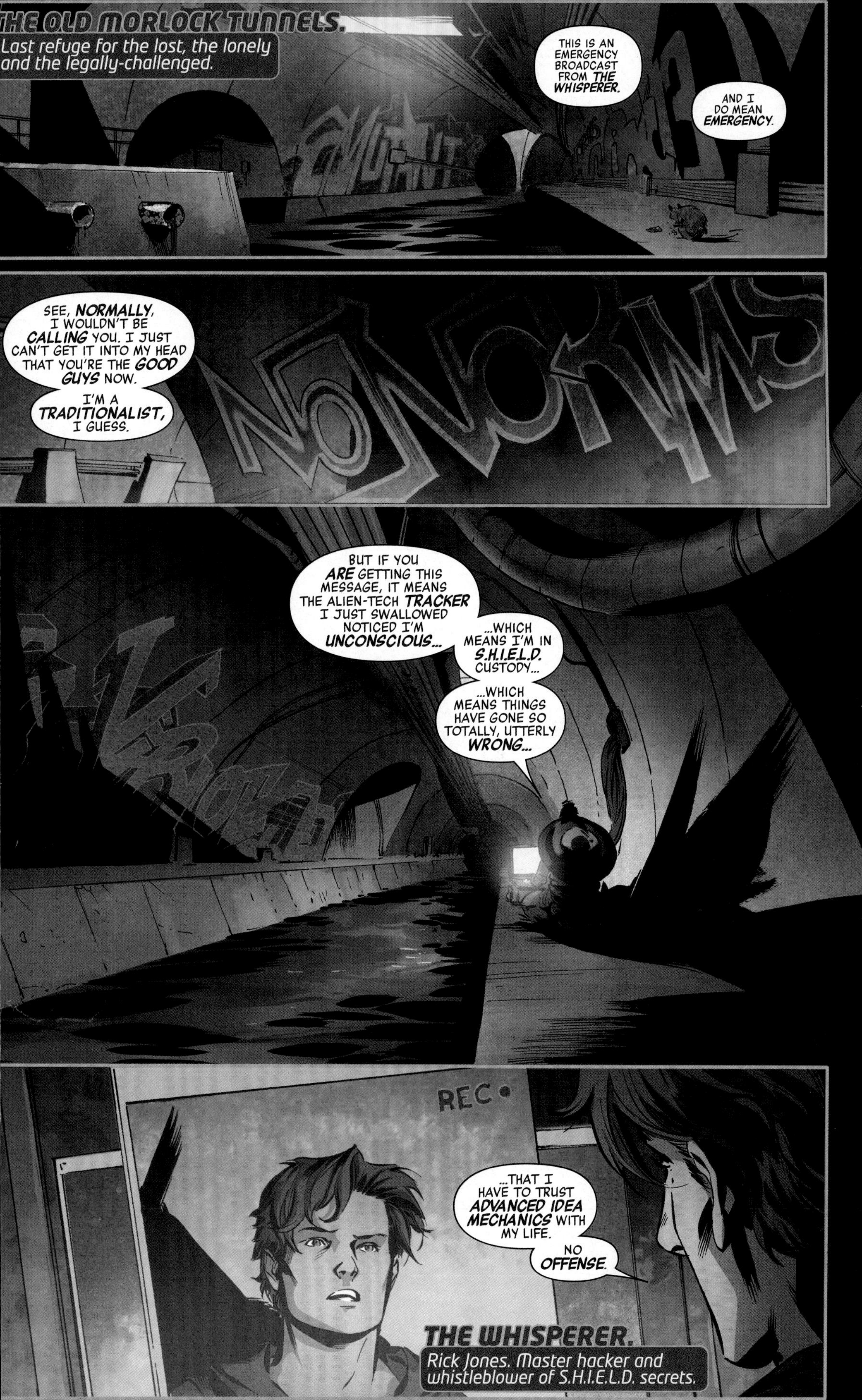

THE OLD MORLOCK TUNNELS.
Last refuge for the lost, the lonely and the legally-challenged.
THIS IS AN EMERGENCY BROADCAST FROM THE WHISPERER.
AND I DO MEAN EMERGENCY.
SEE, NORMALLY, I WOULDN'T BE CALLING YOU. I JUST CAN'T GET IT INTO MY HEAD THAT YOU'RE THE GOOD GUYS NOW.
I'M A TRADITIONALIST, I GUESS.
BUT IF YOU ARE GETTING THIS MESSAGE, IT MEANS THE ALIEN-TECH TRACKER I JUST SWALLOWED NOTICED I'M UNCONSCIOUS...
...WHICH MEANS I'M IN S.H.I.E.L.D. CUSTODY...
...WHICH MEANS THINGS HAVE GONE SO TOTALLY, UTTERLY WRONG...
REC
...THAT I HAVE TO TRUST ADVANCED IDEA MECHANICS WITH MY LIFE.
NO OFFENSE.
THE WHISPERER.
Rick Jones. Master hacker and whistleblower of S.H.I.E.L.D. secrets.

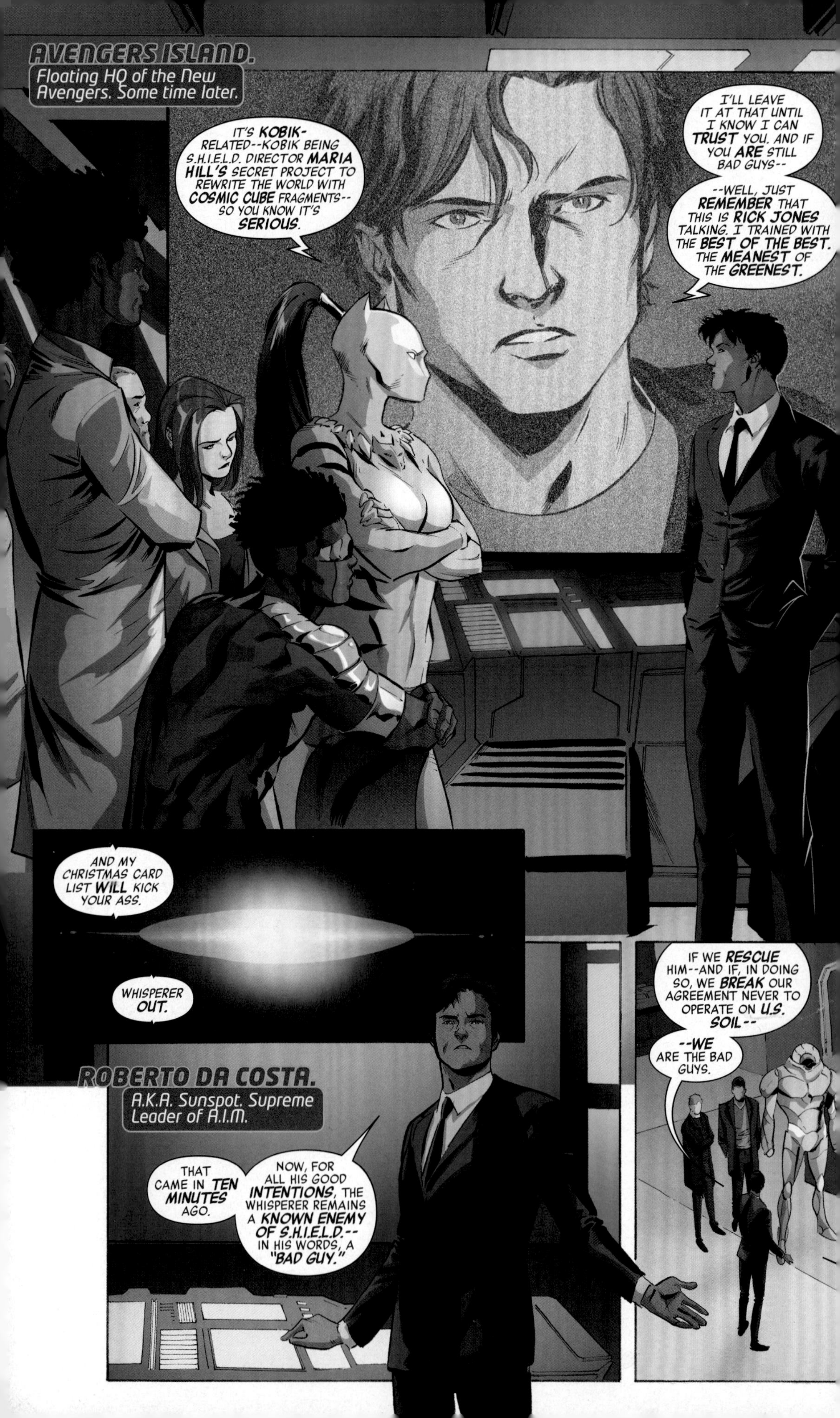

AVENGERS ISLAND.
Floating HQ of the New Avengers. Some time later.
IT'S KOBIK-RELATED--KOBIK BEING S.H.I.E.L.D. DIRECTOR MARIA HILL'S SECRET PROJECT TO REWRITE THE WORLD WITH COSMIC CUBE FRAGMENTS--SO YOU KNOW IT'S SERIOUS.
I'LL LEAVE IT AT THAT UNTIL I KNOW I CAN TRUST YOU. AND IF YOU ARE STILL BAD GUYS--
--WELL, JUST REMEMBER THAT THIS IS RICK JONES TALKING. I TRAINED WITH THE BEST OF THE BEST. THE MEANEST OF THE GREENEST.
AND MY CHRISTMAS CARD LIST WILL KICK YOUR ASS.
WHISPERER OUT.
ROBERTO DA COSTA.
A.K.A. Sunspot. Supreme Leader of A.I.M.
THAT CAME IN TEN MINUTES AGO.
NOW, FOR ALL HIS GOOD INTENTIONS, THE WHISPERER REMAINS A KNOWN ENEMY OF S.H.I.E.L.D.--IN HIS WORDS, A "BAD GUY."
IF WE RESCUE HIM--AND IF, IN DOING SO, WE BREAK OUR AGREEMENT NEVER TO OPERATE ON U.S. SOIL--
--WE ARE THE BAD GUYS.

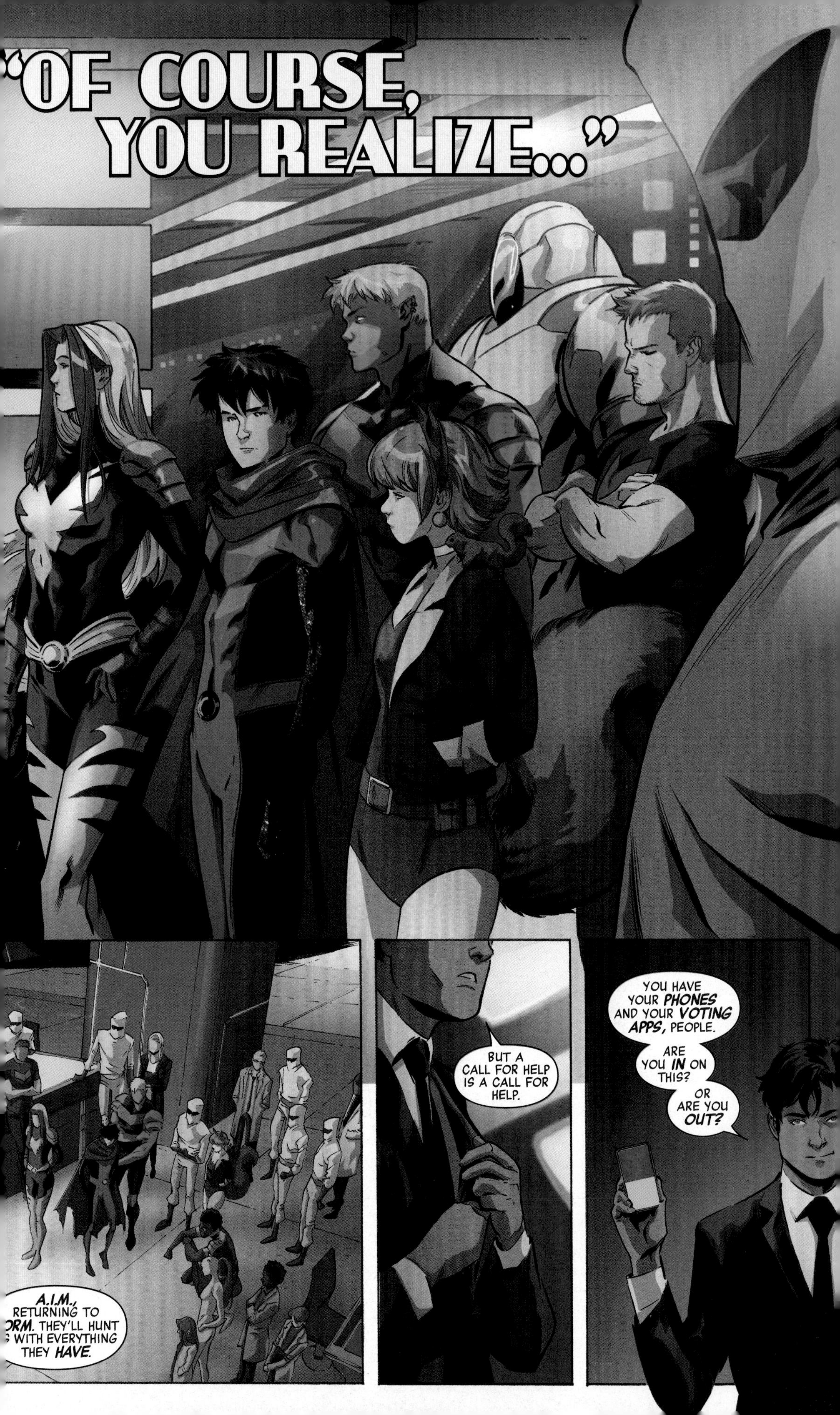
"OF COURSE, YOU REALIZE..."
A.I.M., RETURNING TO ORM. THEY'LL HUNT WITH EVERYTHING THEY HAVE.
BUT A CALL FOR HELP IS A CALL FOR HELP.
YOU HAVE YOUR PHONES AND YOUR VOTING APPS, PEOPLE.
ARE YOU IN ON THIS?
OR ARE YOU OUT?

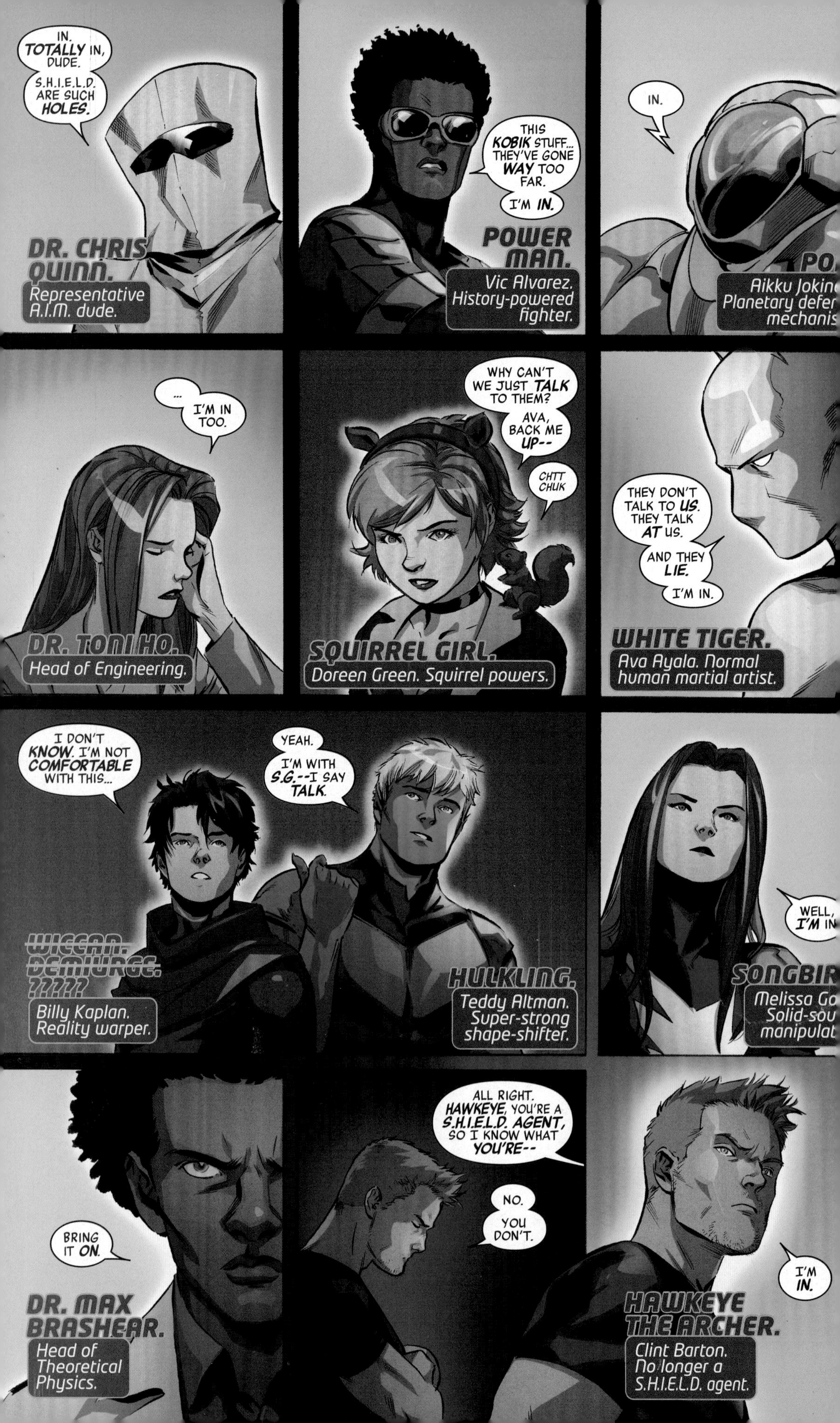

IN. TOTALLY IN, DUDE.
S.H.I.E.L.D. ARE SUCH HOLES.
DR. CHRIS QUINN.
Representative A.I.M. dude.
THIS KOBIK STUFF... THEY'VE GONE WAY TOO FAR.
I'M IN.
POWER MAN.
Vic Alvarez. History-powered fighter.
IN.
PO
Aikku Jokin
Planetary defe
mechanis
...
I'M IN TOO.
DR. TONI HO.
Head of Engineering.
WHY CAN'T WE JUST TALK TO THEM?
AVA, BACK ME UP--
CHTT CHUK
SQUIRREL GIRL.
Doreen Green. Squirrel powers.
THEY DON'T TALK TO US. THEY TALK AT US.
AND THEY LIE.
I'M IN.
WHITE TIGER.
Ava Ayala. Normal human martial artist.
I DON'T KNOW. I'M NOT COMFORTABLE WITH THIS...
YEAH.
I'M WITH S.G.--I SAY TALK.
WICCAN. DEMIURGE. ?????
Billy Kaplan. Reality warper.
HULKLING.
Teddy Altman. Super-strong shape-shifter.
WELL, I'M IN
SONGBIR
Melissa Go
Solid-sou
manipulat
BRING IT ON.
DR. MAX BRASHEAR.
Head of Theoretical Physics.
ALL RIGHT. HAWKEYE, YOU'RE A S.H.I.E.L.D. AGENT, SO I KNOW WHAT YOU'RE--
NO.
YOU DON'T.
I'M IN.
HAWKEYE THE ARCHER.
Clint Barton. No longer a S.H.I.E.L.D. agent.

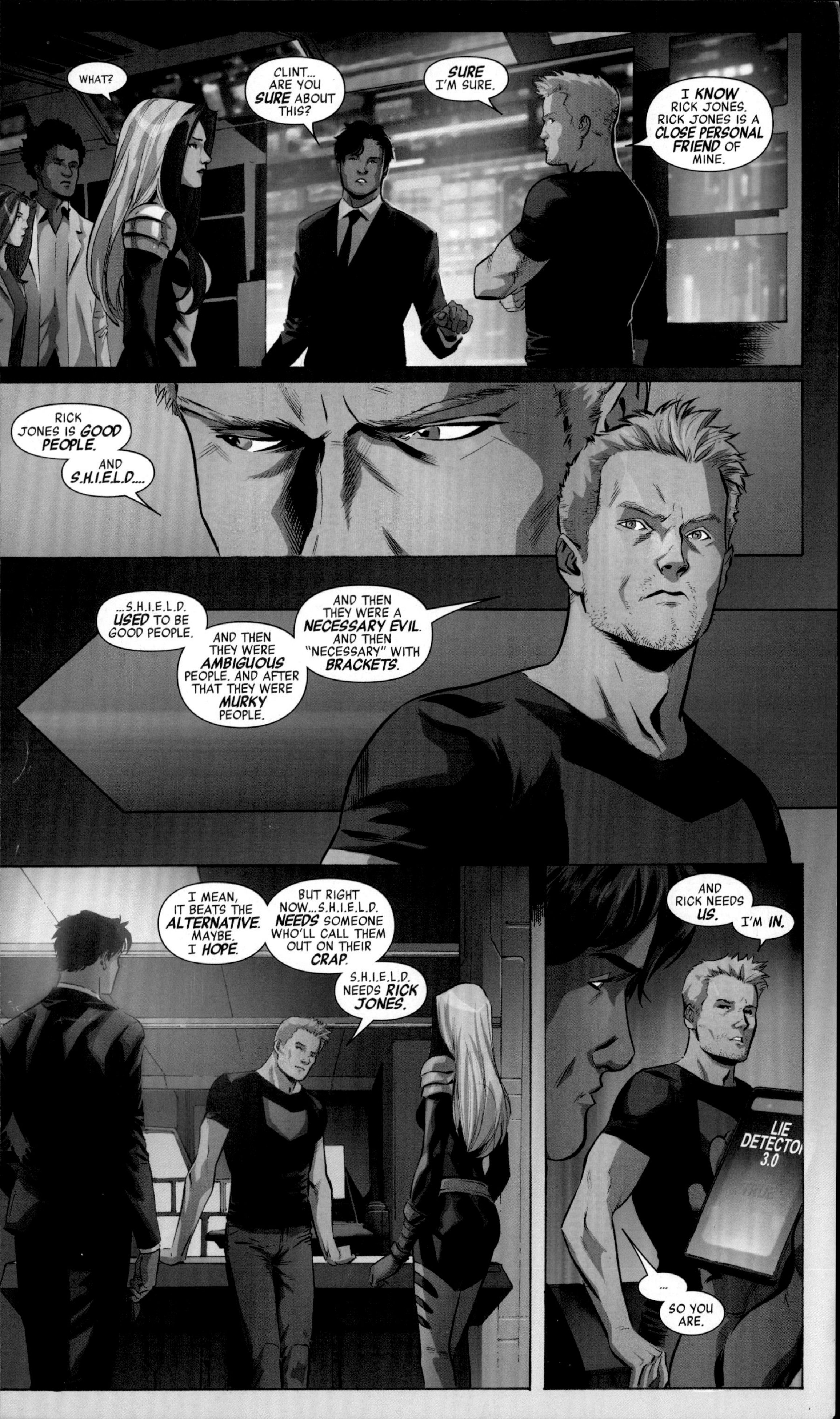
WHAT?
CLINT... ARE YOU SURE ABOUT THIS?
SURE I'M SURE.
I KNOW RICK JONES. RICK JONES IS A CLOSE PERSONAL FRIEND OF MINE.
RICK JONES IS GOOD PEOPLE.
AND S.H.I.E.L.D....
...S.H.I.E.L.D. USED TO BE GOOD PEOPLE.
AND THEN THEY WERE AMBIGUOUS PEOPLE. AND AFTER THAT THEY WERE MURKY PEOPLE.
AND THEN THEY WERE A NECESSARY EVIL. AND THEN "NECESSARY" WITH BRACKETS.
I MEAN, IT BEATS THE ALTERNATIVE. MAYBE. I HOPE.
BUT RIGHT NOW...S.H.I.E.L.D. NEEDS SOMEONE WHO'LL CALL THEM OUT ON THEIR CRAP.
S.H.I.E.L.D. NEEDS RICK JONES.
AND RICK NEEDS US.
I'M IN.
LIE DETECTOR 3.0
TRUE
...
SO YOU ARE.

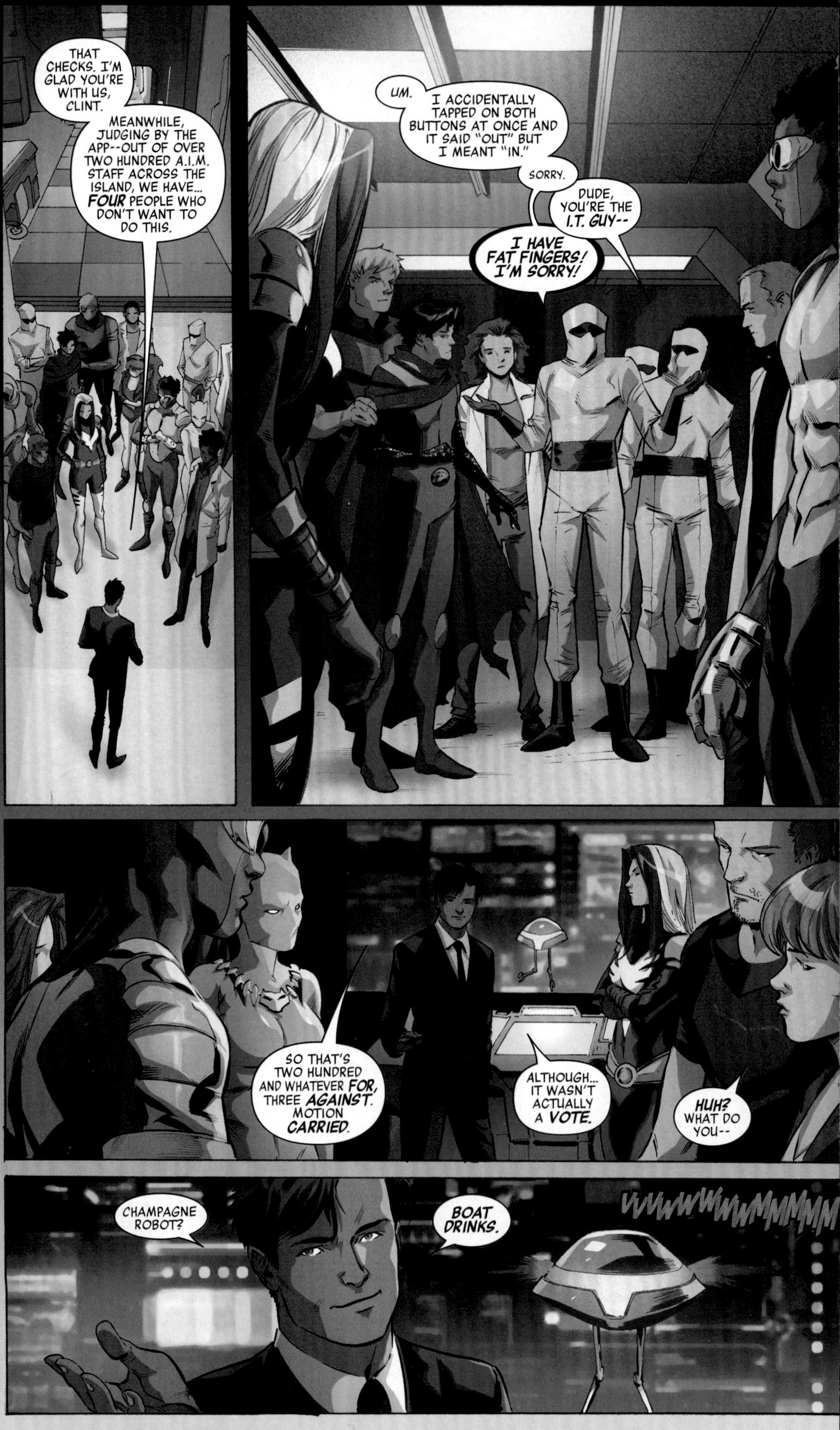
THAT CHECKS. I'M GLAD YOU'RE WITH US, CLINT.
MEANWHILE, JUDGING BY THE APP--OUT OF OVER TWO HUNDRED A.I.M. STAFF ACROSS THE ISLAND, WE HAVE... FOUR PEOPLE WHO DON'T WANT TO DO THIS.
UM.
I ACCIDENTALLY TAPPED ON BOTH BUTTONS AT ONCE AND IT SAID "OUT" BUT I MEANT "IN."
SORRY.
DUDE, YOU'RE THE I.T. GUY--
I HAVE FAT FINGERS! I'M SORRY!
SO THAT'S TWO HUNDRED AND WHATEVER FOR, THREE AGAINST. MOTION CARRIED.
ALTHOUGH... IT WASN'T ACTUALLY A VOTE.
HUH? WHAT DO YOU--
CHAMPAGNE ROBOT?
BOAT DRINKS.
VVVVWWWVVVVMMMMM

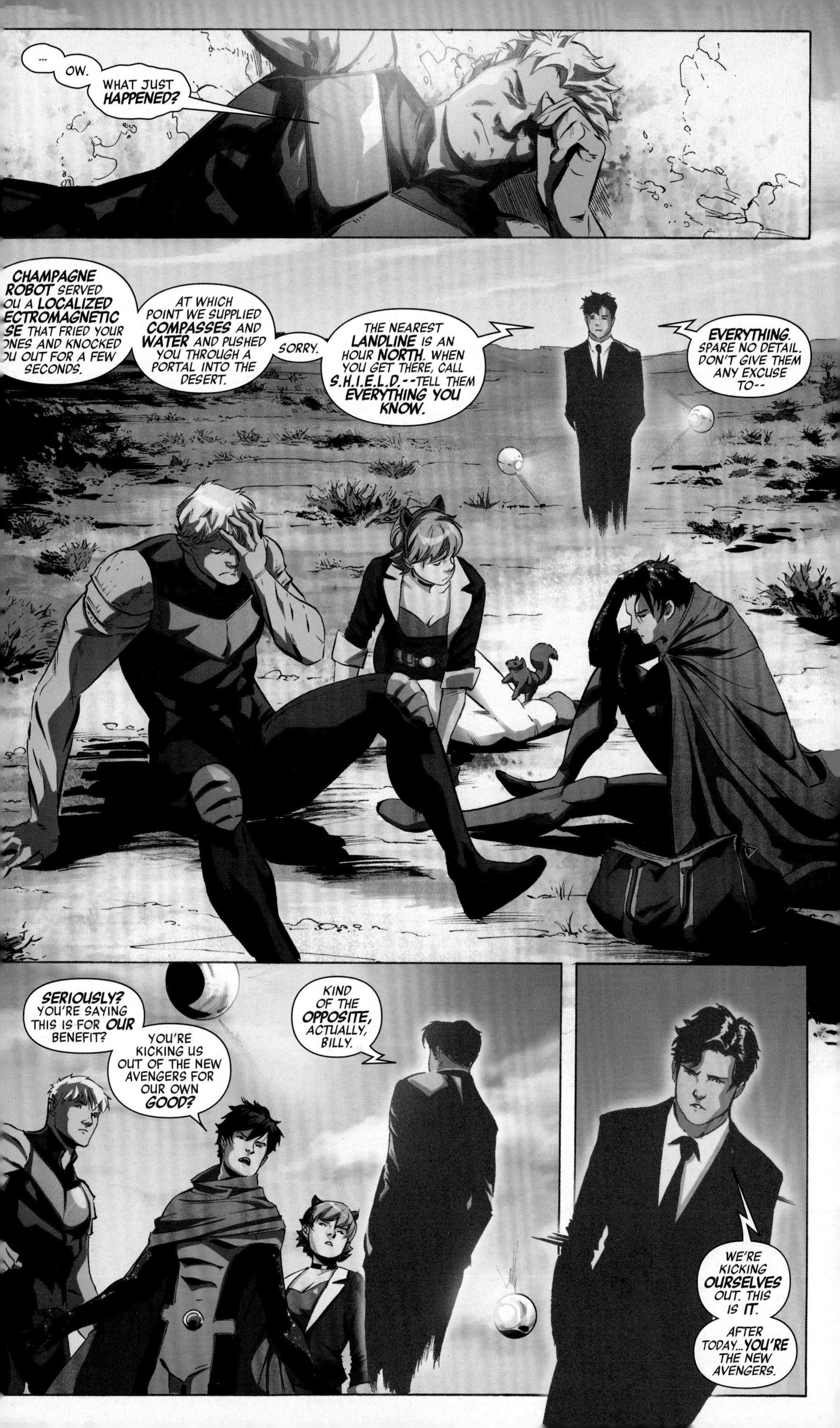
...
OW.
WHAT JUST HAPPENED?
CHAMPAGNE ROBOT SERVED OU A LOCALIZED ECTROMAGNETIC SE THAT FRIED YOUR ONES AND KNOCKED OU OUT FOR A FEW SECONDS.
AT WHICH POINT WE SUPPLIED COMPASSES AND WATER AND PUSHED YOU THROUGH A PORTAL INTO THE DESERT.
SORRY.
THE NEAREST LANDLINE IS AN HOUR NORTH. WHEN YOU GET THERE, CALL S.H.I.E.L.D.--TELL THEM EVERYTHING YOU KNOW.
EVERYTHING. SPARE NO DETAIL. DON'T GIVE THEM ANY EXCUSE TO--
SERIOUSLY? YOU'RE SAYING THIS IS FOR OUR BENEFIT?
YOU'RE KICKING US OUT OF THE NEW AVENGERS FOR OUR OWN GOOD?
KIND OF THE OPPOSITE, ACTUALLY, BILLY.
WE'RE KICKING OURSELVES OUT. THIS IS IT.
AFTER TODAY...YOU'RE THE NEW AVENGERS.

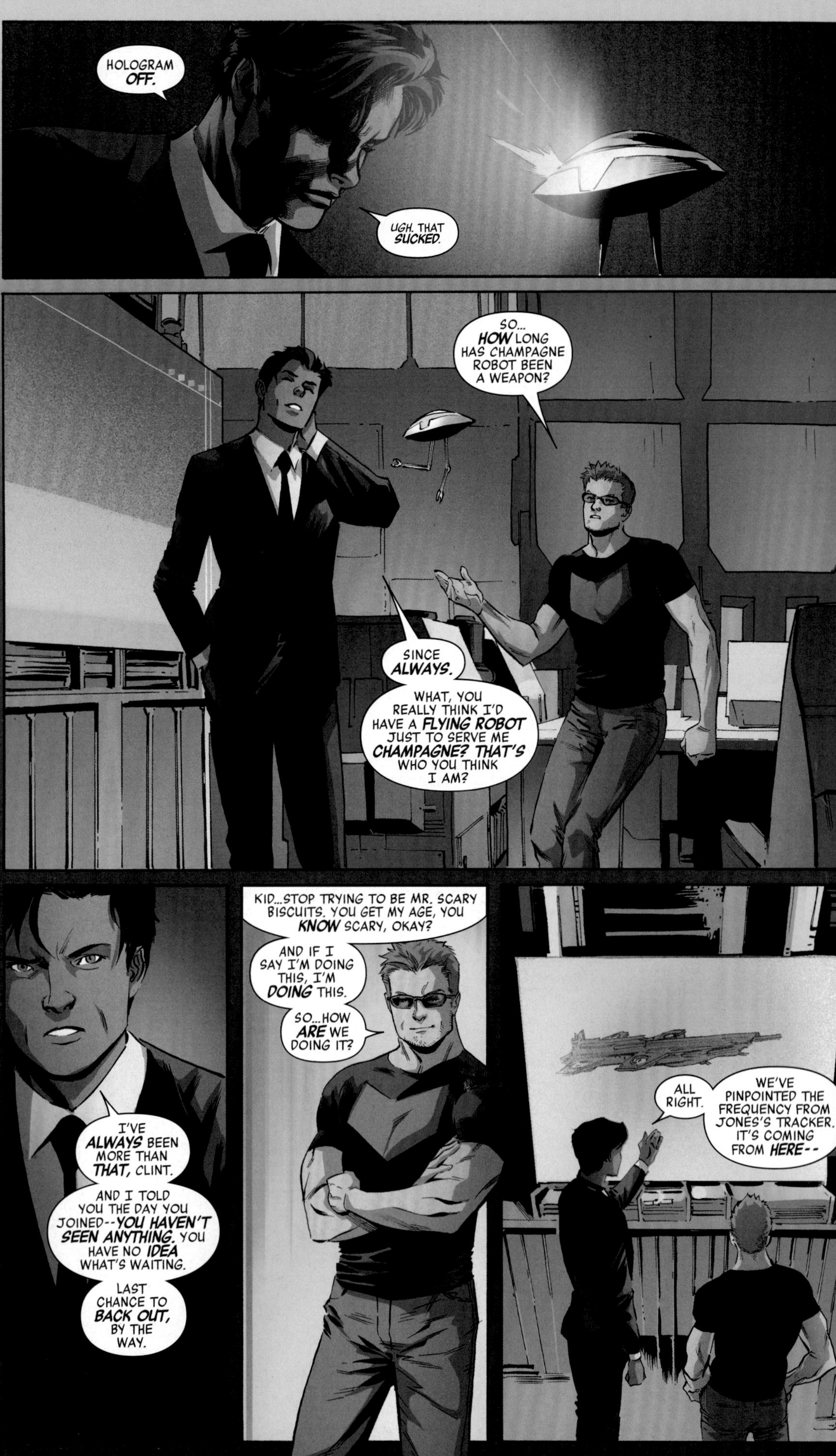
HOLOGRAM OFF.
UGH. THAT SUCKED.
SO... HOW LONG HAS CHAMPAGNE ROBOT BEEN A WEAPON?
SINCE ALWAYS.
WHAT, YOU REALLY THINK I'D HAVE A FLYING ROBOT JUST TO SERVE ME CHAMPAGNE? THAT'S WHO YOU THINK I AM?
I'VE ALWAYS BEEN MORE THAN THAT, CLINT.
AND I TOLD YOU THE DAY YOU JOINED--YOU HAVEN'T SEEN ANYTHING. YOU HAVE NO IDEA WHAT'S WAITING.
LAST CHANCE TO BACK OUT, BY THE WAY.
KID...STOP TRYING TO BE MR. SCARY BISCUITS. YOU GET MY AGE, YOU KNOW SCARY, OKAY?
AND IF I SAY I'M DOING THIS, I'M DOING THIS.
SO...HOW ARE WE DOING IT?
ALL RIGHT.
WE'VE PINPOINTED THE FREQUENCY FROM JONES'S TRACKER. IT'S COMING FROM HERE--

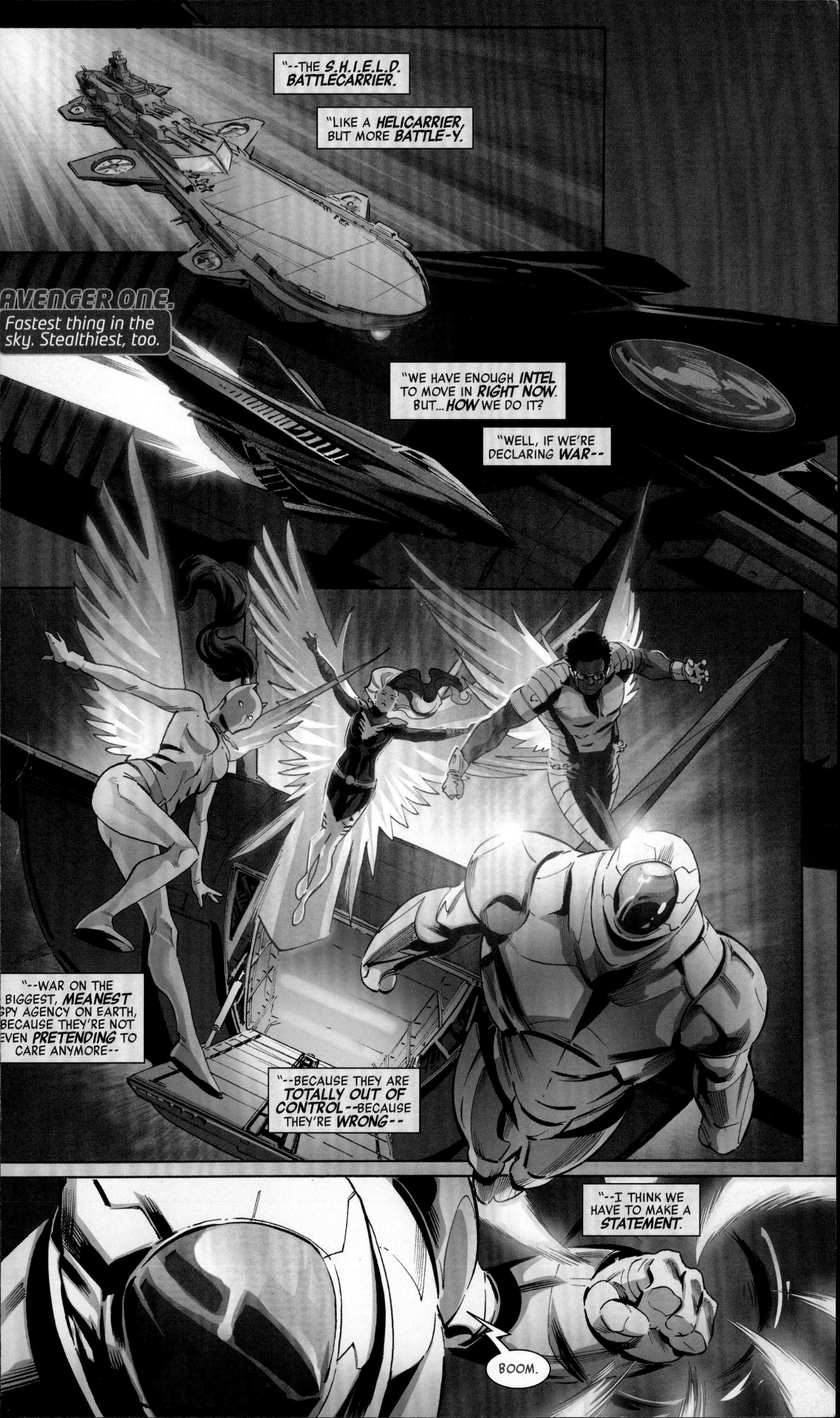
"--THE S.H.I.E.L.D. BATTLECARRIER.
"LIKE A HELICARRIER, BUT MORE BATTLE-Y.
AVENGER ONE.
Fastest thing in the sky. Stealthiest, too.
"WE HAVE ENOUGH INTEL TO MOVE IN RIGHT NOW. BUT... HOW WE DO IT?
"WELL, IF WE'RE DECLARING WAR--
"--WAR ON THE BIGGEST, MEANEST SPY AGENCY ON EARTH, BECAUSE THEY'RE NOT EVEN PRETENDING TO CARE ANYMORE--
"--BECAUSE THEY ARE TOTALLY OUT OF CONTROL--BECAUSE THEY'RE WRONG--
"--I THINK WE HAVE TO MAKE A STATEMENT.
BOOM.

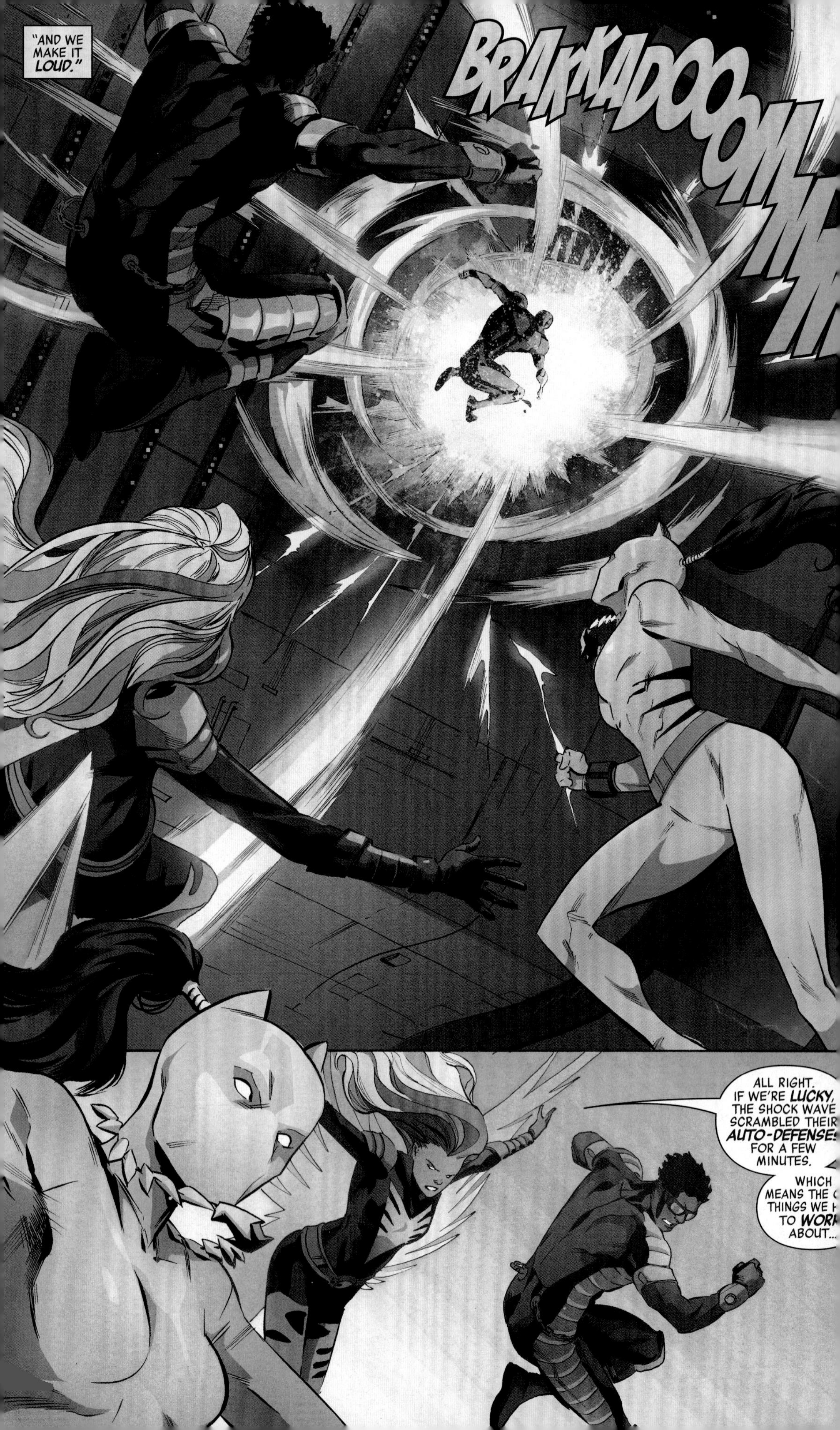
"AND WE MAKE IT LOUD."
BRAKKADOOOOM
ALL RIGHT. IF WE'RE LUCKY, THE SHOCK WAVE SCRAMBLED THEIR AUTO-DEFENSES FOR A FEW MINUTES.
WHICH MEANS THE THINGS WE TO WORK ABOUT...

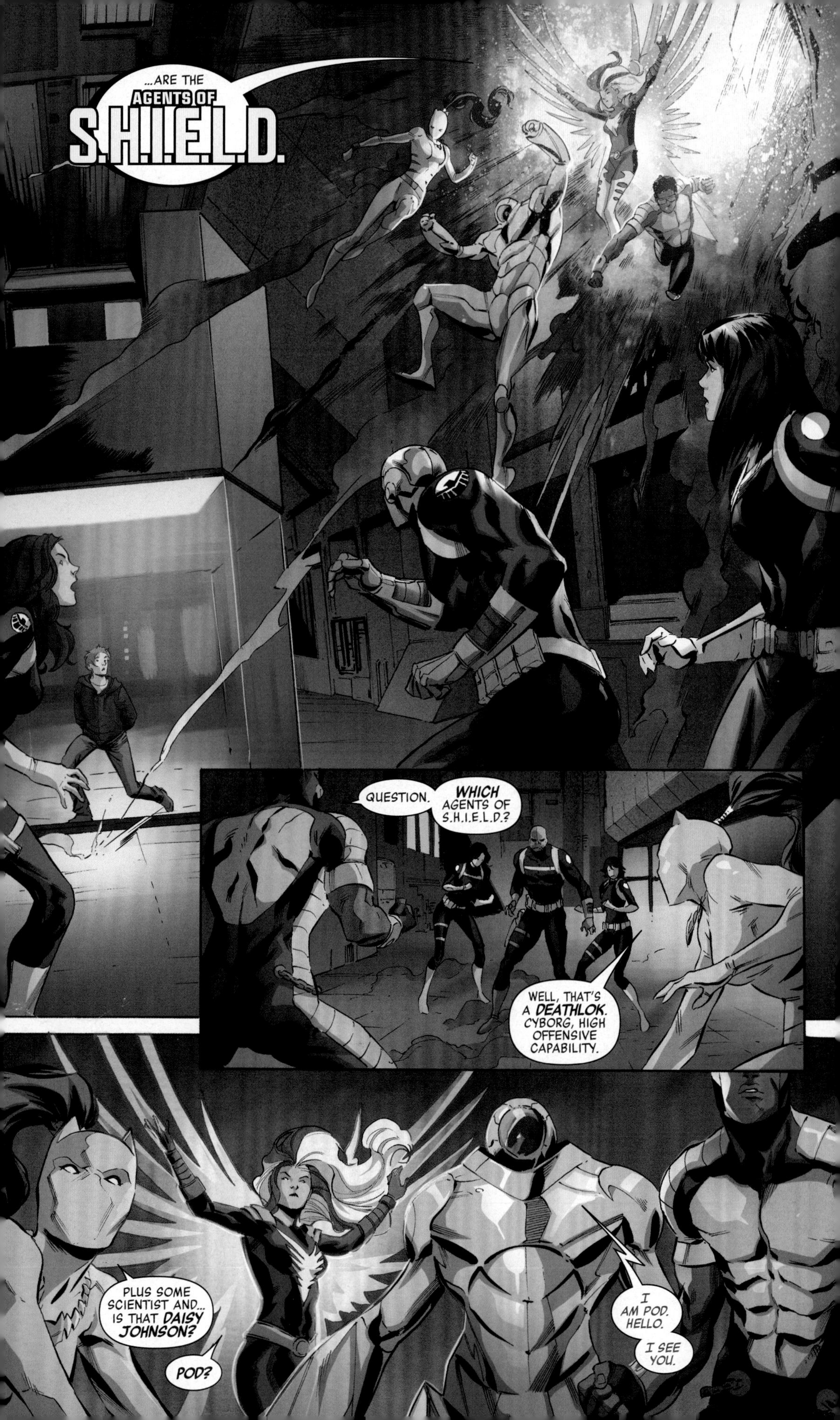
...ARE THE AGENTS OF S.H.I.E.L.D.
QUESTION.
WHICH AGENTS OF S.H.I.E.L.D.?
WELL, THAT'S A DEATHLOK. CYBORG, HIGH OFFENSIVE CAPABILITY.
PLUS SOME SCIENTIST AND... IS THAT DAISY JOHNSON?
POD?
I AM POD. HELLO.
I SEE YOU.

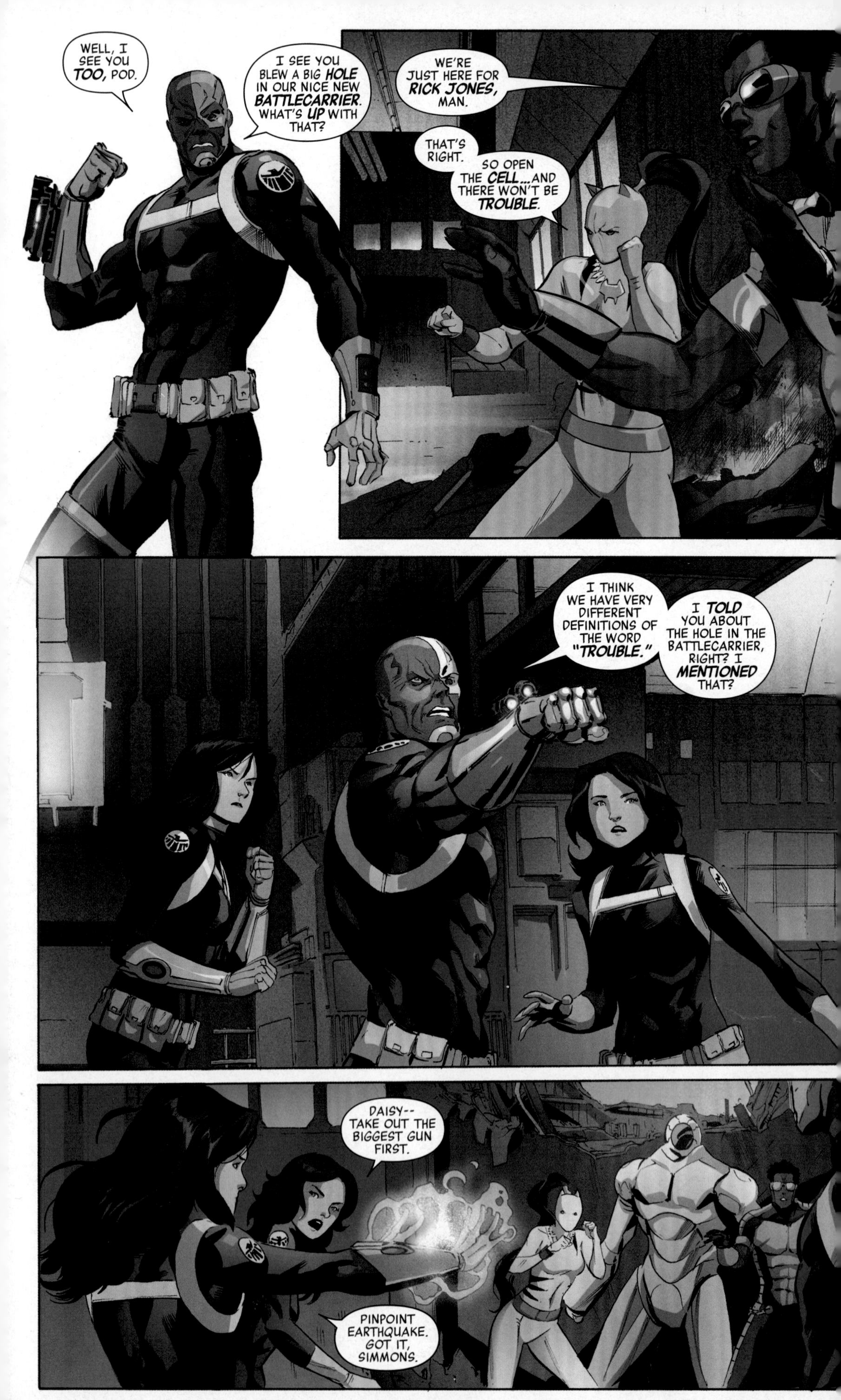
WELL, I SEE YOU TOO, POD.
I SEE YOU BLEW A BIG HOLE IN OUR NICE NEW BATTLECARRIER. WHAT'S UP WITH THAT?
WE'RE JUST HERE FOR RICK JONES, MAN.
THAT'S RIGHT.
SO OPEN THE CELL...AND THERE WON'T BE TROUBLE.
I THINK WE HAVE VERY DIFFERENT DEFINITIONS OF THE WORD "TROUBLE."
I TOLD YOU ABOUT THE HOLE IN THE BATTLECARRIER, RIGHT? I MENTIONED THAT?
DAISY--TAKE OUT THE BIGGEST GUN FIRST.
PINPOINT EARTHQUAKE. GOT IT, SIMMONS.

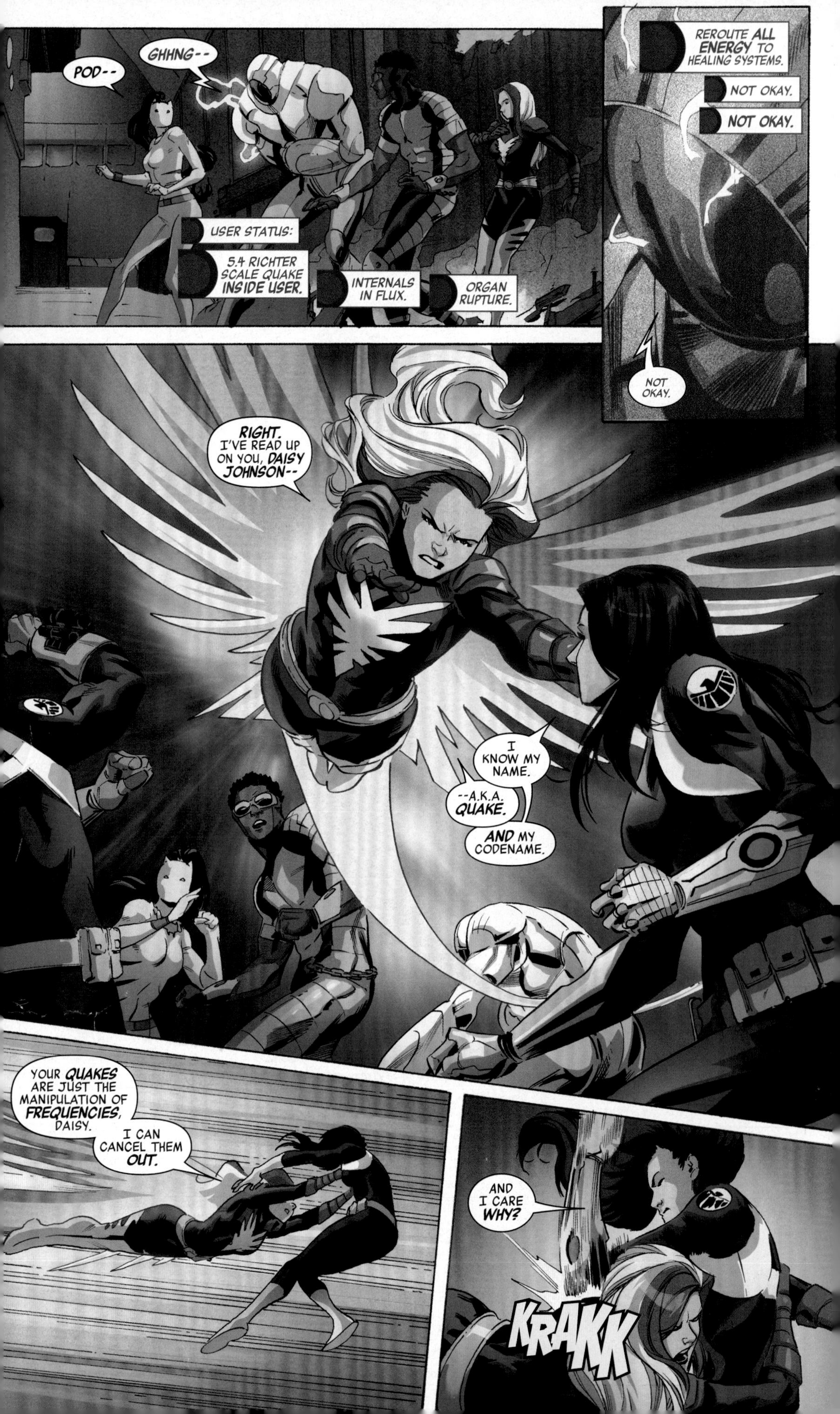

POD--
GHHNG--
USER STATUS:
5.4 RICHTER SCALE QUAKE INSIDE USER.
INTERNALS IN FLUX.
ORGAN RUPTURE.
REROUTE ALL ENERGY TO HEALING SYSTEMS.
NOT OKAY.
NOT OKAY.
NOT OKAY.
RIGHT. I'VE READ UP ON YOU, DAISY JOHNSON--
--A.K.A. QUAKE.
I KNOW MY NAME.
AND MY CODENAME.
YOUR QUAKES ARE JUST THE MANIPULATION OF FREQUENCIES, DAISY.
I CAN CANCEL THEM OUT.
AND I CARE WHY?
KRAKK

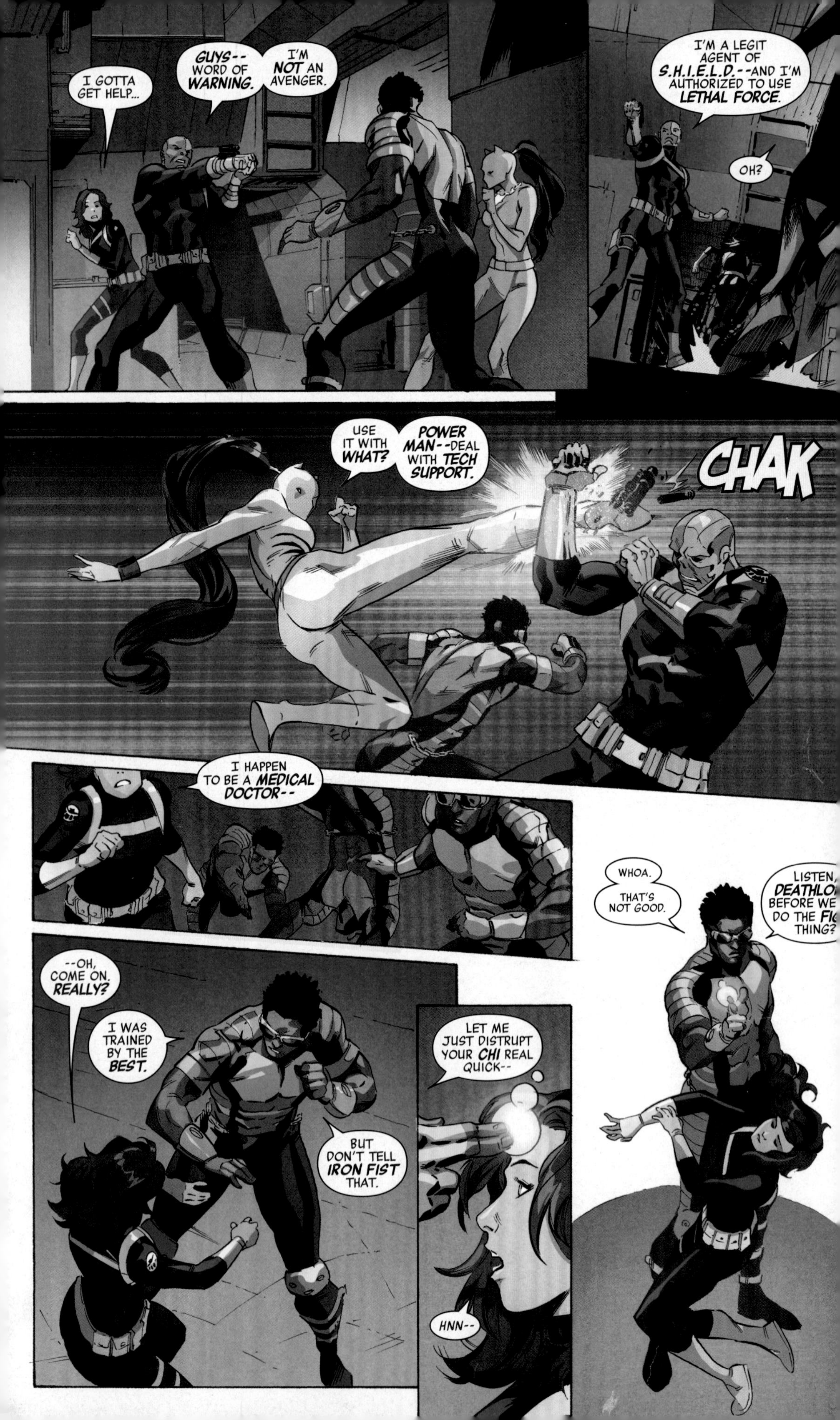

I GOTTA GET HELP...
GUYS--WORD OF WARNING.
I'M NOT AN AVENGER.
I'M A LEGIT AGENT OF S.H.I.E.L.D.--AND I'M AUTHORIZED TO USE LETHAL FORCE.
OH?
USE IT WITH WHAT?
POWER MAN--DEAL WITH TECH SUPPORT.
CHAK
I HAPPEN TO BE A MEDICAL DOCTOR--
--OH, COME ON. REALLY?
I WAS TRAINED BY THE BEST.
BUT DON'T TELL IRON FIST THAT.
LET ME JUST DISTRUPT YOUR CHI REAL QUICK--
HNN--
WHOA.
THAT'S NOT GOOD.

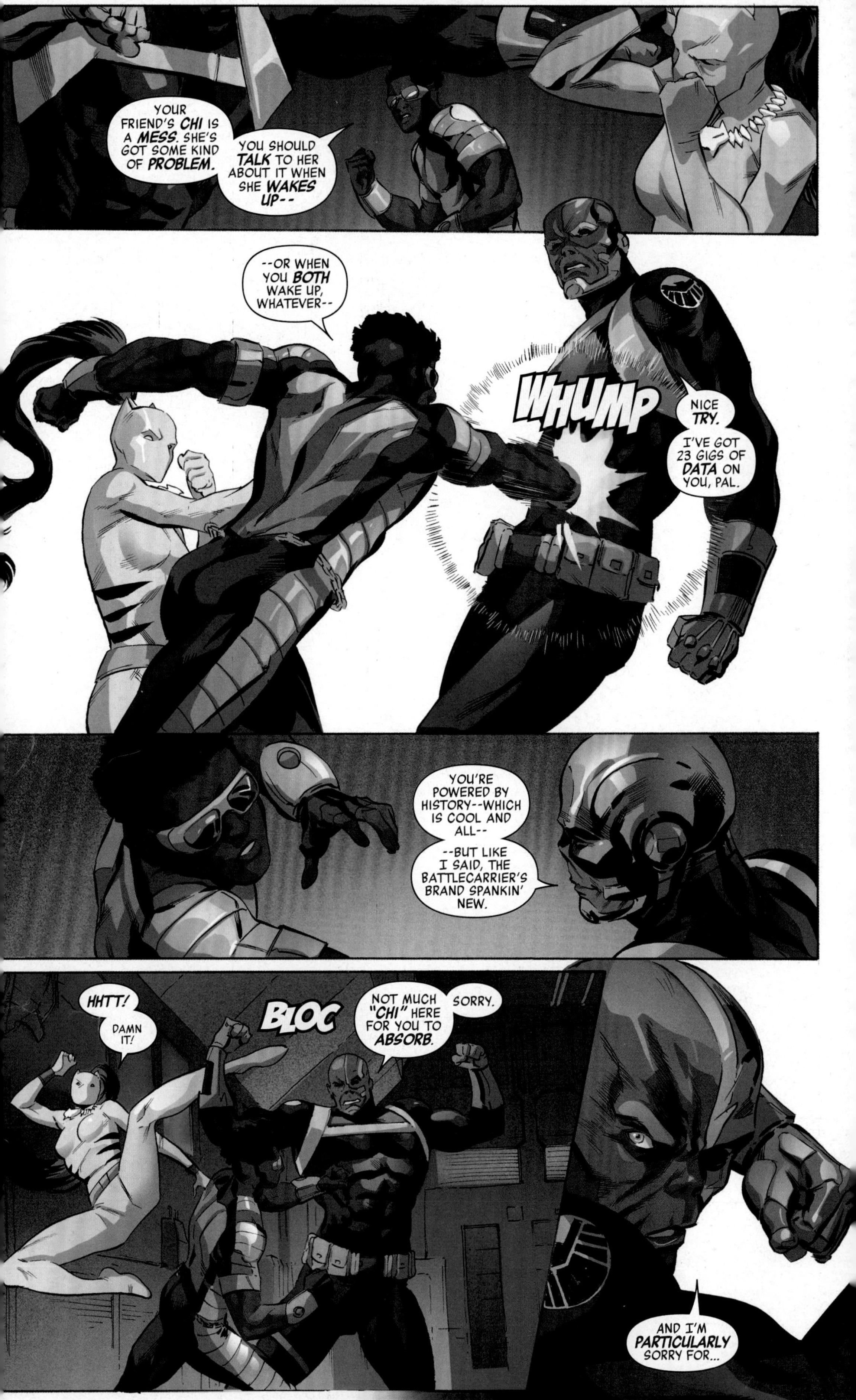
YOUR FRIEND'S CHI IS A MESS. SHE'S GOT SOME KIND OF PROBLEM.
YOU SHOULD TALK TO HER ABOUT IT WHEN SHE WAKES UP--
--OR WHEN YOU BOTH WAKE UP, WHATEVER--
WHUMP
NICE TRY.
I'VE GOT 23 GIGS OF DATA ON YOU, PAL.
YOU'RE POWERED BY HISTORY--WHICH IS COOL AND ALL--
--BUT LIKE I SAID, THE BATTLECARRIER'S BRAND SPANKIN' NEW.
HHTT!
DAMN IT!
BLOC
NOT MUCH "CHI" HERE FOR YOU TO ABSORB.
SORRY.
AND I'M PARTICULARLY SORRY FOR...

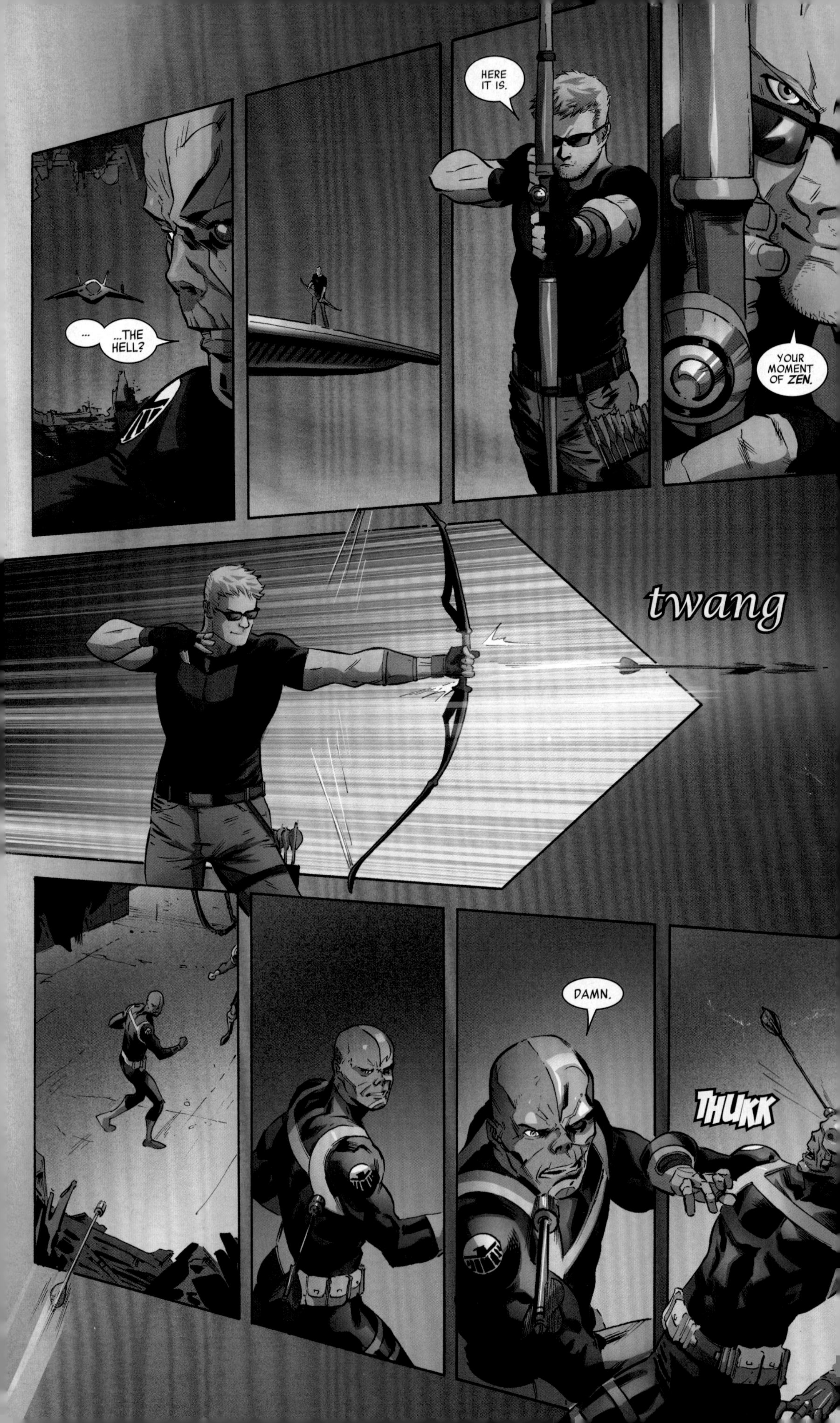
... ...THE HELL?
HERE IT IS.
YOUR MOMENT OF ZEN.
twang
DAMN.
THUKK

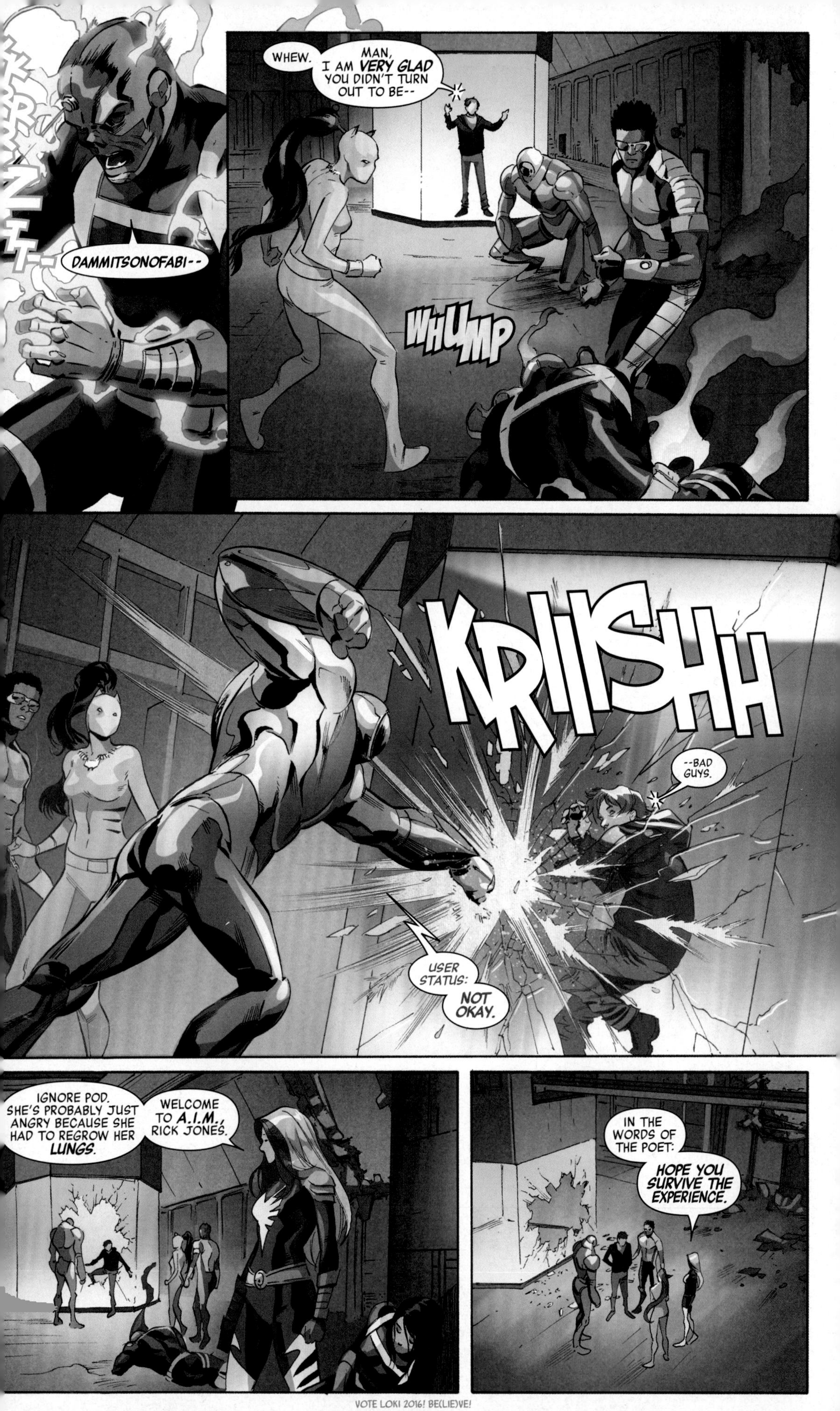

ZZRRZZZTT--
DAMMITSONOFABI--
WHEW.
MAN, I AM VERY GLAD YOU DIDN'T TURN OUT TO BE--
WHUMP
KRIIISHH
--BAD GUYS.
USER STATUS: NOT OKAY.
IGNORE POD. SHE'S PROBABLY JUST ANGRY BECAUSE SHE HAD TO REGROW HER LUNGS.
WELCOME TO A.I.M., RICK JONES.
IN THE WORDS OF THE POET:
HOPE YOU SURVIVE THE EXPERIENCE.

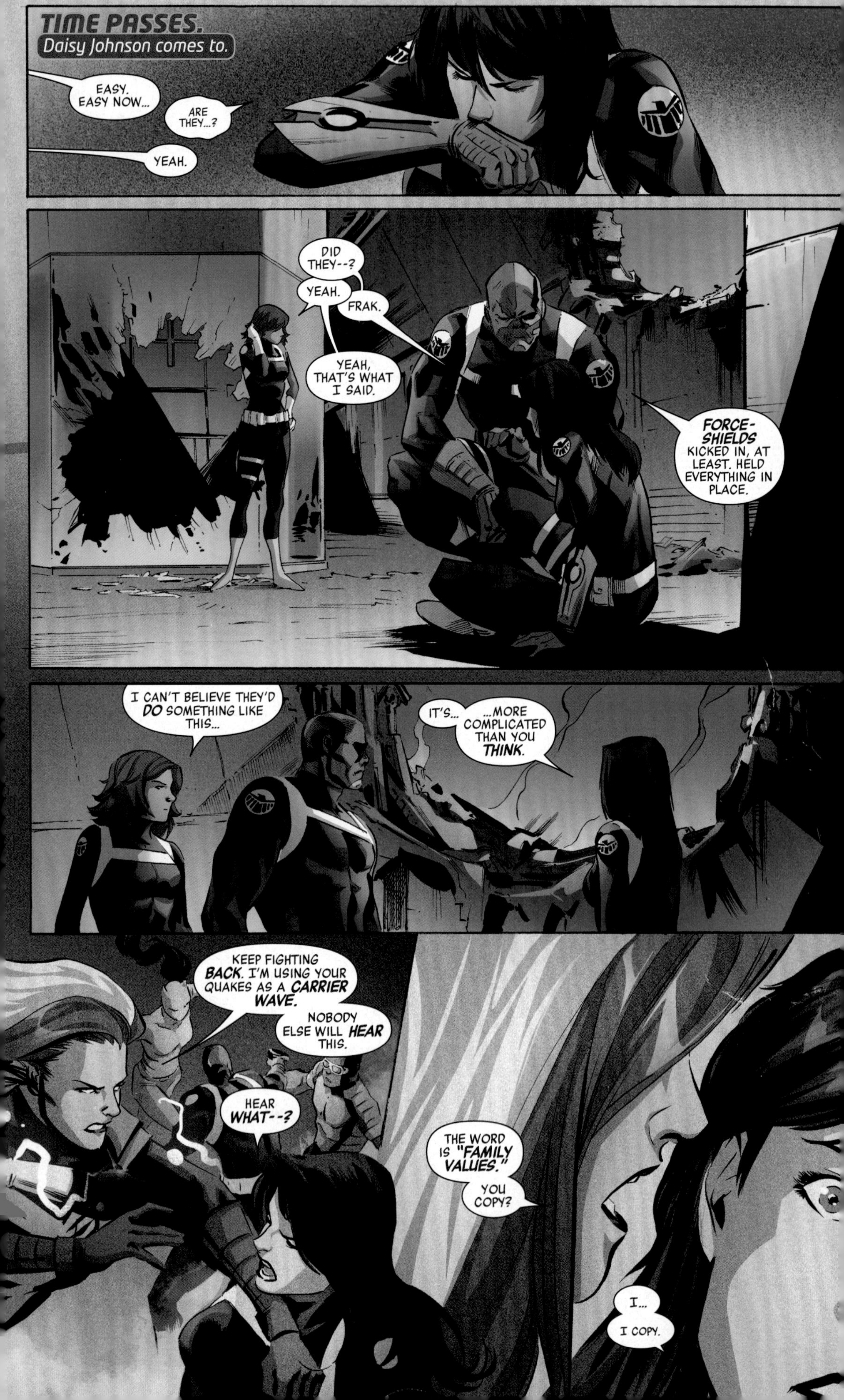
TIME PASSES.
Daisy Johnson comes to.
EASY. EASY NOW...
ARE THEY...?
YEAH.
DID THEY--?
YEAH.
FRAK.
YEAH, THAT'S WHAT I SAID.
FORCE-SHIELDS KICKED IN, AT LEAST. HELD EVERYTHING IN PLACE.
I CAN'T BELIEVE THEY'D DO SOMETHING LIKE THIS...
IT'S...
...MORE COMPLICATED THAN YOU THINK.
KEEP FIGHTING BACK. I'M USING YOUR QUAKES AS A CARRIER WAVE.
NOBODY ELSE WILL HEAR THIS.
HEAR WHAT--?
THE WORD IS "FAMILY VALUES."
YOU COPY?
I...
I COPY.

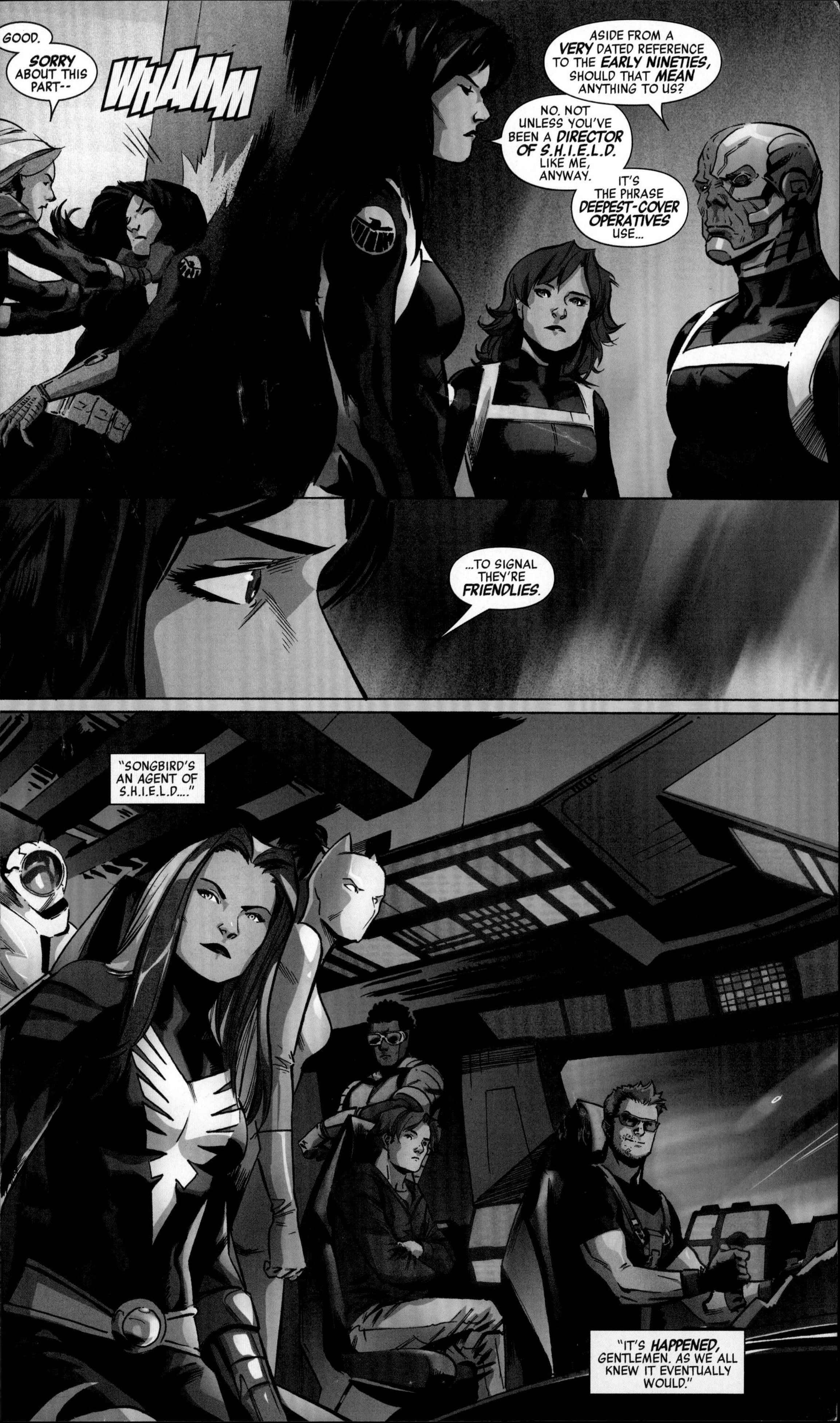
GOOD. SORRY ABOUT THIS PART--
WHAMM
ASIDE FROM A VERY DATED REFERENCE TO THE EARLY NINETIES, SHOULD THAT MEAN ANYTHING TO US?
NO. NOT UNLESS YOU'VE BEEN A DIRECTOR OF S.H.I.E.L.D. LIKE ME, ANYWAY.
IT'S THE PHRASE DEEPEST-COVER OPERATIVES USE...
...TO SIGNAL THEY'RE FRIENDLIES.
"SONGBIRD'S AN AGENT OF S.H.I.E.L.D...."
"IT'S HAPPENED, GENTLEMEN. AS WE ALL KNEW IT EVENTUALLY WOULD."

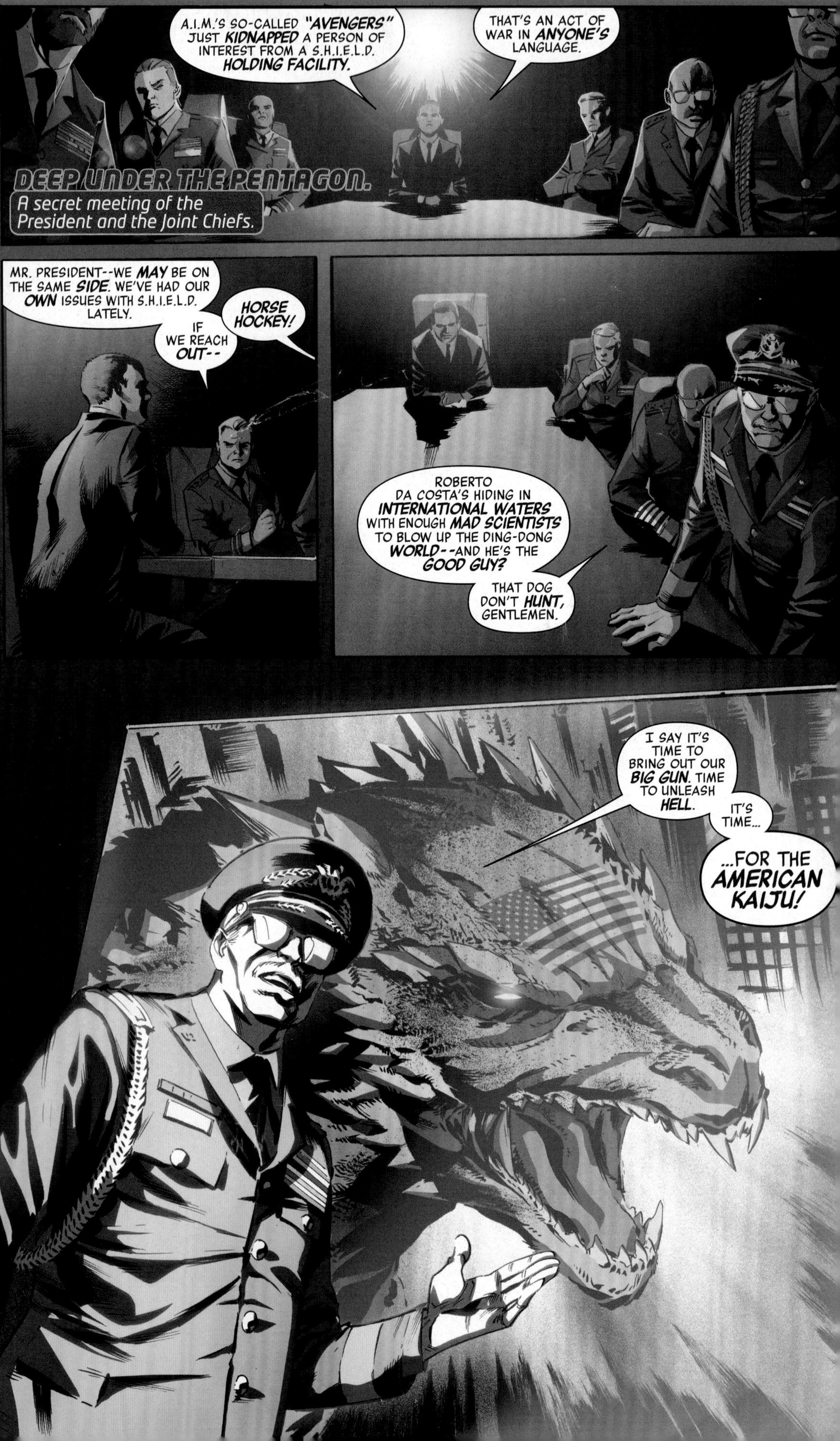
A.I.M.'S SO-CALLED "AVENGERS" JUST KIDNAPPED A PERSON OF INTEREST FROM A S.H.I.E.L.D. HOLDING FACILITY.
THAT'S AN ACT OF WAR IN ANYONE'S LANGUAGE.
DEEP UNDER THE PENTAGON.
A secret meeting of the President and the Joint Chiefs.
MR. PRESIDENT--WE MAY BE ON THE SAME SIDE. WE'VE HAD OUR OWN ISSUES WITH S.H.I.E.L.D. LATELY.
IF WE REACH OUT--
HORSE HOCKEY!
ROBERTO DA COSTA'S HIDING IN INTERNATIONAL WATERS WITH ENOUGH MAD SCIENTISTS TO BLOW UP THE DING-DONG WORLD--AND HE'S THE GOOD GUY?
THAT DOG DON'T HUNT, GENTLEMEN.
I SAY IT'S TIME TO BRING OUT OUR BIG GUN. TIME TO UNLEASH HELL.
IT'S TIME...
...FOR THE AMERICAN KAIJU!

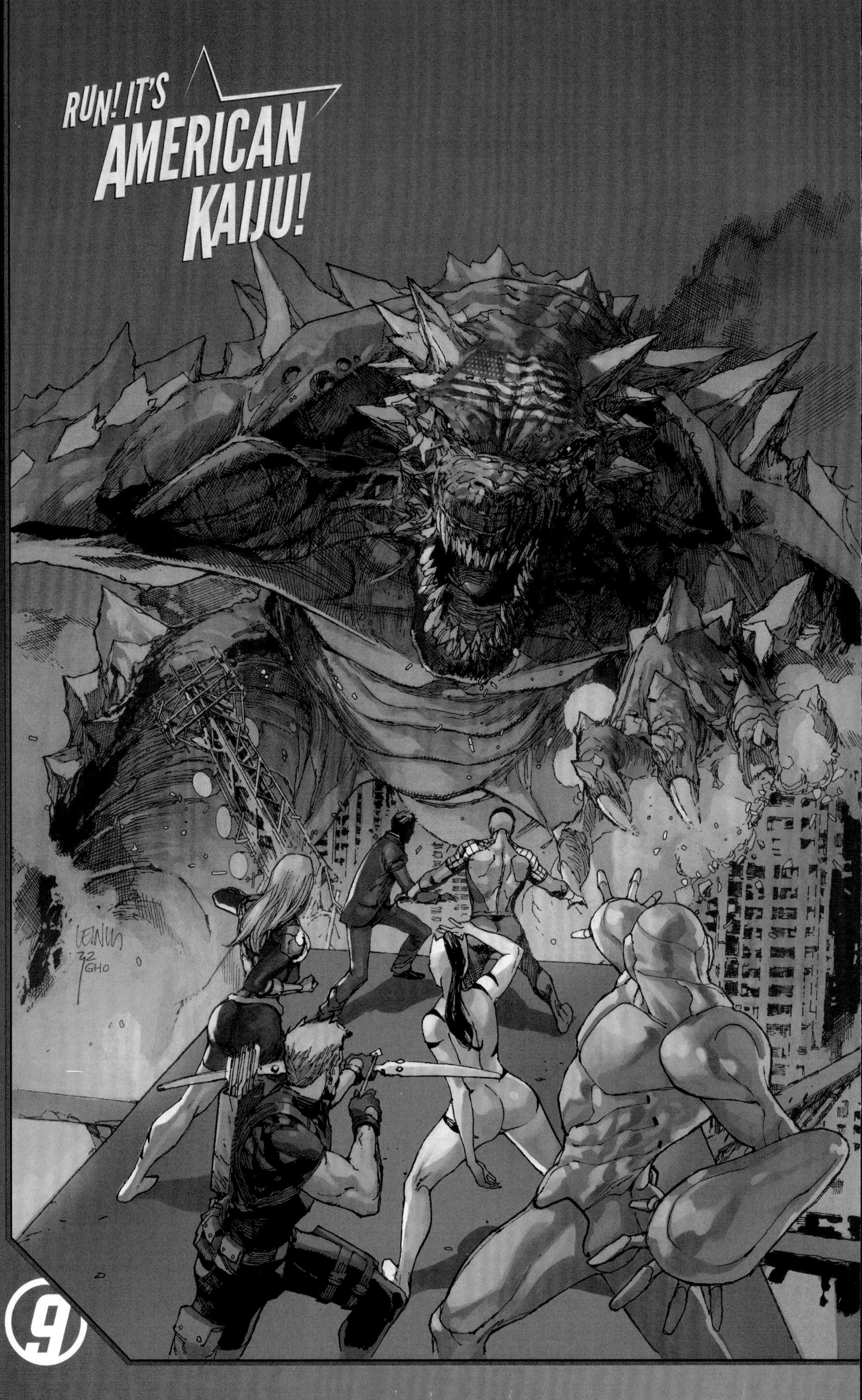
RUN! IT'S
AMERICAN
KAIJU!
9

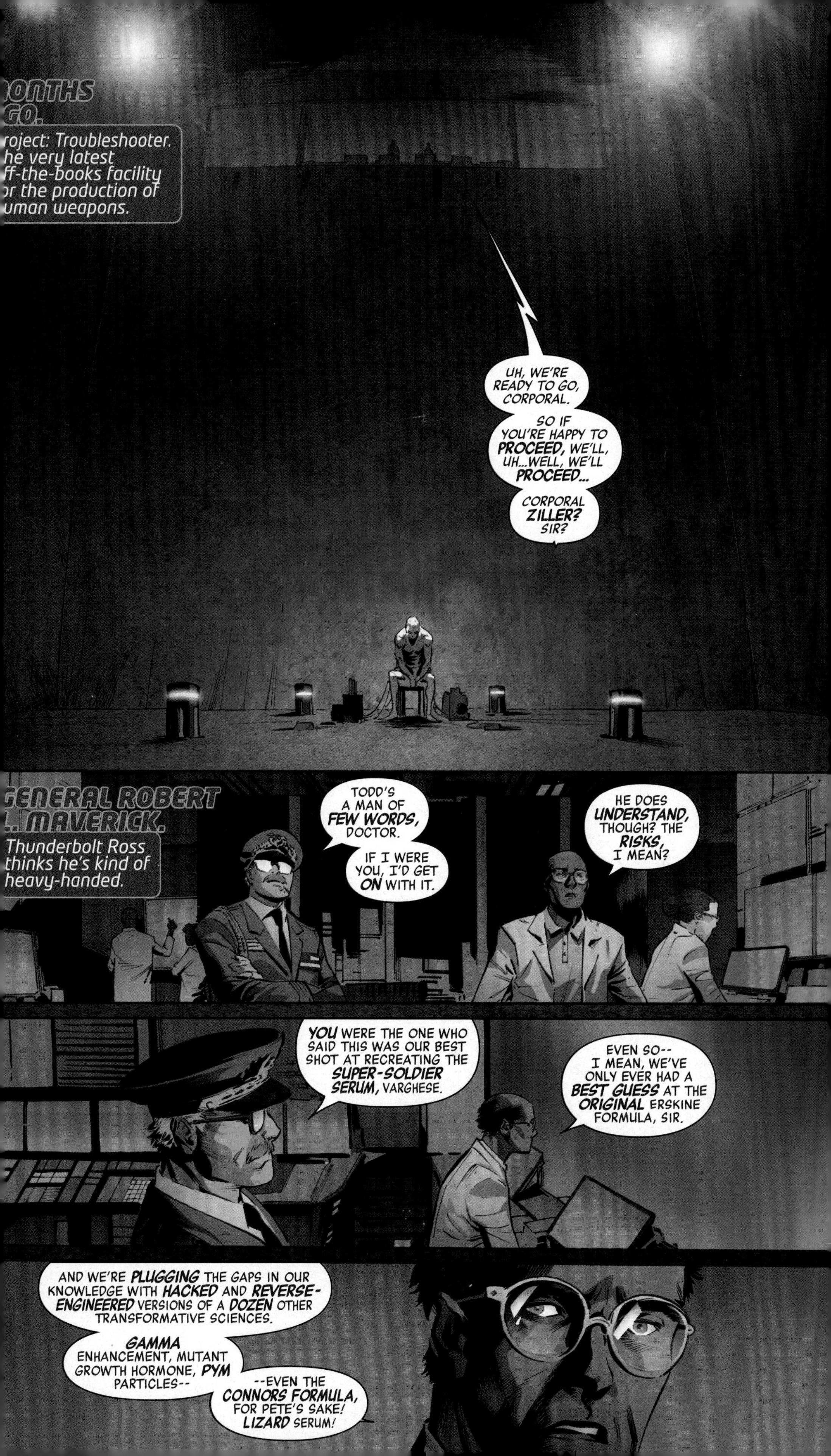

ONTHS
GO.
roject: Troubleshooter. he very latest ff-the-books facility or the production of uman weapons.
UH, WE'RE READY TO GO, CORPORAL.
SO IF YOU'RE HAPPY TO PROCEED, WE'LL, UH...WELL, WE'LL PROCEED...
CORPORAL ZILLER? SIR?
GENERAL ROBERT L. MAVERICK.
Thunderbolt Ross thinks he's kind of heavy-handed.
TODD'S A MAN OF FEW WORDS, DOCTOR.
IF I WERE YOU, I'D GET ON WITH IT.
HE DOES UNDERSTAND, THOUGH? THE RISKS, I MEAN?
YOU WERE THE ONE WHO SAID THIS WAS OUR BEST SHOT AT RECREATING THE SUPER-SOLDIER SERUM, VARGHESE.
EVEN SO-- I MEAN, WE'VE ONLY EVER HAD A BEST GUESS AT THE ORIGINAL ERSKINE FORMULA, SIR.
AND WE'RE PLUGGING THE GAPS IN OUR KNOWLEDGE WITH HACKED AND REVERSE-ENGINEERED VERSIONS OF A DOZEN OTHER TRANSFORMATIVE SCIENCES.
GAMMA ENHANCEMENT, MUTANT GROWTH HORMONE, PYM PARTICLES--
--EVEN THE CONNORS FORMULA, FOR PETE'S SAKE! LIZARD SERUM!

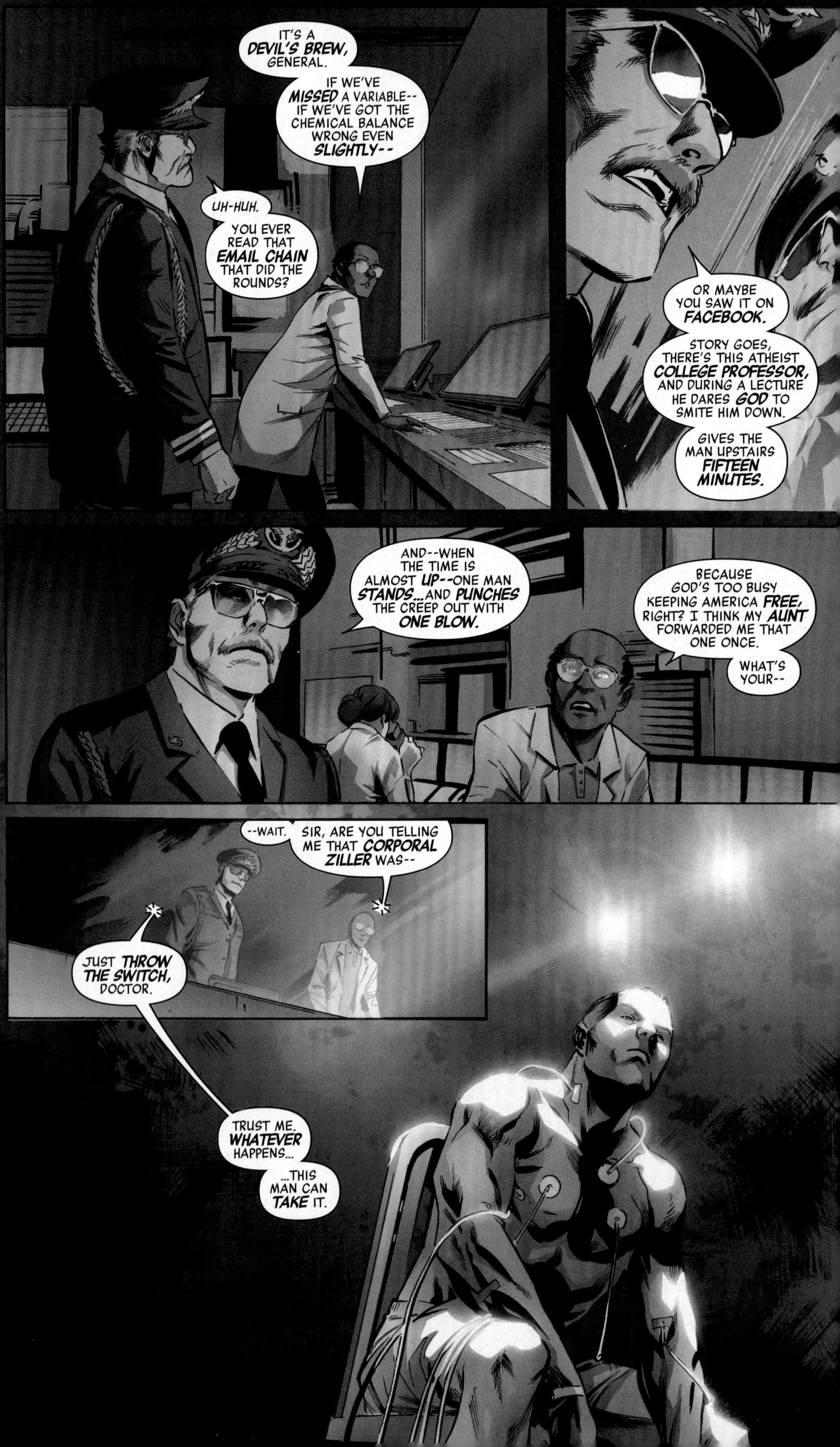
IT'S A DEVIL'S BREW, GENERAL.
IF WE'VE MISSED A VARIABLE-- IF WE'VE GOT THE CHEMICAL BALANCE WRONG EVEN SLIGHTLY--
UH-HUH.
YOU EVER READ THAT EMAIL CHAIN THAT DID THE ROUNDS?
OR MAYBE YOU SAW IT ON FACEBOOK.
STORY GOES, THERE'S THIS ATHEIST COLLEGE PROFESSOR, AND DURING A LECTURE HE DARES GOD TO SMITE HIM DOWN.
GIVES THE MAN UPSTAIRS FIFTEEN MINUTES.
AND--WHEN THE TIME IS ALMOST UP--ONE MAN STANDS...AND PUNCHES THE CREEP OUT WITH ONE BLOW.
BECAUSE GOD'S TOO BUSY KEEPING AMERICA FREE, RIGHT? I THINK MY AUNT FORWARDED ME THAT ONE ONCE.
WHAT'S YOUR--
--WAIT.
SIR, ARE YOU TELLING ME THAT CORPORAL ZILLER WAS--
JUST THROW THE SWITCH, DOCTOR.
TRUST ME. WHATEVER HAPPENS...
...THIS MAN CAN TAKE IT.

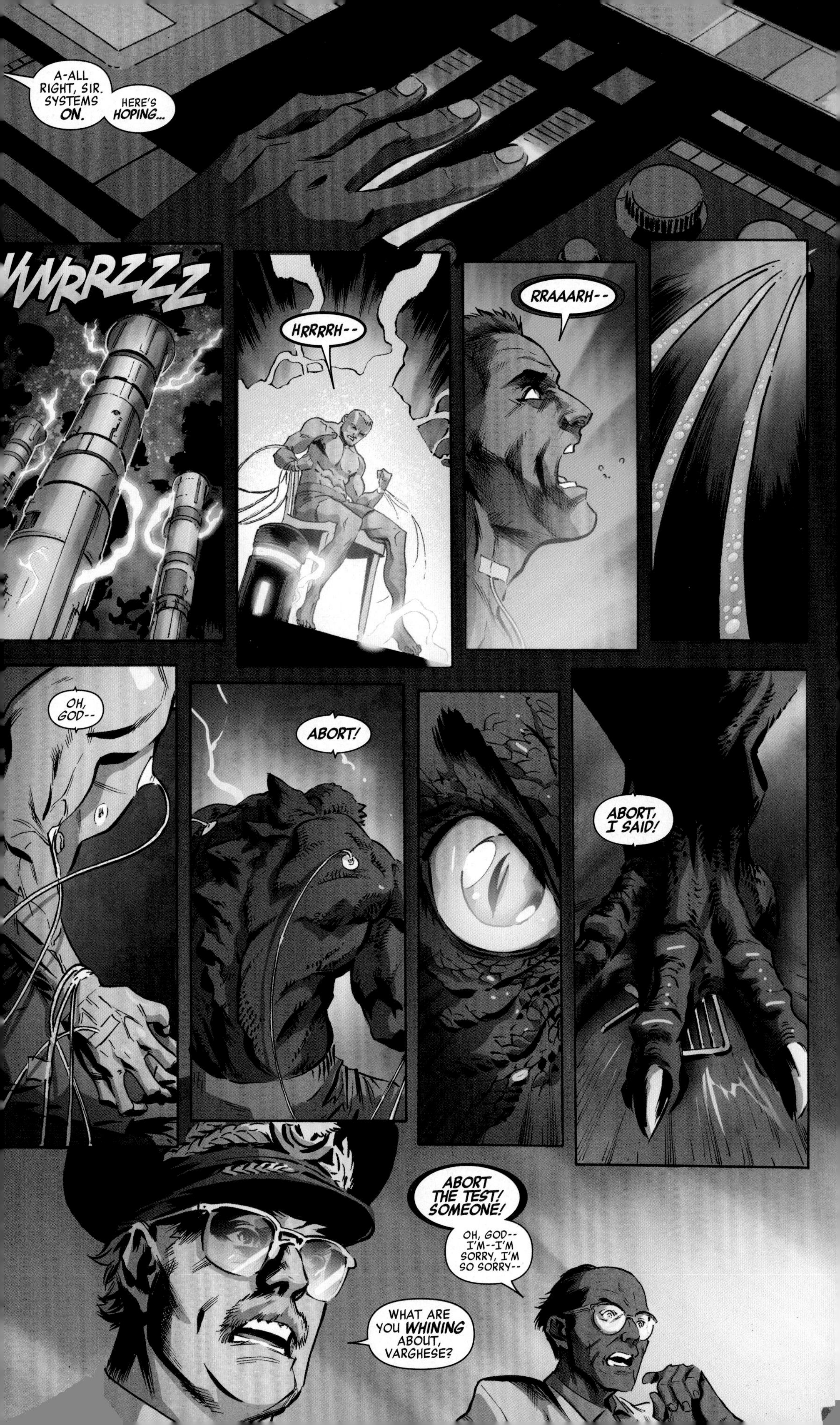
A-ALL RIGHT, SIR. SYSTEMS ON.
HERE'S HOPING...
WWRRZZZZ
HRRRRH--
RRAAARH--
OH, GOD--
ABORT!
ABORT, I SAID!
ABORT THE TEST! SOMEONE!
OH, GOD-- I'M--I'M SORRY, I'M SO SORRY--
WHAT ARE YOU WHINING ABOUT, VARGHESE?

UP FROM THE DEPTHS

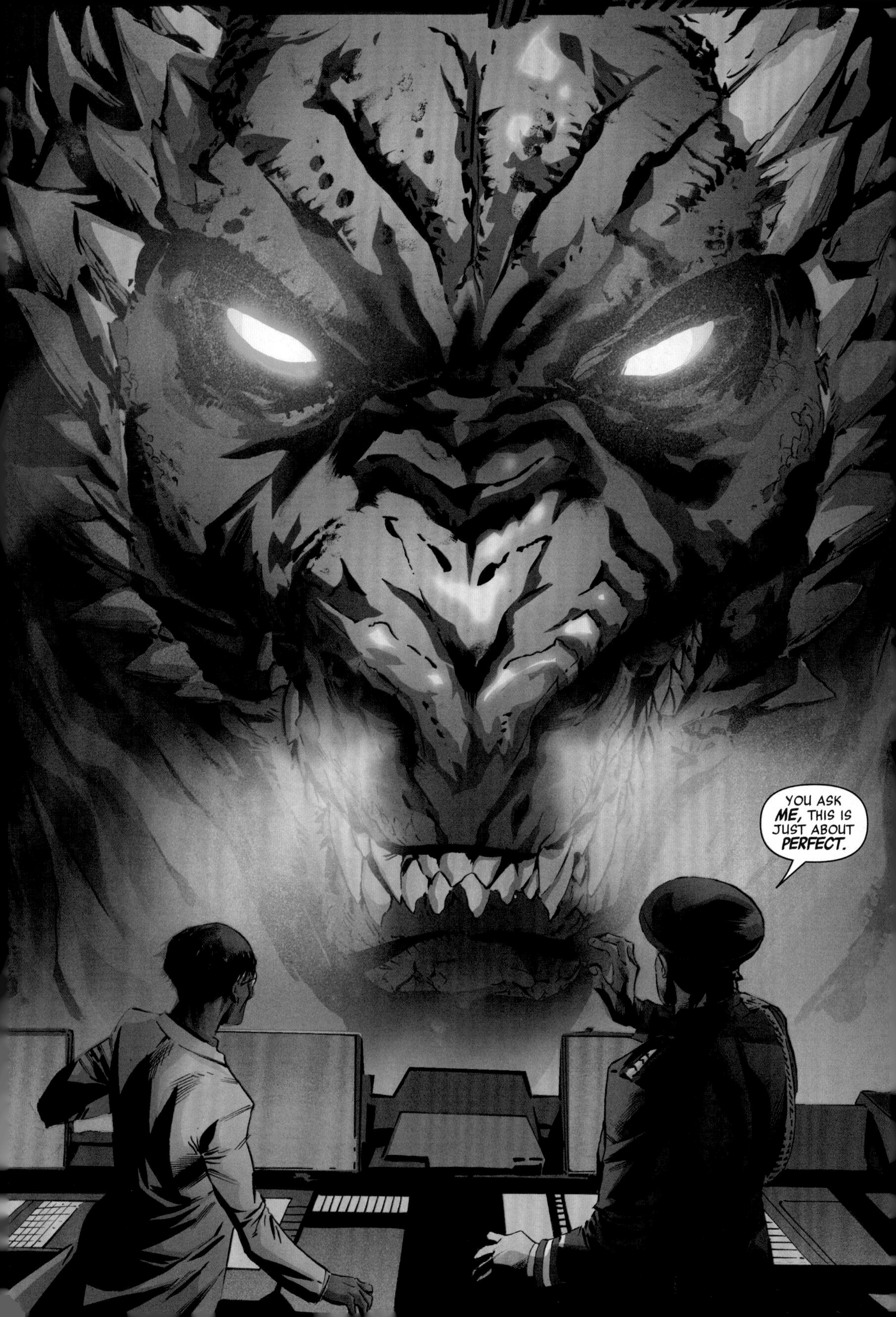
YOU ASK ME, THIS IS JUST ABOUT PERFECT.

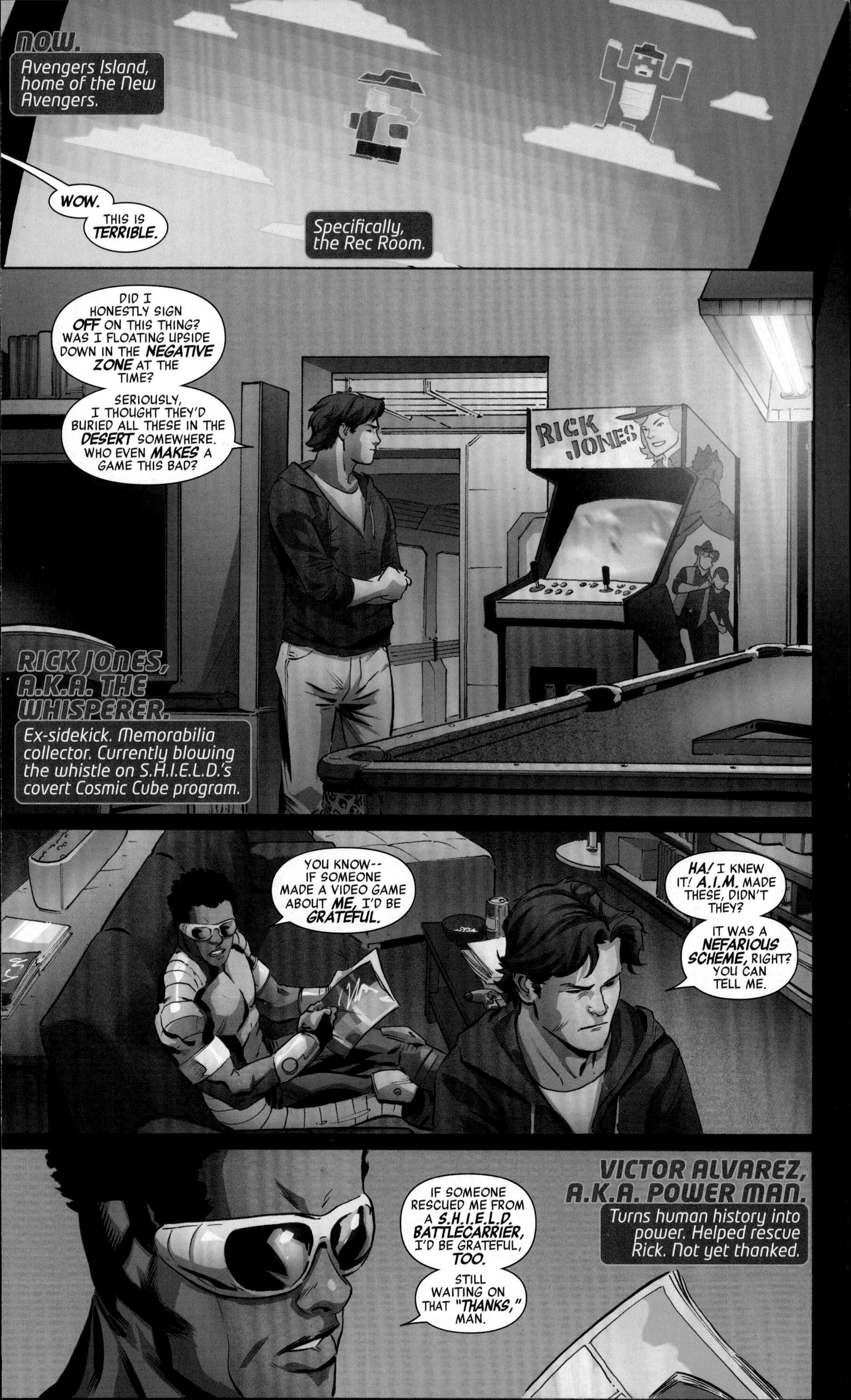
NOW.
Avengers Island, home of the New Avengers.
WOW. THIS IS TERRIBLE.
Specifically, the Rec Room.
DID I HONESTLY SIGN OFF ON THIS THING? WAS I FLOATING UPSIDE DOWN IN THE NEGATIVE ZONE AT THE TIME?
SERIOUSLY, I THOUGHT THEY'D BURIED ALL THESE IN THE DESERT SOMEWHERE. WHO EVEN MAKES A GAME THIS BAD?
RICK JONES
RICK JONES, A.K.A. THE WHISPERER.
Ex-sidekick. Memorabilia collector. Currently blowing the whistle on S.H.I.E.L.D.'s covert Cosmic Cube program.
YOU KNOW-- IF SOMEONE MADE A VIDEO GAME ABOUT ME, I'D BE GRATEFUL.
HA! I KNEW IT! A.I.M. MADE THESE, DIDN'T THEY?
IT WAS A NEFARIOUS SCHEME, RIGHT? YOU CAN TELL ME.
VICTOR ALVAREZ, A.K.A. POWER MAN.
Turns human history into power. Helped rescue Rick. Not yet thanked.
IF SOMEONE RESCUED ME FROM A S.H.I.E.L.D. BATTLECARRIER, I'D BE GRATEFUL, TOO.
STILL WAITING ON THAT "THANKS," MAN.

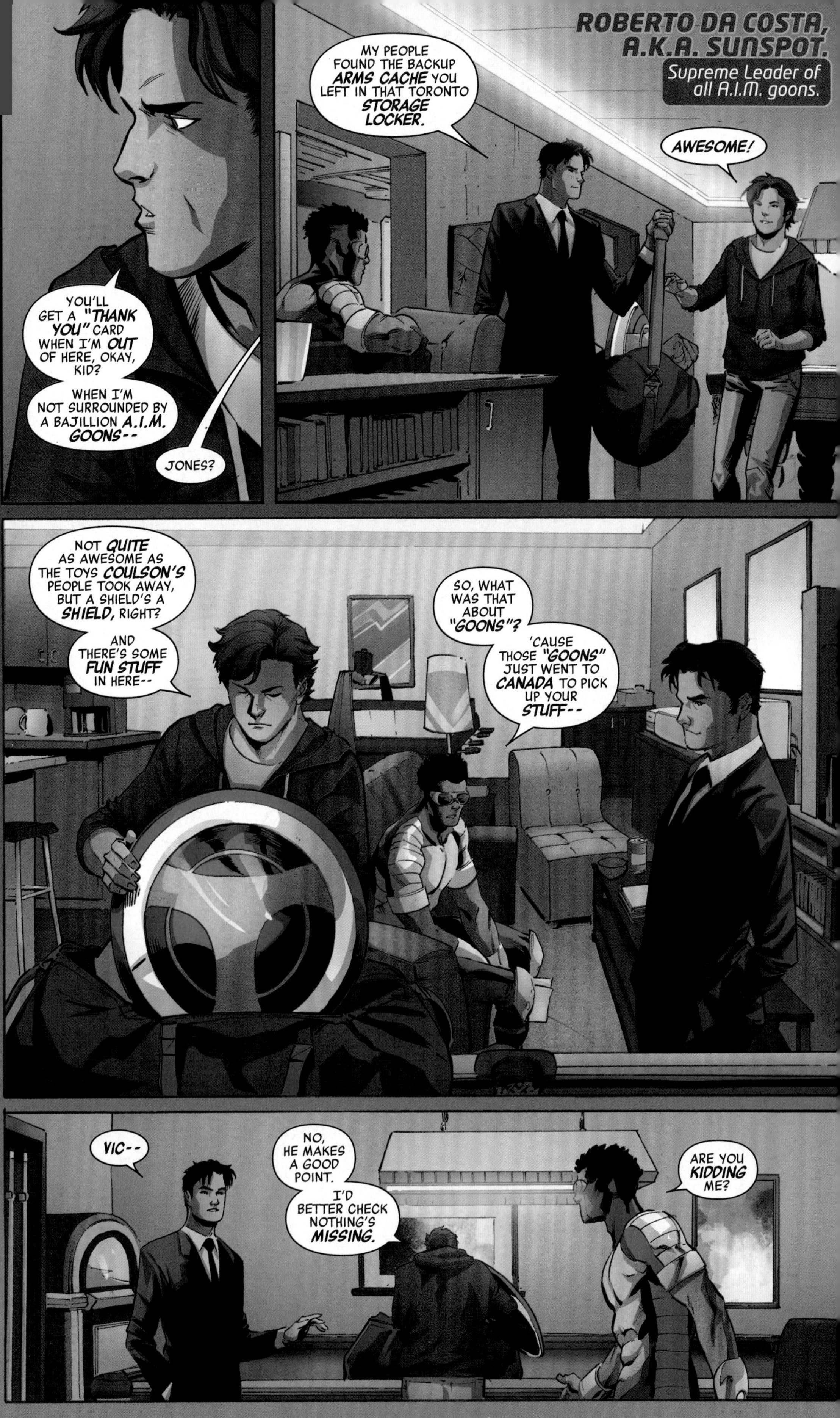
ROBERTO DA COSTA, A.K.A. SUNSPOT.
Supreme Leader of all A.I.M. goons.
MY PEOPLE FOUND THE BACKUP ARMS CACHE YOU LEFT IN THAT TORONTO STORAGE LOCKER.
AWESOME!
YOU'LL GET A "THANK YOU" CARD WHEN I'M OUT OF HERE, OKAY, KID?
WHEN I'M NOT SURROUNDED BY A BAJILLION A.I.M. GOONS--
JONES?
NOT QUITE AS AWESOME AS THE TOYS COULSON'S PEOPLE TOOK AWAY, BUT A SHIELD'S A SHIELD, RIGHT?
AND THERE'S SOME FUN STUFF IN HERE--
SO, WHAT WAS THAT ABOUT "GOONS"?
'CAUSE THOSE "GOONS" JUST WENT TO CANADA TO PICK UP YOUR STUFF--
VIC--
NO, HE MAKES A GOOD POINT.
I'D BETTER CHECK NOTHING'S MISSING.
ARE YOU KIDDING ME?

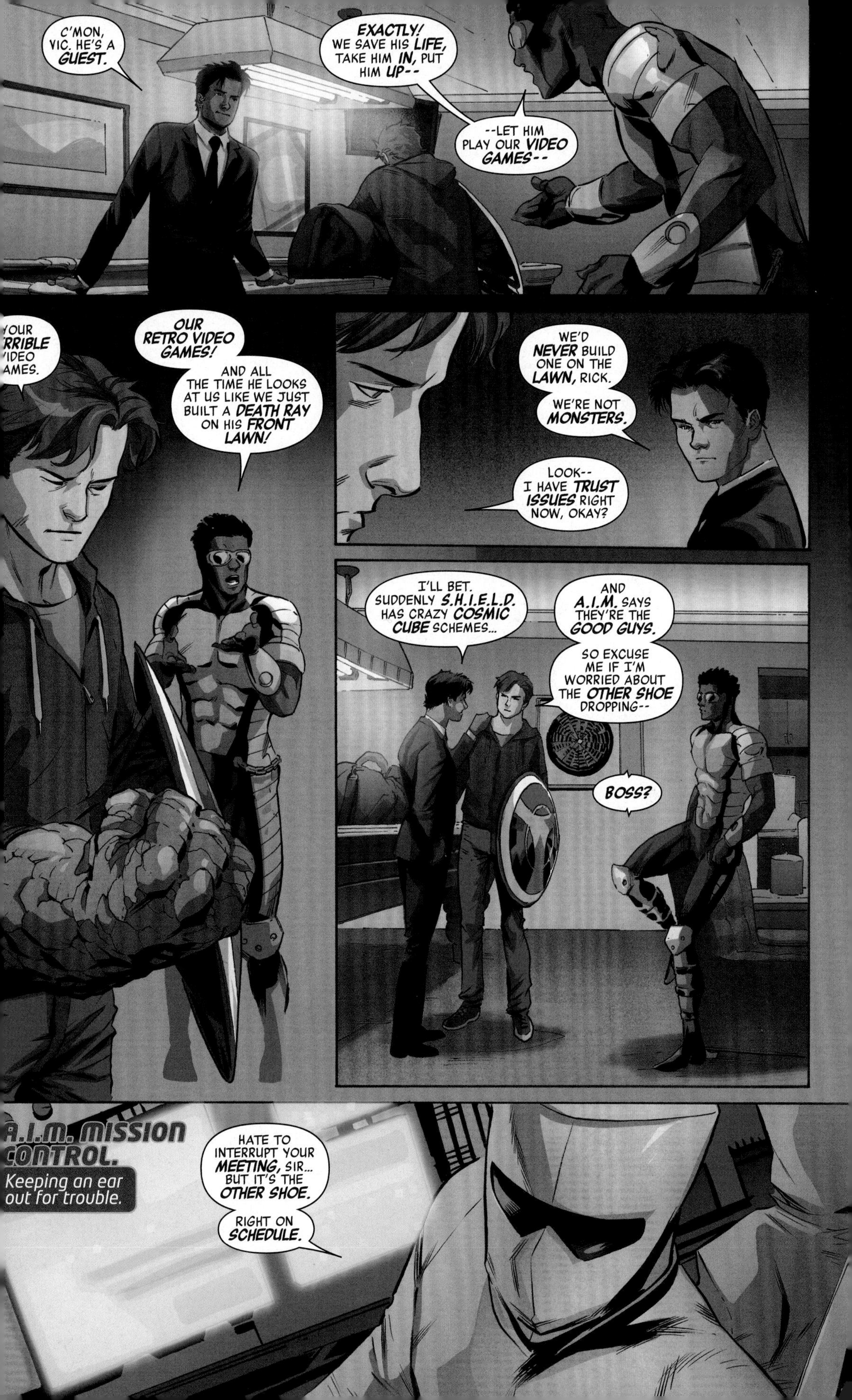
C'MON, VIC. HE'S A GUEST.
EXACTLY! WE SAVE HIS LIFE, TAKE HIM IN, PUT HIM UP--
--LET HIM PLAY OUR VIDEO GAMES--
YOUR ...RRIBLE VIDEO ...AMES.
OUR RETRO VIDEO GAMES!
AND ALL THE TIME HE LOOKS AT US LIKE WE JUST BUILT A DEATH RAY ON HIS FRONT LAWN!
WE'D NEVER BUILD ONE ON THE LAWN, RICK.
WE'RE NOT MONSTERS.
LOOK-- I HAVE TRUST ISSUES RIGHT NOW, OKAY?
I'LL BET. SUDDENLY S.H.I.E.L.D. HAS CRAZY COSMIC CUBE SCHEMES...
AND A.I.M. SAYS THEY'RE THE GOOD GUYS.
SO EXCUSE ME IF I'M WORRIED ABOUT THE OTHER SHOE DROPPING--
BOSS?
A.I.M. MISSION CONTROL.
Keeping an ear out for trouble.
HATE TO INTERRUPT YOUR MEETING, SIR... BUT IT'S THE OTHER SHOE.
RIGHT ON SCHEDULE.

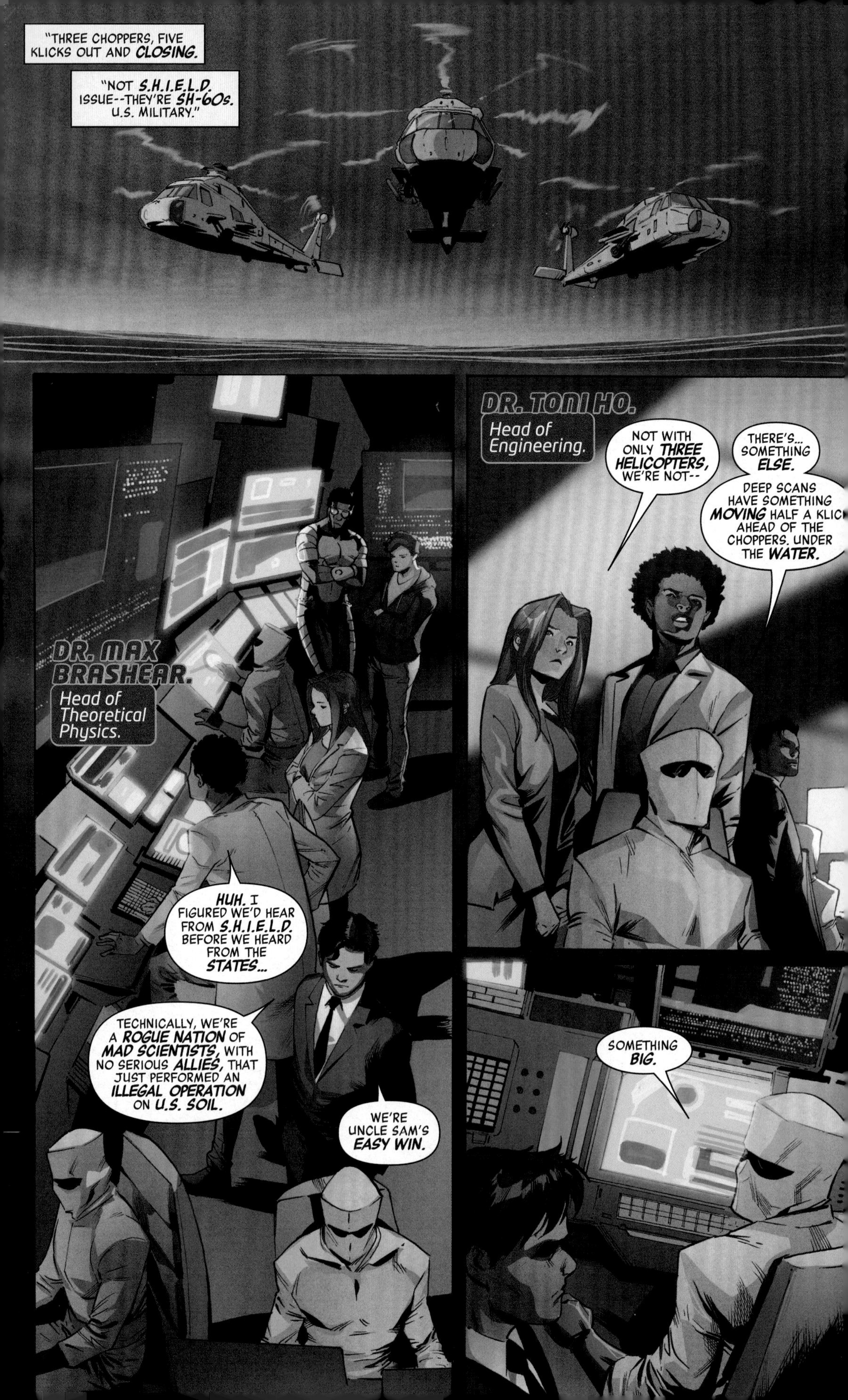
"THREE CHOPPERS, FIVE KLICKS OUT AND CLOSING.
"NOT S.H.I.E.L.D. ISSUE--THEY'RE SH-60s. U.S. MILITARY."
DR. MAX BRASHEAR.
Head of Theoretical Physics.
HUH. I FIGURED WE'D HEAR FROM S.H.I.E.L.D. BEFORE WE HEARD FROM THE STATES...
TECHNICALLY, WE'RE A ROGUE NATION OF MAD SCIENTISTS, WITH NO SERIOUS ALLIES, THAT JUST PERFORMED AN ILLEGAL OPERATION ON U.S. SOIL.
WE'RE UNCLE SAM'S EASY WIN.
DR. TONI HO.
Head of Engineering.
NOT WITH ONLY THREE HELICOPTERS, WE'RE NOT--
THERE'S... SOMETHING ELSE.
DEEP SCANS HAVE SOMETHING MOVING HALF A KLICK AHEAD OF THE CHOPPERS. UNDER THE WATER.
SOMETHING BIG.

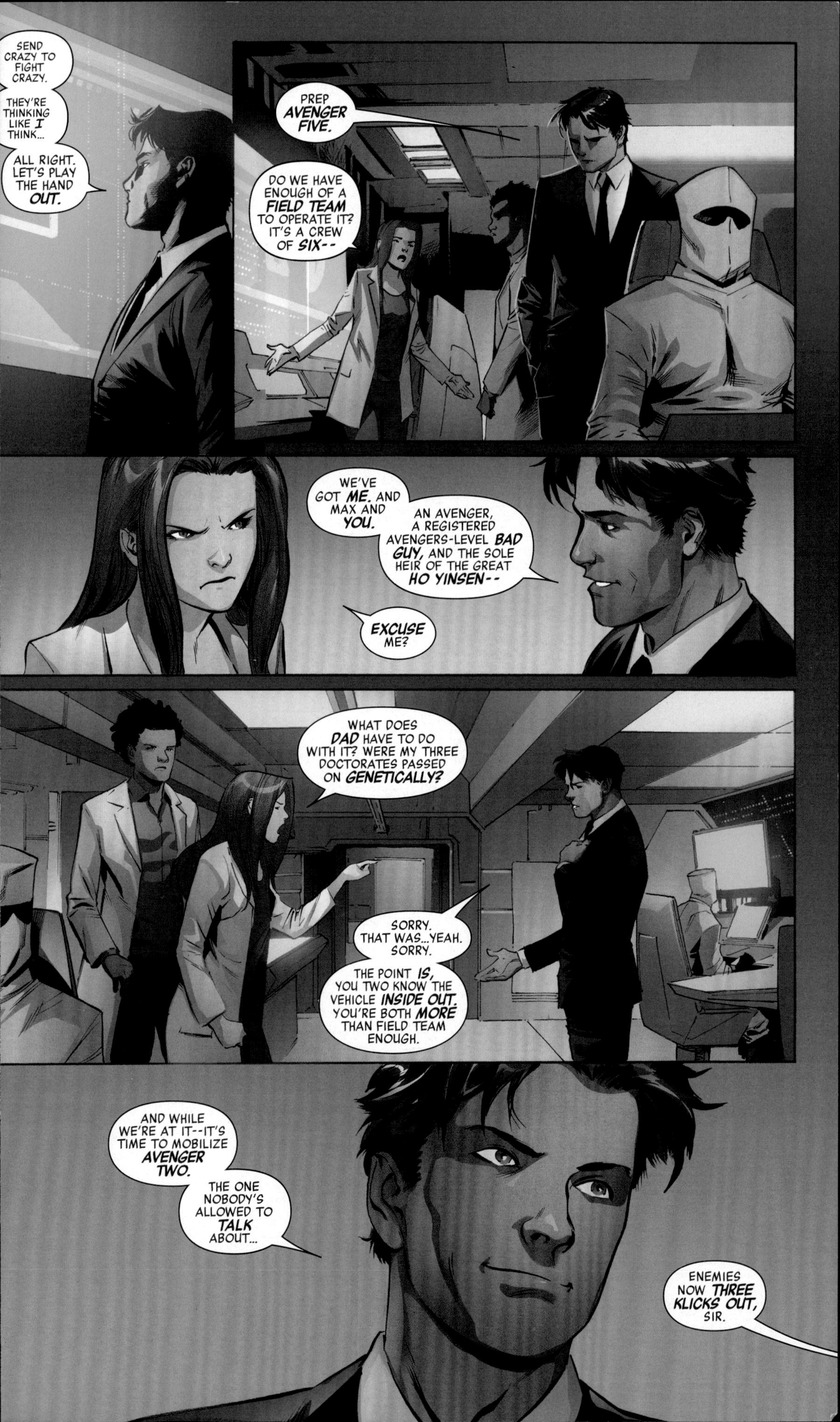
SEND CRAZY TO FIGHT CRAZY.
THEY'RE THINKING LIKE I THINK...
ALL RIGHT. LET'S PLAY THE HAND OUT.
PREP AVENGER FIVE.
DO WE HAVE ENOUGH OF A FIELD TEAM TO OPERATE IT? IT'S A CREW OF SIX--
WE'VE GOT ME. AND MAX AND YOU.
AN AVENGER, A REGISTERED AVENGERS-LEVEL BAD GUY, AND THE SOLE HEIR OF THE GREAT HO YINSEN--
EXCUSE ME?
WHAT DOES DAD HAVE TO DO WITH IT? WERE MY THREE DOCTORATES PASSED ON GENETICALLY?
SORRY. THAT WAS...YEAH. SORRY.
THE POINT IS, YOU TWO KNOW THE VEHICLE INSIDE OUT. YOU'RE BOTH MORE THAN FIELD TEAM ENOUGH.
AND WHILE WE'RE AT IT--IT'S TIME TO MOBILIZE AVENGER TWO.
THE ONE NOBODY'S ALLOWED TO TALK ABOUT...
ENEMIES NOW THREE KLICKS OUT, SIR.

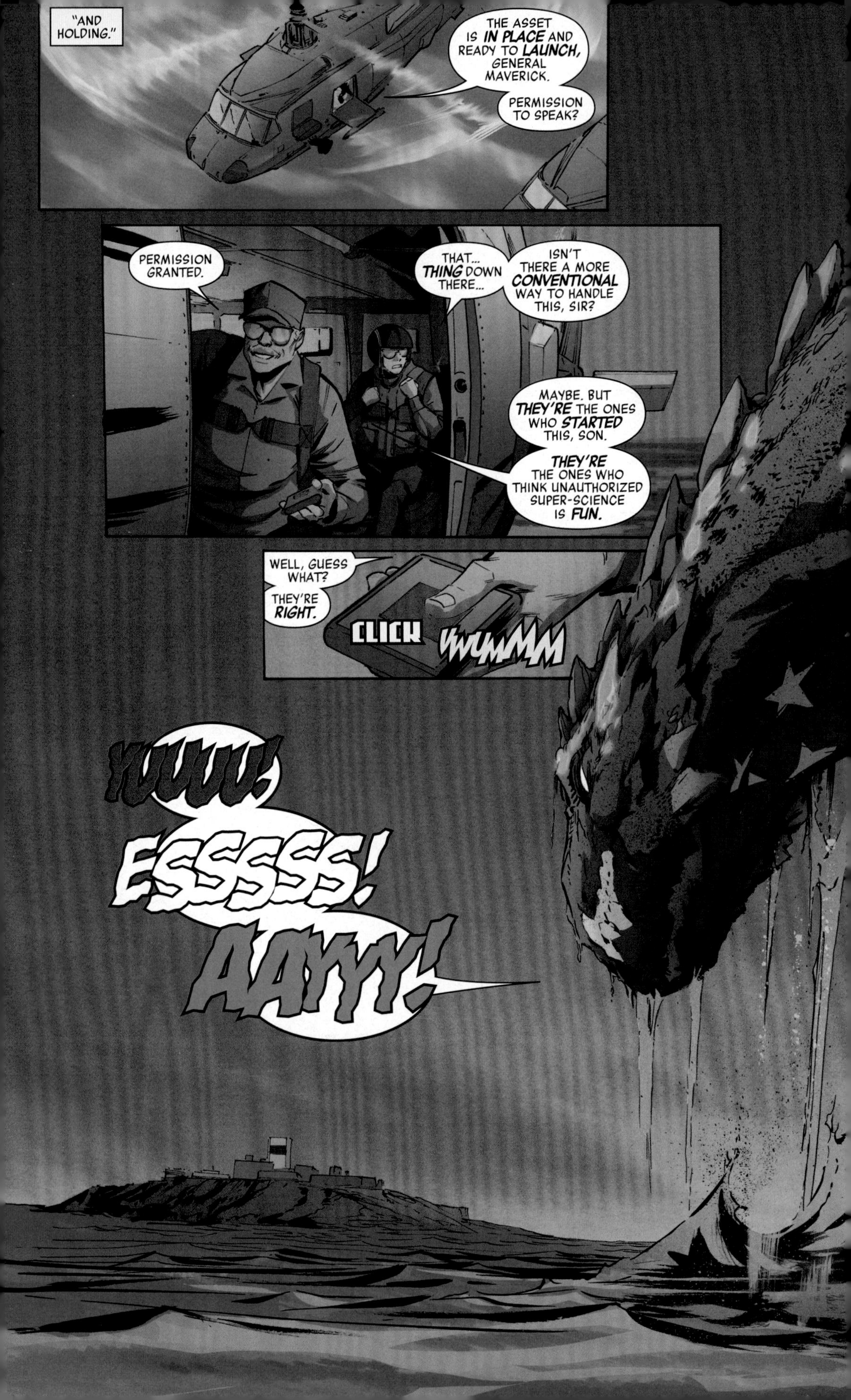
"AND HOLDING."
THE ASSET IS IN PLACE AND READY TO LAUNCH, GENERAL MAVERICK.
PERMISSION TO SPEAK?
PERMISSION GRANTED.
THAT... THING DOWN THERE...
ISN'T THERE A MORE CONVENTIONAL WAY TO HANDLE THIS, SIR?
MAYBE. BUT THEY'RE THE ONES WHO STARTED THIS, SON.
THEY'RE THE ONES WHO THINK UNAUTHORIZED SUPER-SCIENCE IS FUN.
WELL, GUESS WHAT?
THEY'RE RIGHT.
CLICK
VWUMMM
ESSSSS!
AAYYY!

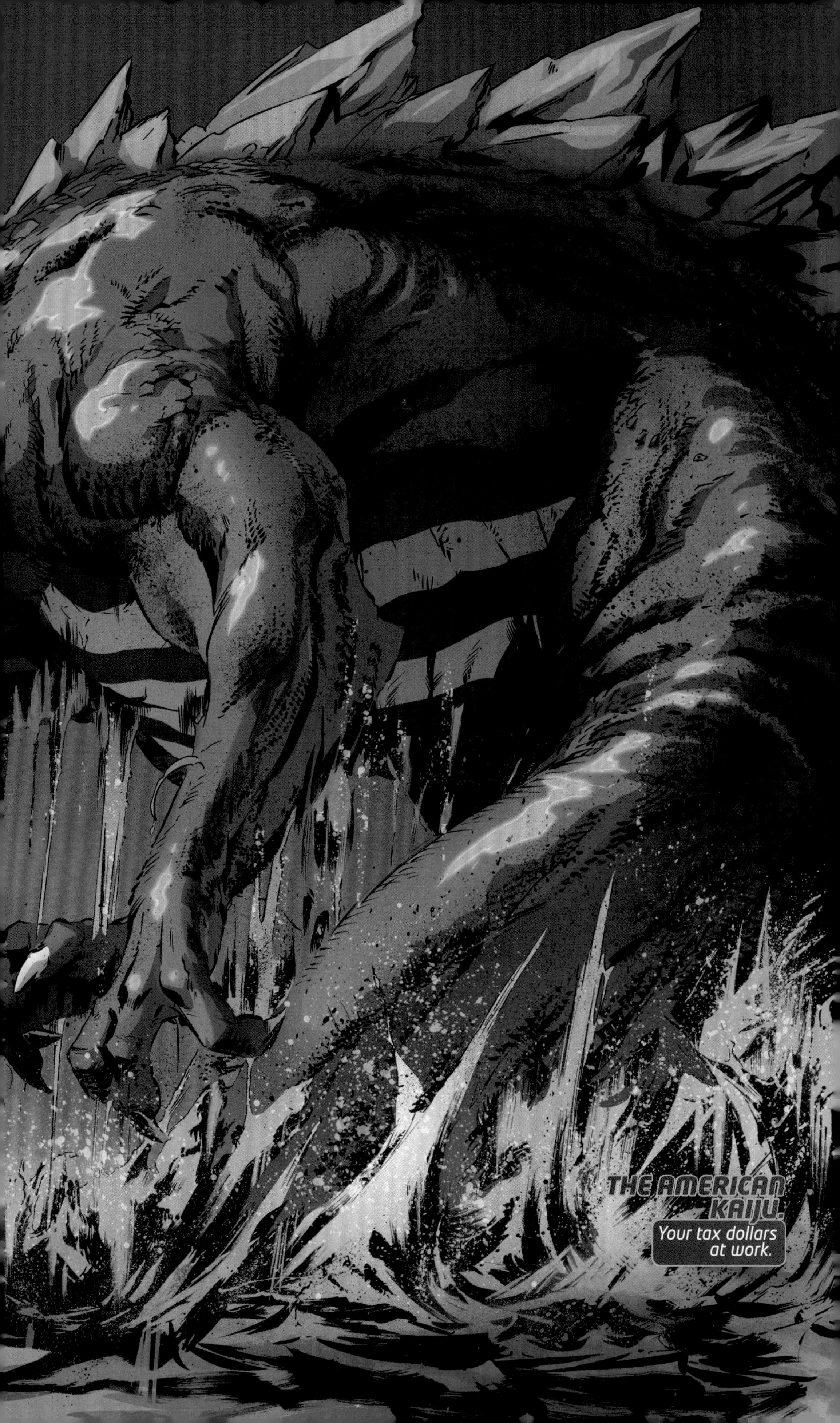
THE AMERICAN KAIJU.
Your tax dollars at work.

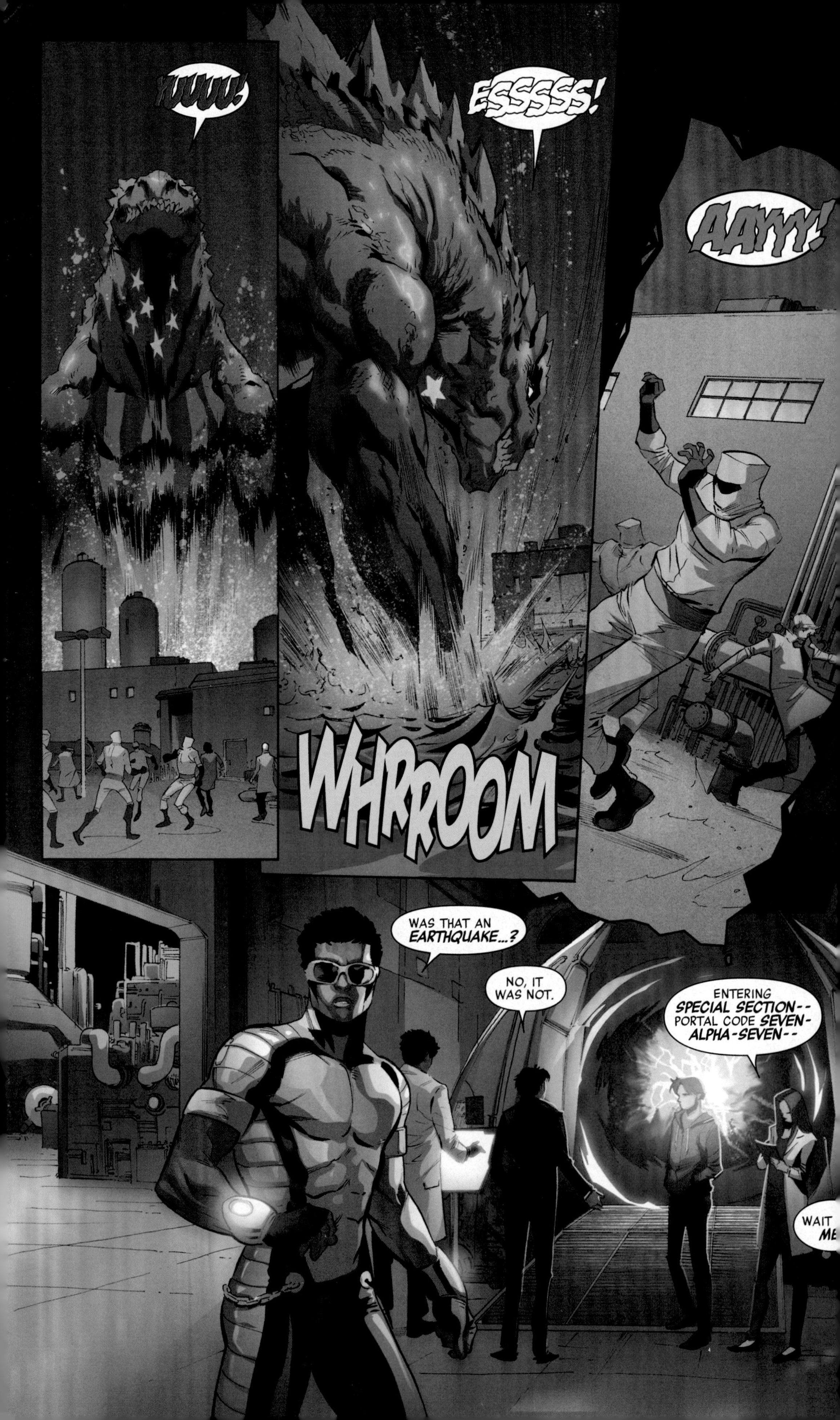
ESSSSS!
AAYYY!
WHROOM
WAS THAT AN EARTHQUAKE...?
NO, IT WAS NOT.
ENTERING SPECIAL SECTION-- PORTAL CODE SEVEN-ALPHA-SEVEN--
WAIT

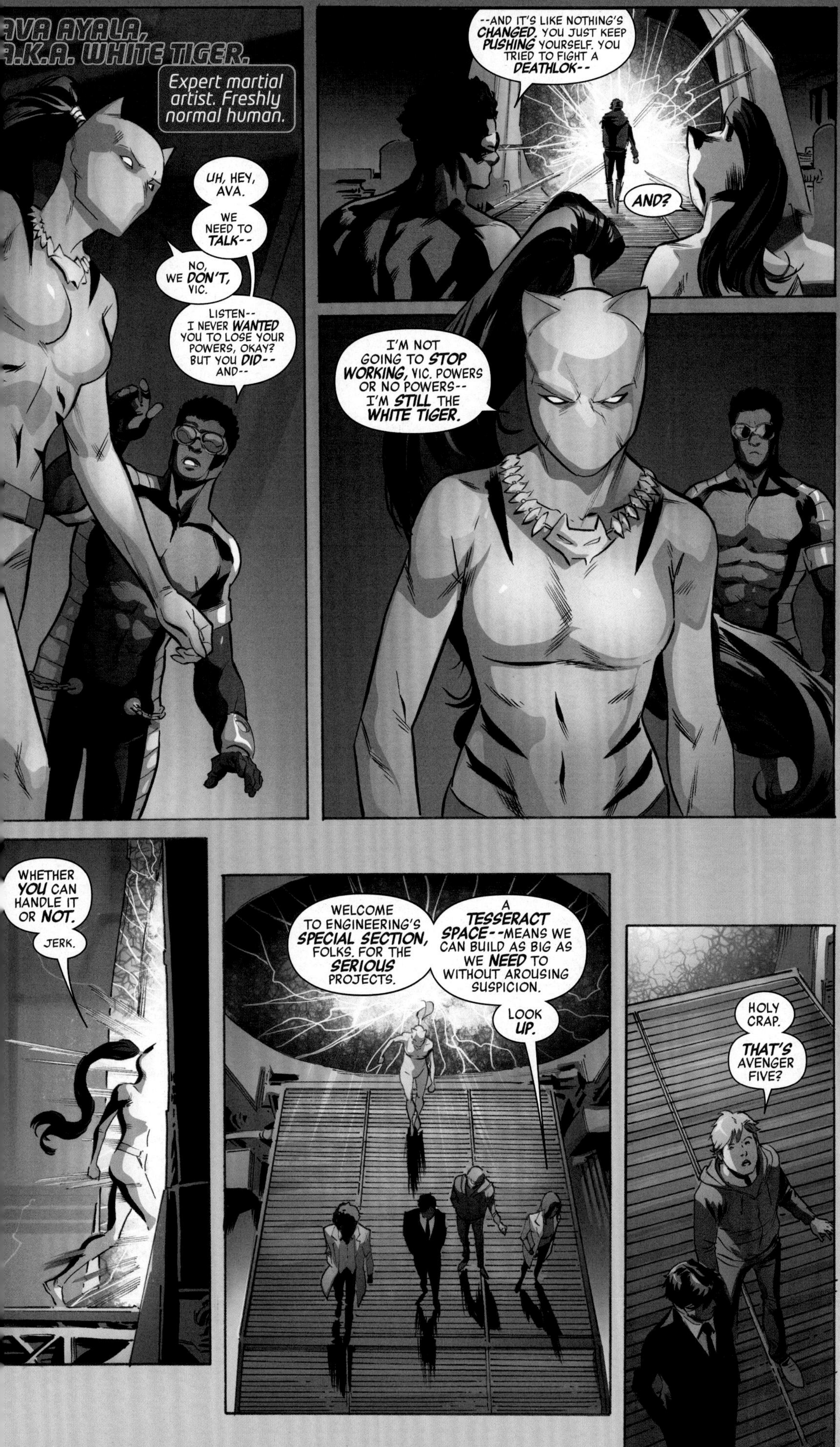
AVA AYALA, A.K.A. WHITE TIGER.
Expert martial artist. Freshly normal human.
UH, HEY, AVA.
WE NEED TO TALK--
NO, WE DON'T, VIC.
LISTEN-- I NEVER WANTED YOU TO LOSE YOUR POWERS, OKAY? BUT YOU DID-- AND--
--AND IT'S LIKE NOTHING'S CHANGED. YOU JUST KEEP PUSHING YOURSELF. YOU TRIED TO FIGHT A DEATHLOK--
AND?
I'M NOT GOING TO STOP WORKING, VIC. POWERS OR NO POWERS-- I'M STILL THE WHITE TIGER.
WHETHER YOU CAN HANDLE IT OR NOT.
JERK.
WELCOME TO ENGINEERING'S SPECIAL SECTION, FOLKS. FOR THE SERIOUS PROJECTS.
A TESSERACT SPACE--MEANS WE CAN BUILD AS BIG AS WE NEED TO WITHOUT AROUSING SUSPICION.
LOOK UP.
HOLY CRAP.
THAT'S AVENGER FIVE?

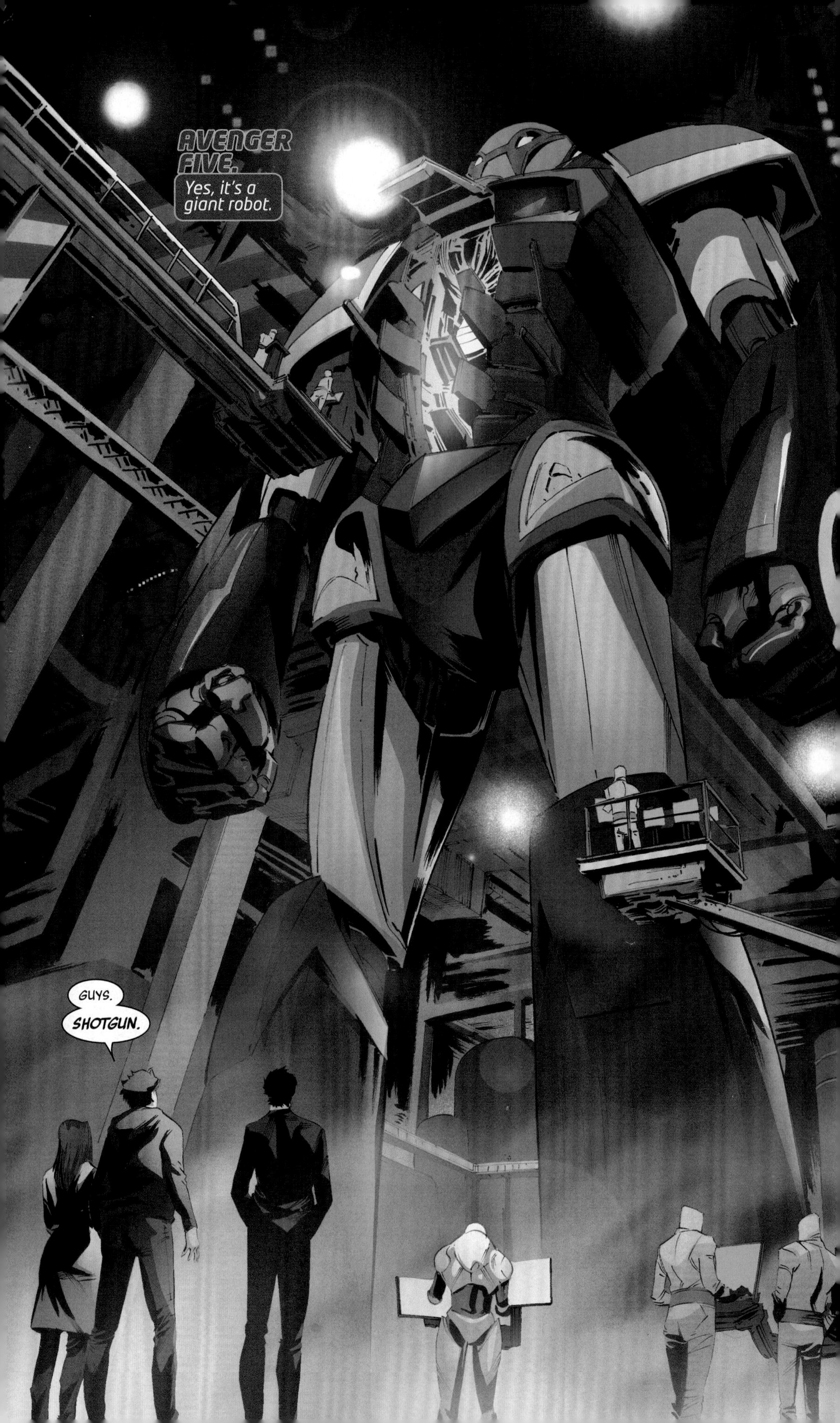
AVENGER FIVE.
Yes, it's a giant robot.
GUYS.
SHOTGUN.

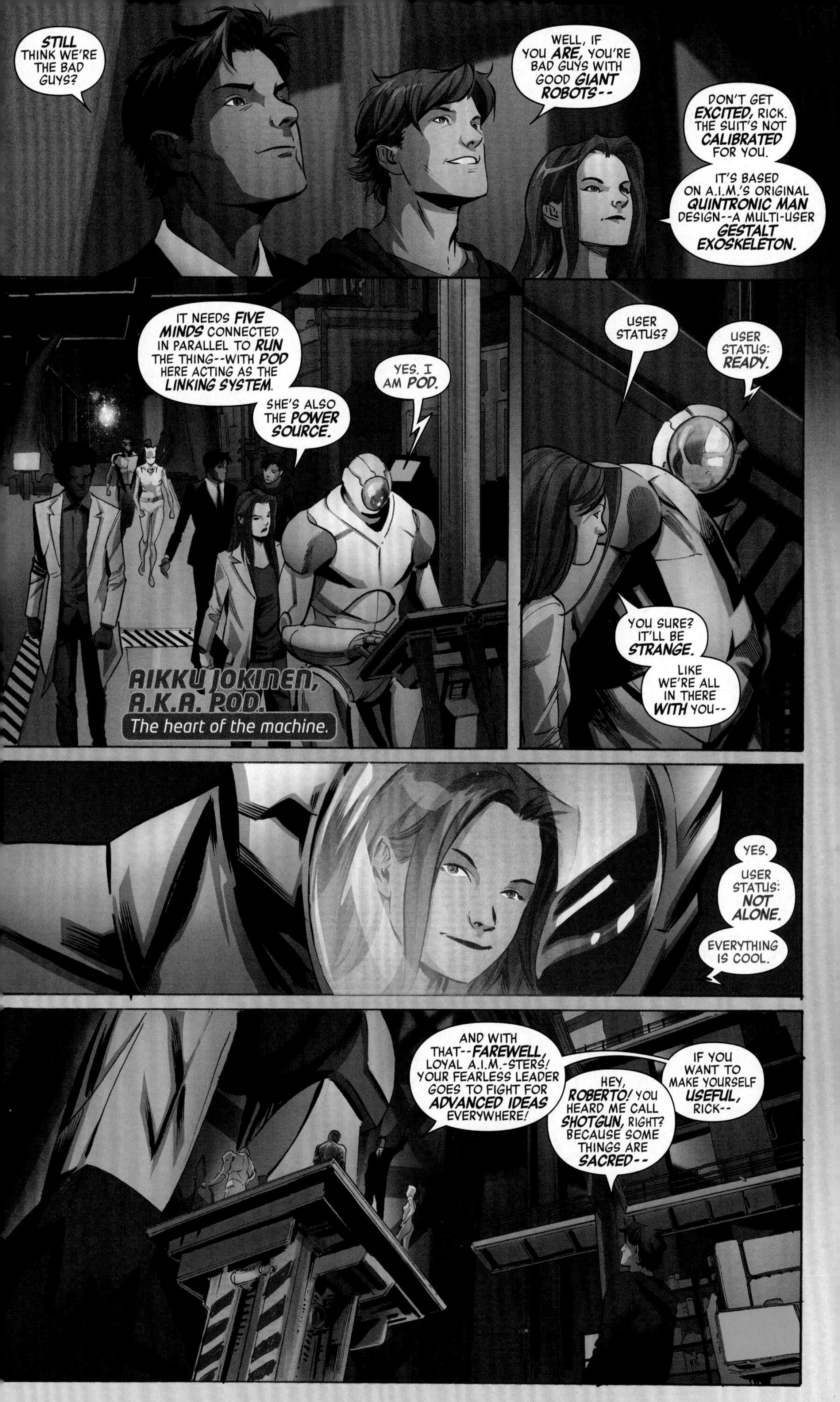
STILL THINK WE'RE THE BAD GUYS?
WELL, IF YOU ARE, YOU'RE BAD GUYS WITH GOOD GIANT ROBOTS--
DON'T GET EXCITED, RICK. THE SUIT'S NOT CALIBRATED FOR YOU.
IT'S BASED ON A.I.M.'S ORIGINAL QUINTRONIC MAN DESIGN--A MULTI-USER GESTALT EXOSKELETON.
IT NEEDS FIVE MINDS CONNECTED IN PARALLEL TO RUN THE THING--WITH POD HERE ACTING AS THE LINKING SYSTEM.
SHE'S ALSO THE POWER SOURCE.
YES. I AM POD.
AIKKU JOKINEN, A.K.A. POD.
The heart of the machine.
USER STATUS?
USER STATUS: READY.
YOU SURE? IT'LL BE STRANGE.
LIKE WE'RE ALL IN THERE WITH YOU--
YES.
USER STATUS: NOT ALONE.
EVERYTHING IS COOL.
AND WITH THAT--FAREWELL, LOYAL A.I.M.-STERS! YOUR FEARLESS LEADER GOES TO FIGHT FOR ADVANCED IDEAS EVERYWHERE!
IF YOU WANT TO MAKE YOURSELF USEFUL, RICK--
HEY, ROBERTO! YOU HEARD ME CALL SHOTGUN, RIGHT? BECAUSE SOME THINGS ARE SACRED--

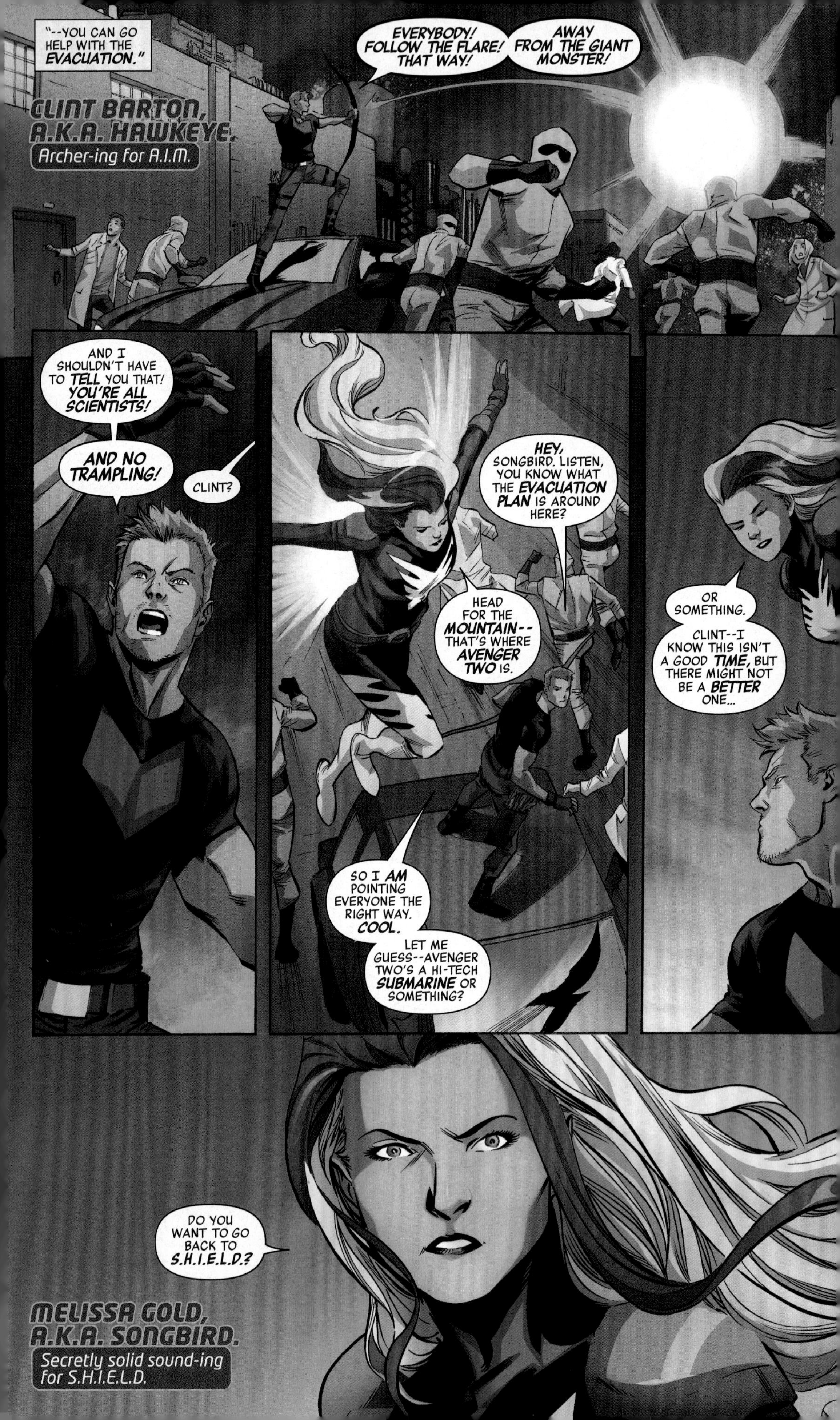
"--YOU CAN GO HELP WITH THE EVACUATION."
EVERYBODY! FOLLOW THE FLARE! THAT WAY!
AWAY FROM THE GIANT MONSTER!
CLINT BARTON, A.K.A. HAWKEYE.
Archer-ing for A.I.M.
AND I SHOULDN'T HAVE TO TELL YOU THAT! YOU'RE ALL SCIENTISTS!
AND NO TRAMPLING!
CLINT?
HEY, SONGBIRD. LISTEN, YOU KNOW WHAT THE EVACUATION PLAN IS AROUND HERE?
HEAD FOR THE MOUNTAIN--THAT'S WHERE AVENGER TWO IS.
SO I AM POINTING EVERYONE THE RIGHT WAY. COOL.
LET ME GUESS--AVENGER TWO'S A HI-TECH SUBMARINE OR SOMETHING?
OR SOMETHING.
CLINT--I KNOW THIS ISN'T A GOOD TIME, BUT THERE MIGHT NOT BE A BETTER ONE...
DO YOU WANT TO GO BACK TO S.H.I.E.L.D.?
MELISSA GOLD, A.K.A. SONGBIRD.
Secretly solid sound-ing for S.H.I.E.L.D.

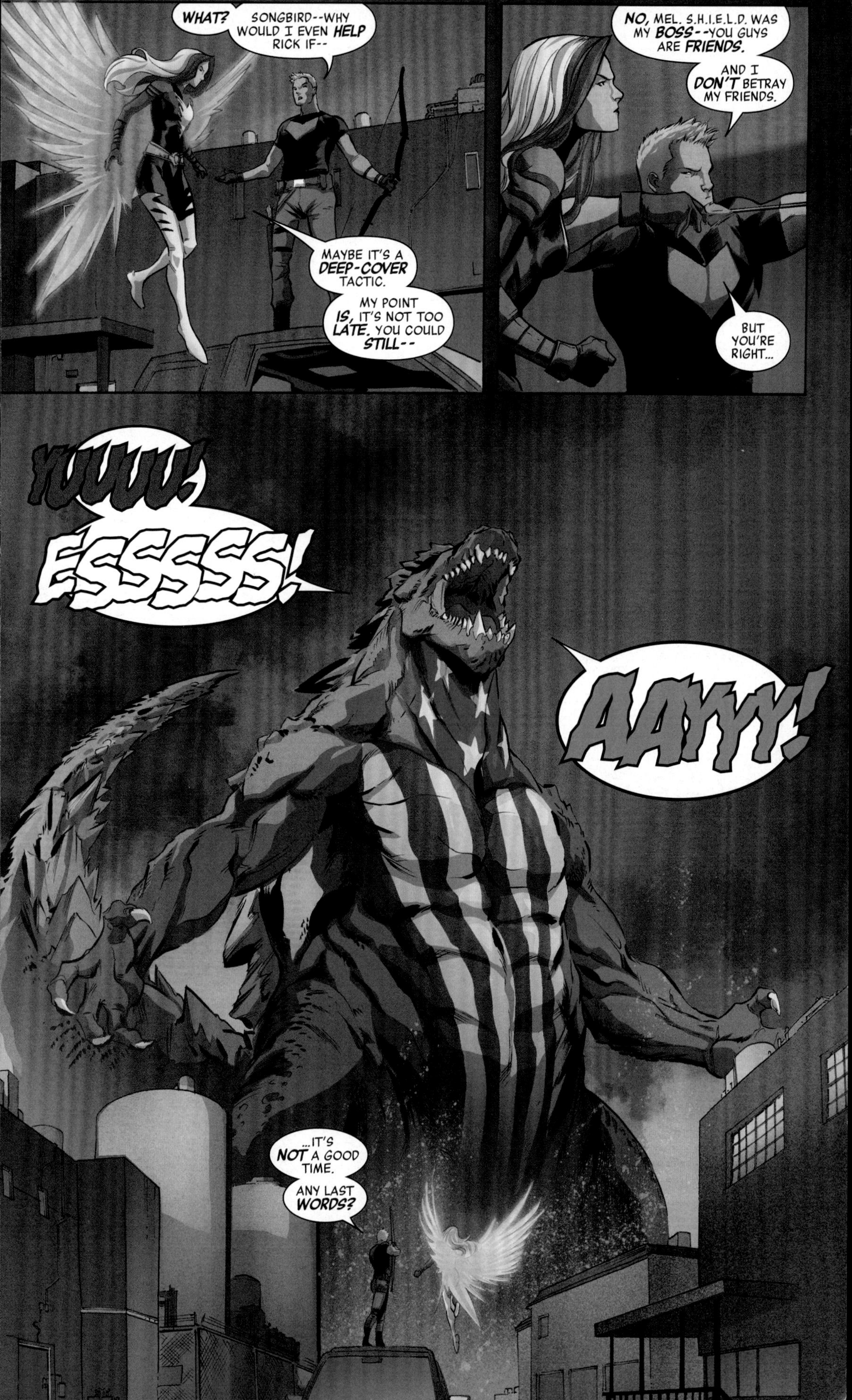
WHAT?
SONGBIRD--WHY WOULD I EVEN HELP RICK IF--
MAYBE IT'S A DEEP-COVER TACTIC.
MY POINT IS, IT'S NOT TOO LATE. YOU COULD STILL--
NO, MEL. S.H.I.E.L.D. WAS MY BOSS--YOU GUYS ARE FRIENDS.
AND I DON'T BETRAY MY FRIENDS.
BUT YOU'RE RIGHT...
ESSSSS!
AAYYY!
...IT'S NOT A GOOD TIME.
ANY LAST WORDS?

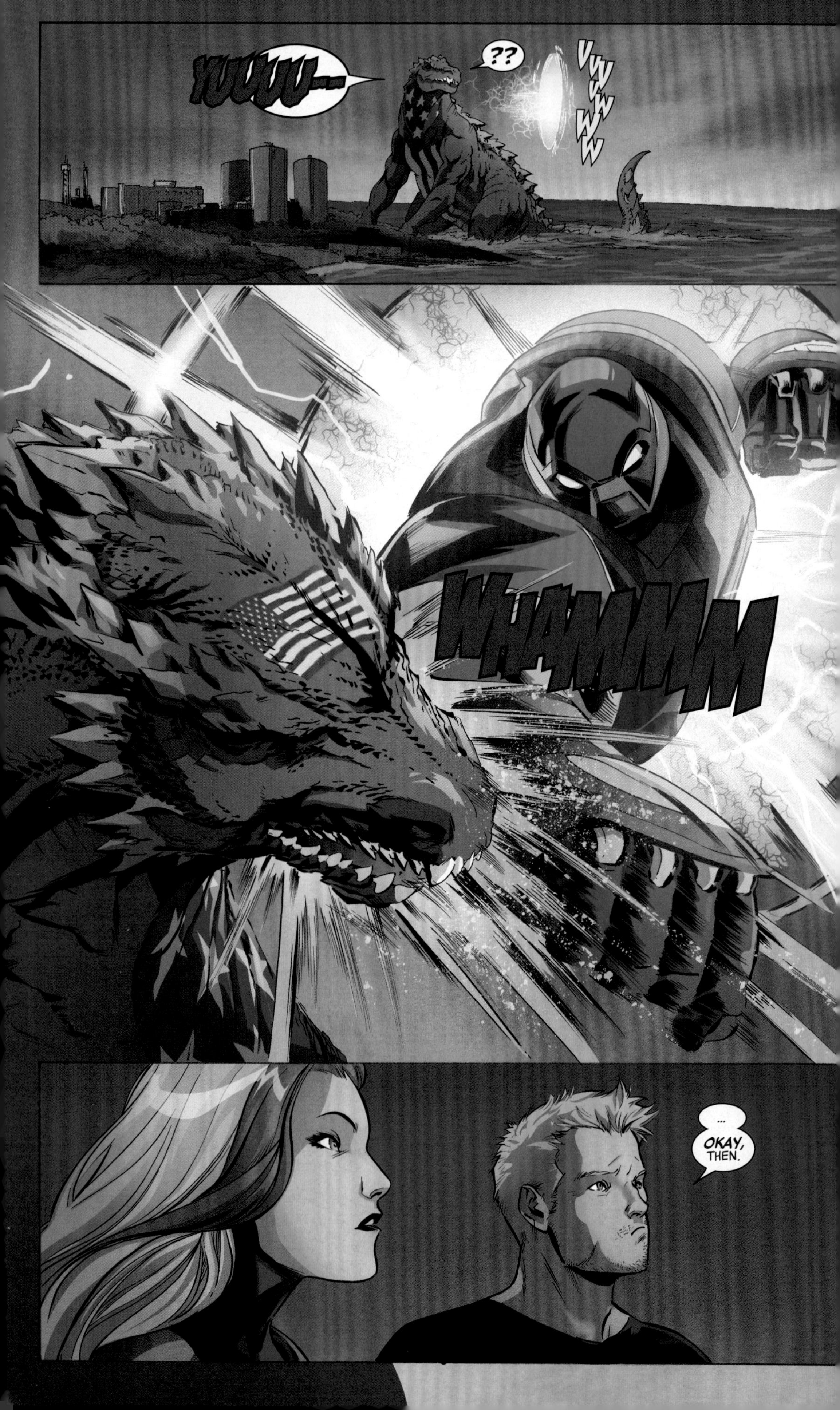
YUUUU--
??
VVVVVVVV
WHAMMMM
... OKAY, THEN.

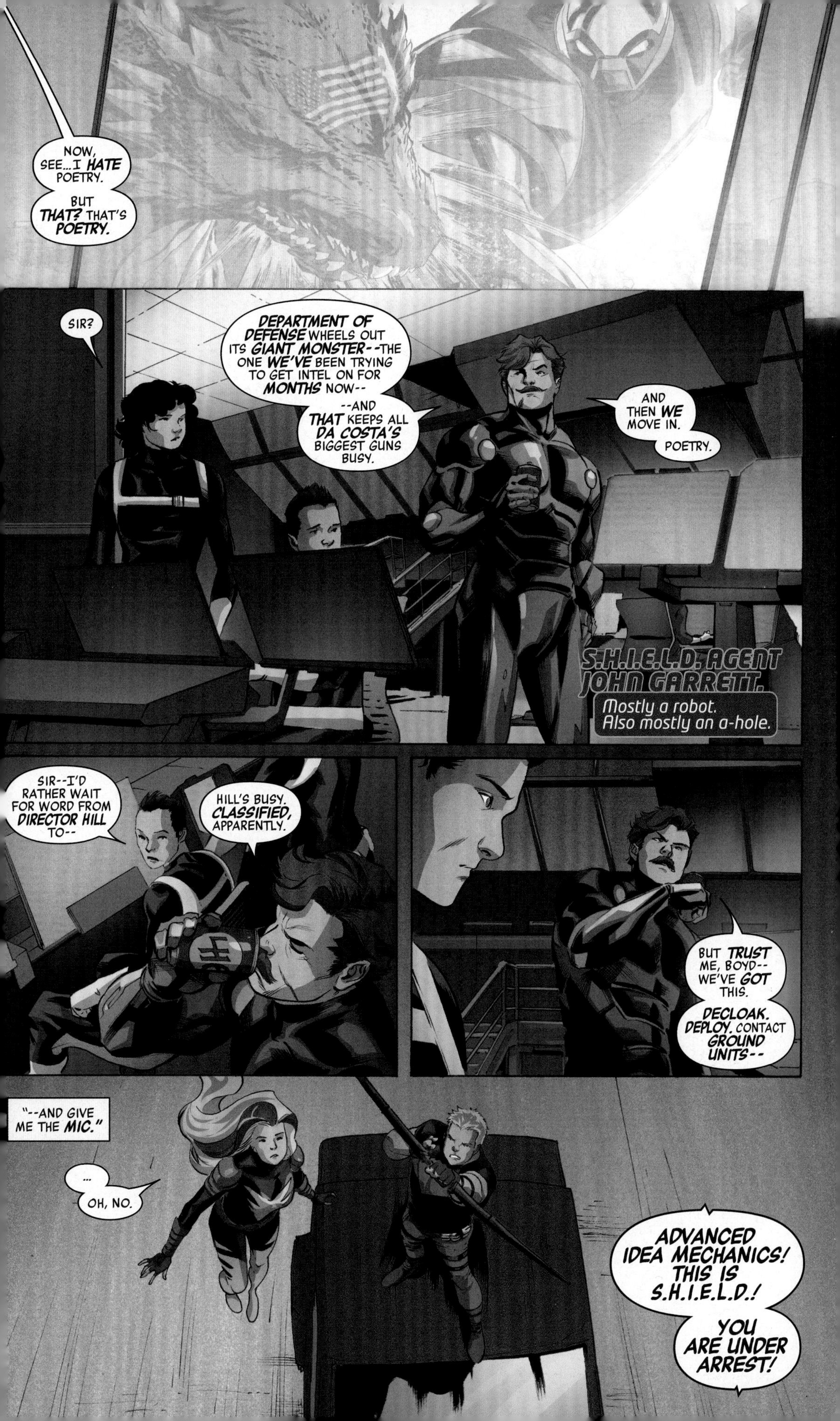
NOW, SEE...I HATE POETRY.
BUT THAT? THAT'S POETRY.
SIR?
DEPARTMENT OF DEFENSE WHEELS OUT ITS GIANT MONSTER--THE ONE WE'VE BEEN TRYING TO GET INTEL ON FOR MONTHS NOW--
--AND THAT KEEPS ALL DA COSTA'S BIGGEST GUNS BUSY.
AND THEN WE MOVE IN.
POETRY.
S.H.I.E.L.D. AGENT JOHN GARRETT.
Mostly a robot. Also mostly an a-hole.
SIR--I'D RATHER WAIT FOR WORD FROM DIRECTOR HILL TO--
HILL'S BUSY. CLASSIFIED, APPARENTLY.
BUT TRUST ME, BOYD--WE'VE GOT THIS.
DECLOAK. DEPLOY. CONTACT GROUND UNITS--
"--AND GIVE ME THE MIC."
... OH, NO.
ADVANCED IDEA MECHANICS! THIS IS S.H.I.E.L.D.!
YOU ARE UNDER ARREST!

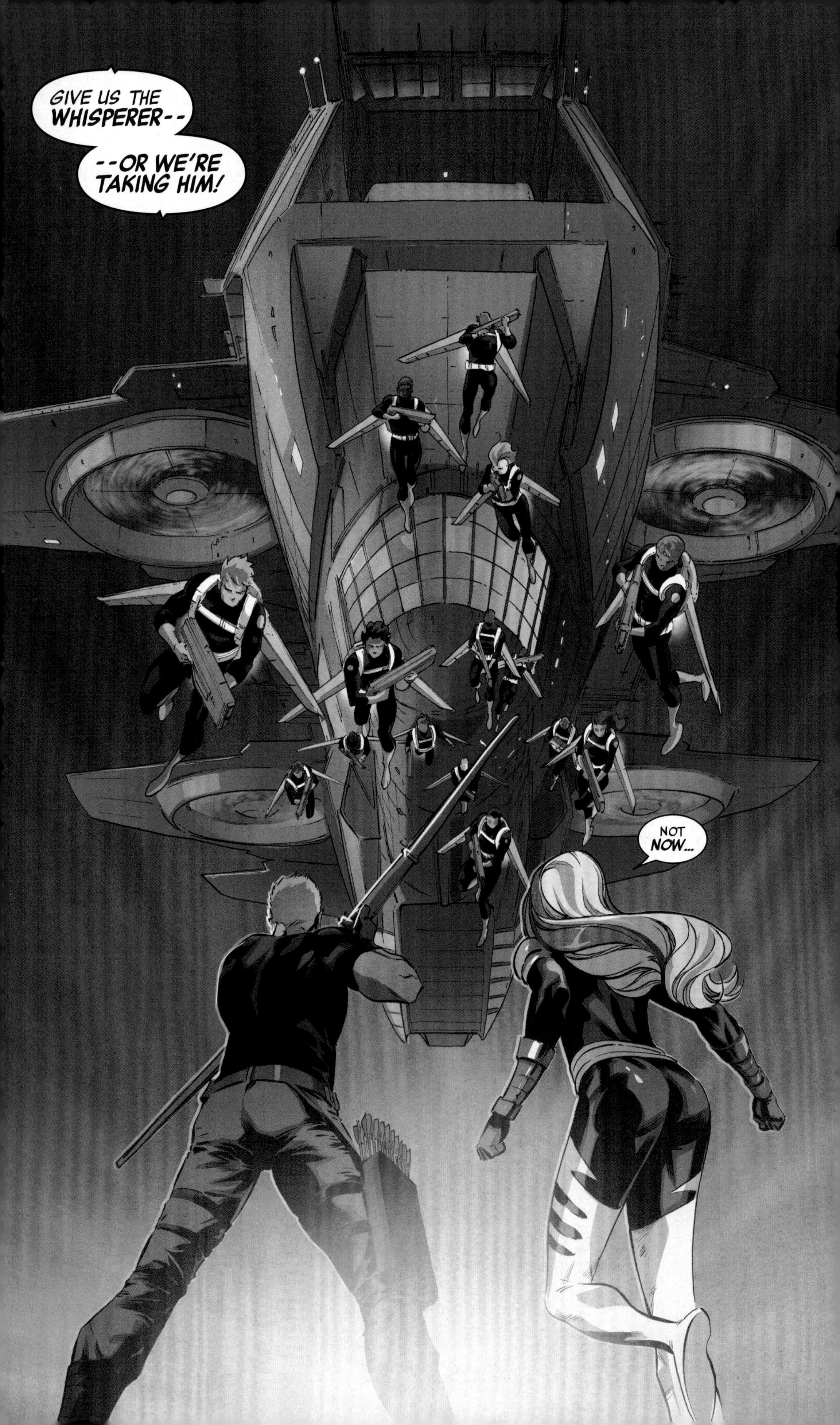
GIVE US THE WHISPERER--
--OR WE'RE TAKING HIM!
NOT NOW...

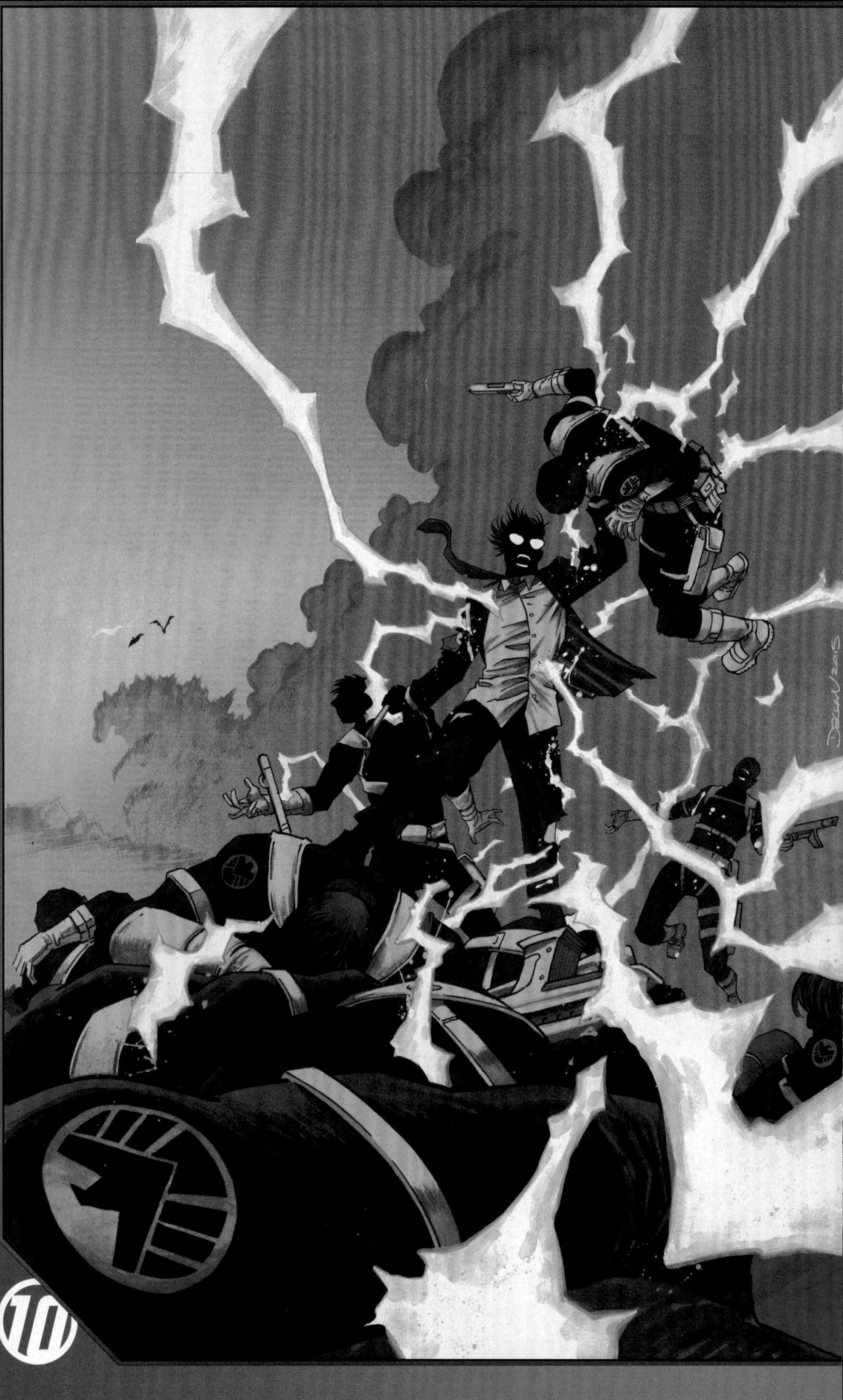

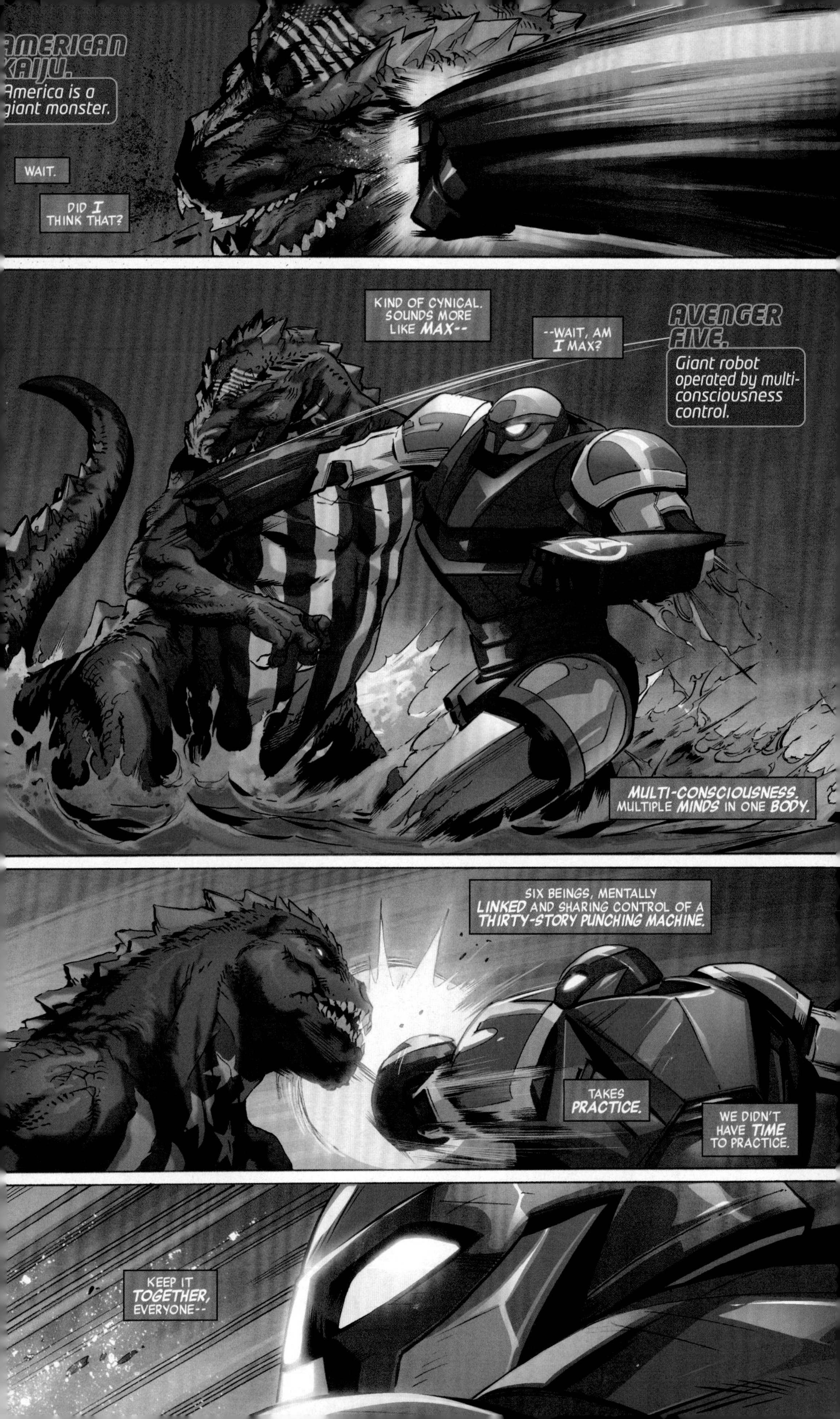
AMERICAN KAIJU.
America is a giant monster.
WAIT.
DID I THINK THAT?
KIND OF CYNICAL. SOUNDS MORE LIKE MAX--
--WAIT, AM I MAX?
AVENGER FIVE.
Giant robot operated by multi-consciousness control.
MULTI-CONSCIOUSNESS. MULTIPLE MINDS IN ONE BODY.
SIX BEINGS, MENTALLY LINKED AND SHARING CONTROL OF A THIRTY-STORY PUNCHING MACHINE.
TAKES PRACTICE.
WE DIDN'T HAVE TIME TO PRACTICE.
KEEP IT TOGETHER, EVERYONE--

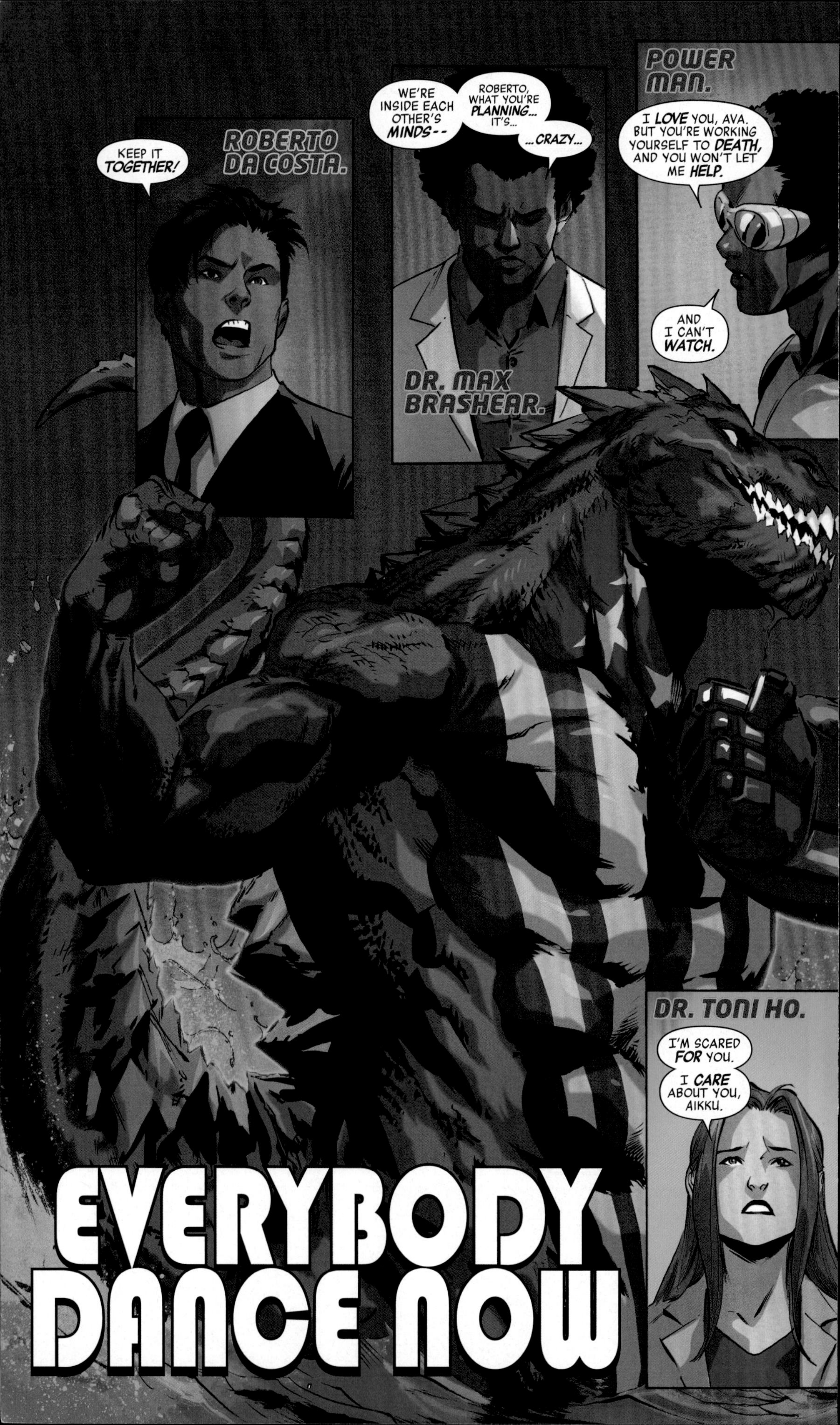
ROBERTO DA COSTA.
KEEP IT TOGETHER!
WE'RE INSIDE EACH OTHER'S MINDS--
ROBERTO, WHAT YOU'RE PLANNING... IT'S...
...CRAZY...
DR. MAX BRASHEAR.
POWER MAN.
I LOVE YOU, AVA. BUT YOU'RE WORKING YOURSELF TO DEATH, AND YOU WON'T LET ME HELP.
AND I CAN'T WATCH.
DR. TONI HO.
I'M SCARED FOR YOU.
I CARE ABOUT YOU, AIKKU.
EVERYBODY DANCE NOW

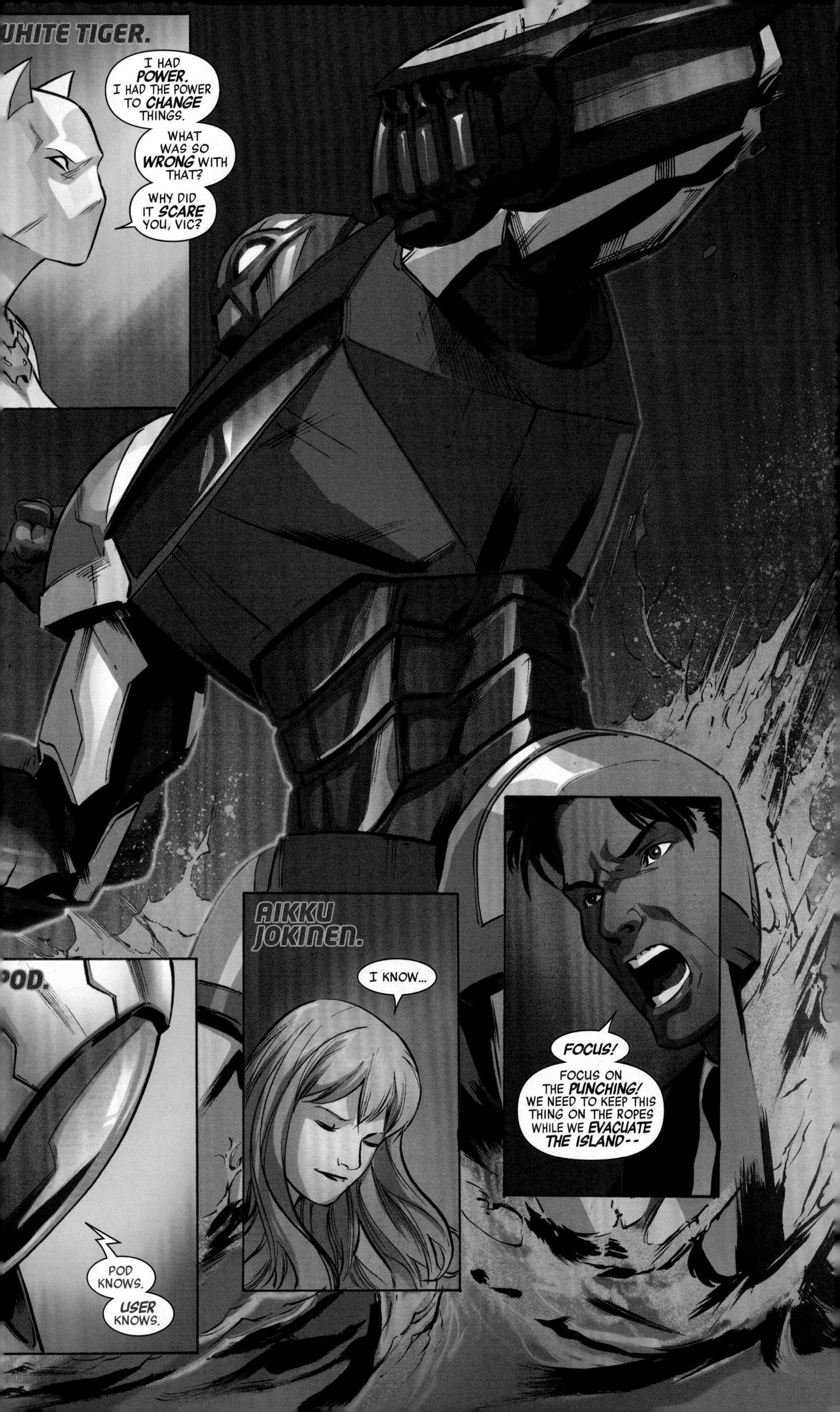
WHITE TIGER.
I HAD POWER. I HAD THE POWER TO CHANGE THINGS.
WHAT WAS SO WRONG WITH THAT?
WHY DID IT SCARE YOU, VIC?
POD.
POD KNOWS.
USER KNOWS.
AIKKU JOKINEN.
I KNOW...
FOCUS!
FOCUS ON THE PUNCHING! WE NEED TO KEEP THIS THING ON THE ROPES WHILE WE EVACUATE THE ISLAND--

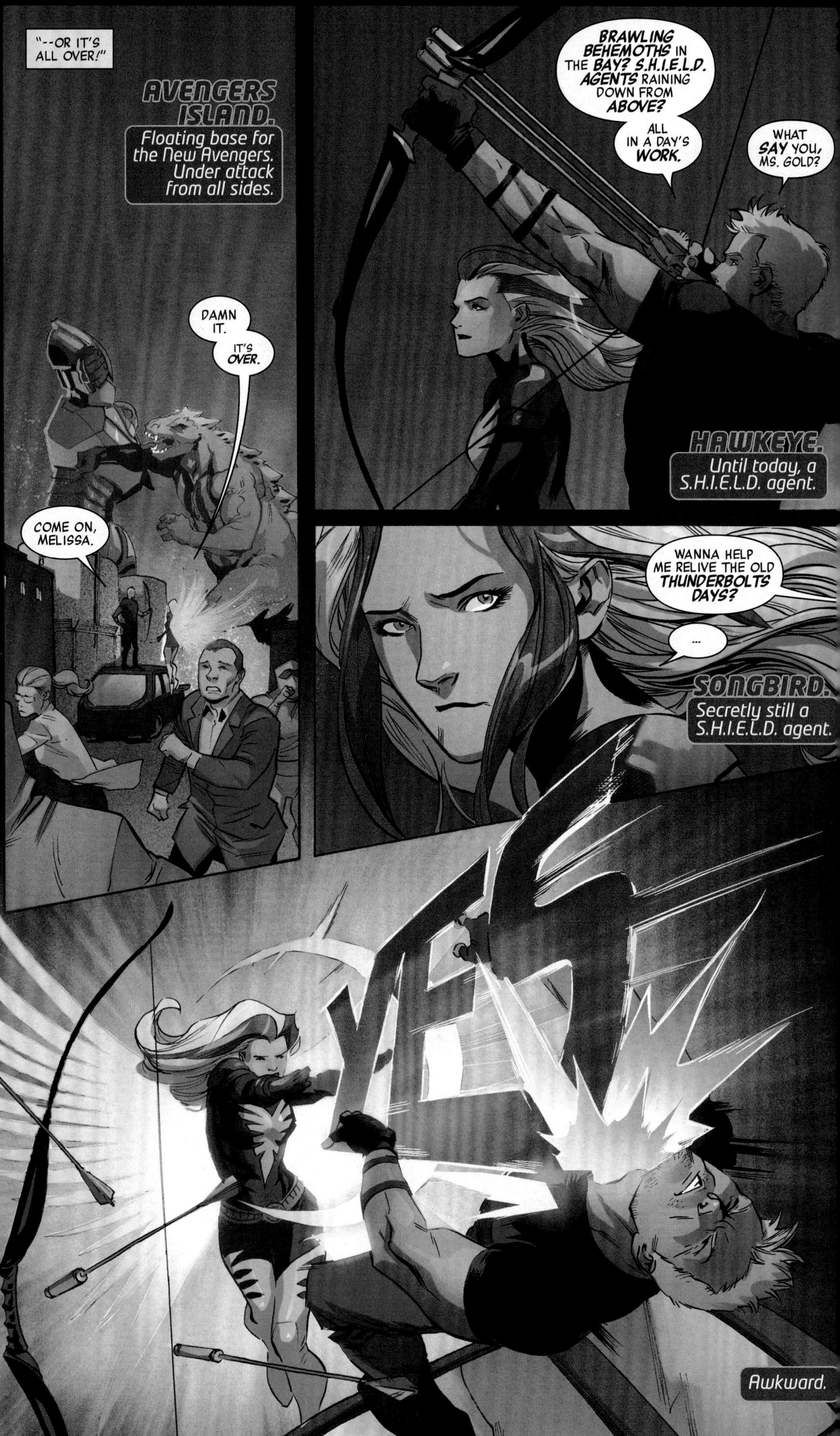
"--OR IT'S ALL OVER!"
AVENGERS ISLAND.
Floating base for the New Avengers. Under attack from all sides.
DAMN IT.
IT'S OVER.
COME ON, MELISSA.
BRAWLING BEHEMOTHS IN THE BAY? S.H.I.E.L.D. AGENTS RAINING DOWN FROM ABOVE?
ALL IN A DAY'S WORK.
WHAT SAY YOU, MS. GOLD?
HAWKEYE.
Until today, a S.H.I.E.L.D. agent.
WANNA HELP ME RELIVE THE OLD THUNDERBOLTS DAYS?
...
SONGBIRD.
Secretly still a S.H.I.E.L.D. agent.
YEEW
Awkward.

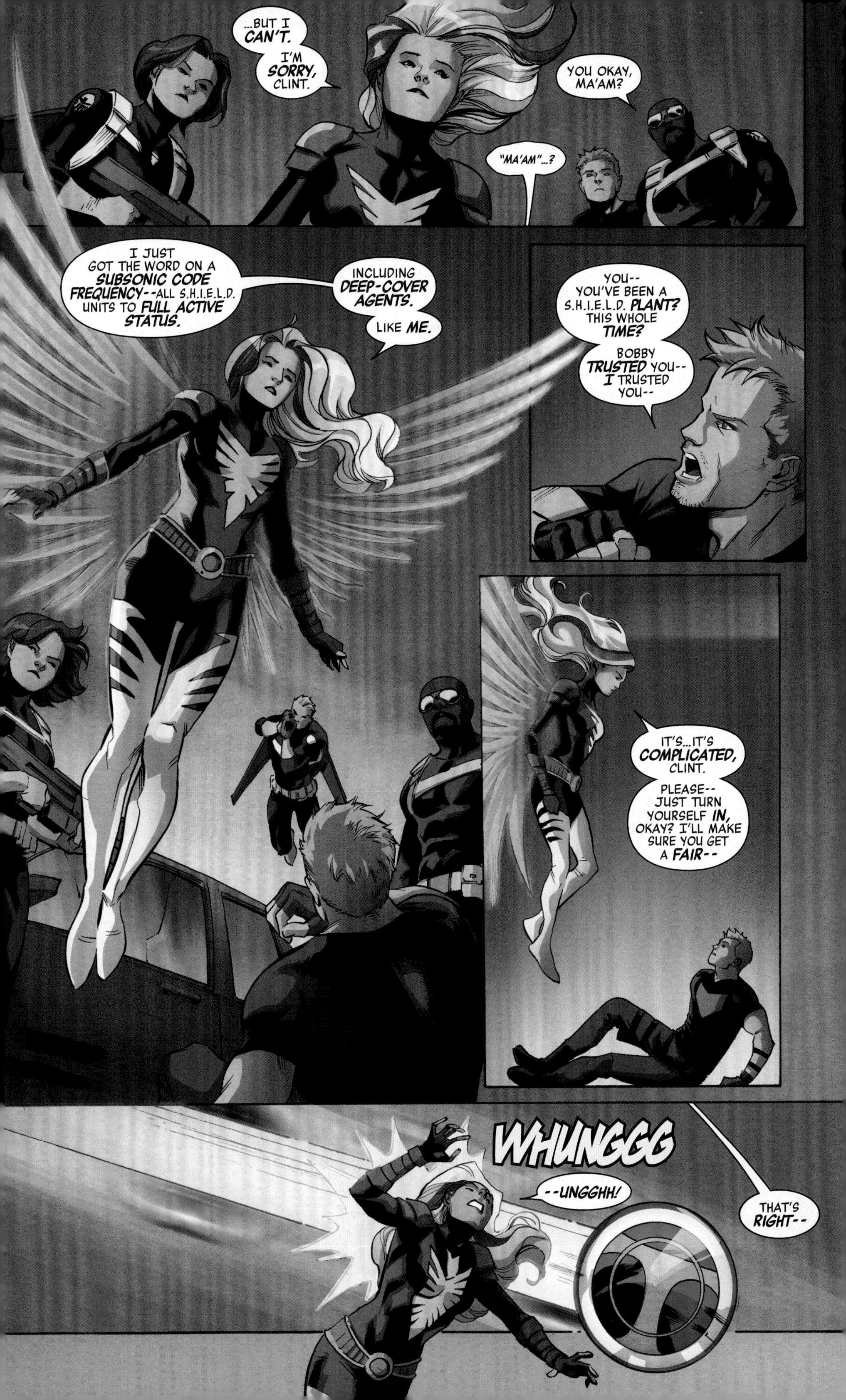
...BUT I CAN'T.
I'M SORRY, CLINT.
YOU OKAY, MA'AM?
"MA'AM"...?
I JUST GOT THE WORD ON A SUBSONIC CODE FREQUENCY--ALL S.H.I.E.L.D. UNITS TO FULL ACTIVE STATUS.
INCLUDING DEEP-COVER AGENTS.
LIKE ME.
YOU-- YOU'VE BEEN A S.H.I.E.L.D. PLANT? THIS WHOLE TIME?
BOBBY TRUSTED YOU-- I TRUSTED YOU--
IT'S...IT'S COMPLICATED, CLINT.
PLEASE-- JUST TURN YOURSELF IN, OKAY? I'LL MAKE SURE YOU GET A FAIR--
WHUNGGG
--UNGGHH!
THAT'S RIGHT--

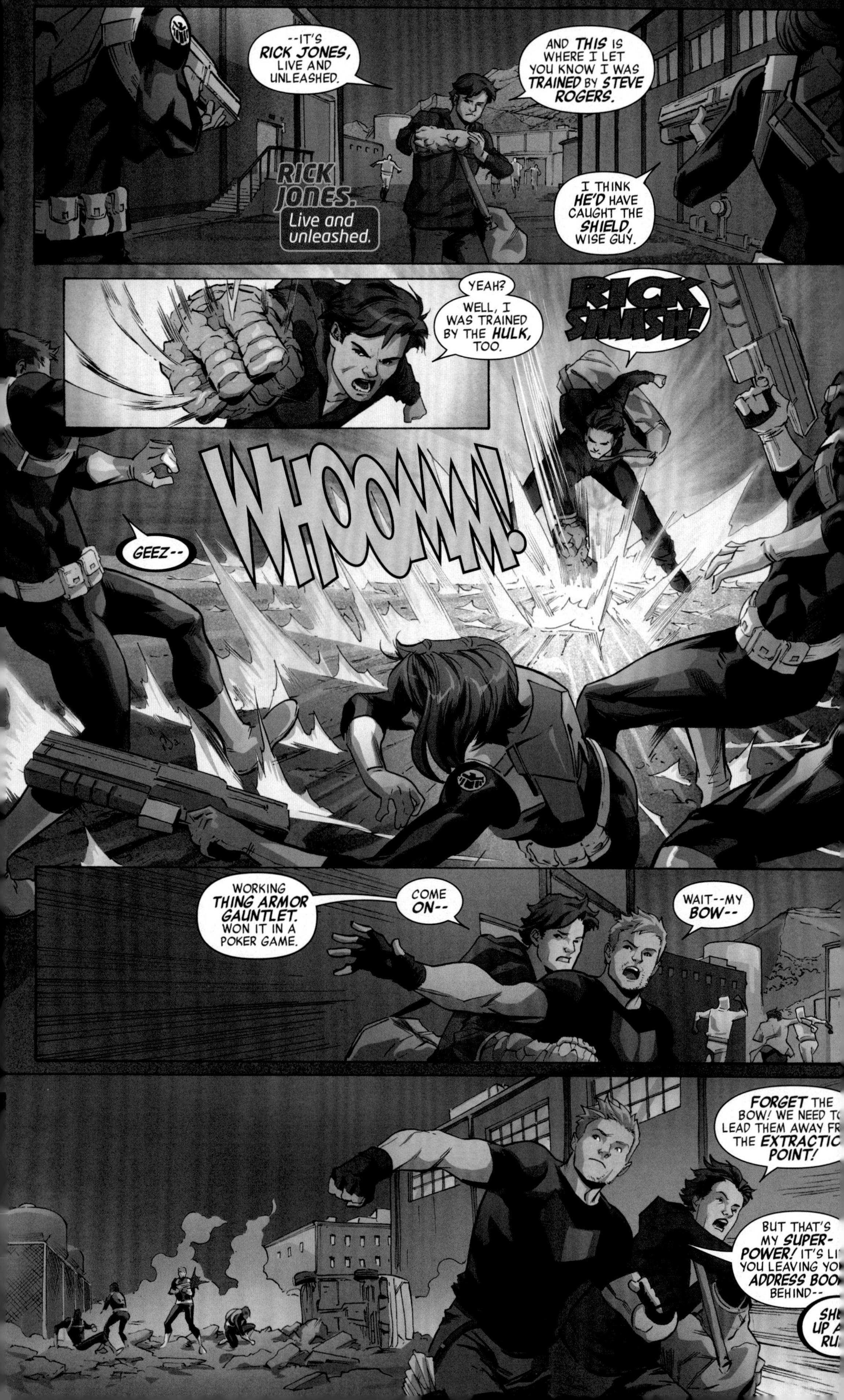

--IT'S RICK JONES, LIVE AND UNLEASHED.
AND THIS IS WHERE I LET YOU KNOW I WAS TRAINED BY STEVE ROGERS.
RICK JONES.
Live and unleashed.
I THINK HE'D HAVE CAUGHT THE SHIELD, WISE GUY.
YEAH? WELL, I WAS TRAINED BY THE HULK, TOO.
RICK SMASH!
WHOOMM!
GEEZ--
WORKING THING ARMOR GAUNTLET. WON IT IN A POKER GAME.
COME ON--
WAIT--MY BOW--
FORGET THE BOW! WE NEED T LEAD THEM AWAY FR THE EXTRACTI POINT!
BUT THAT'S MY SUPER-POWER! IT'S LI YOU LEAVING YO ADDRESS BOO BEHIND--

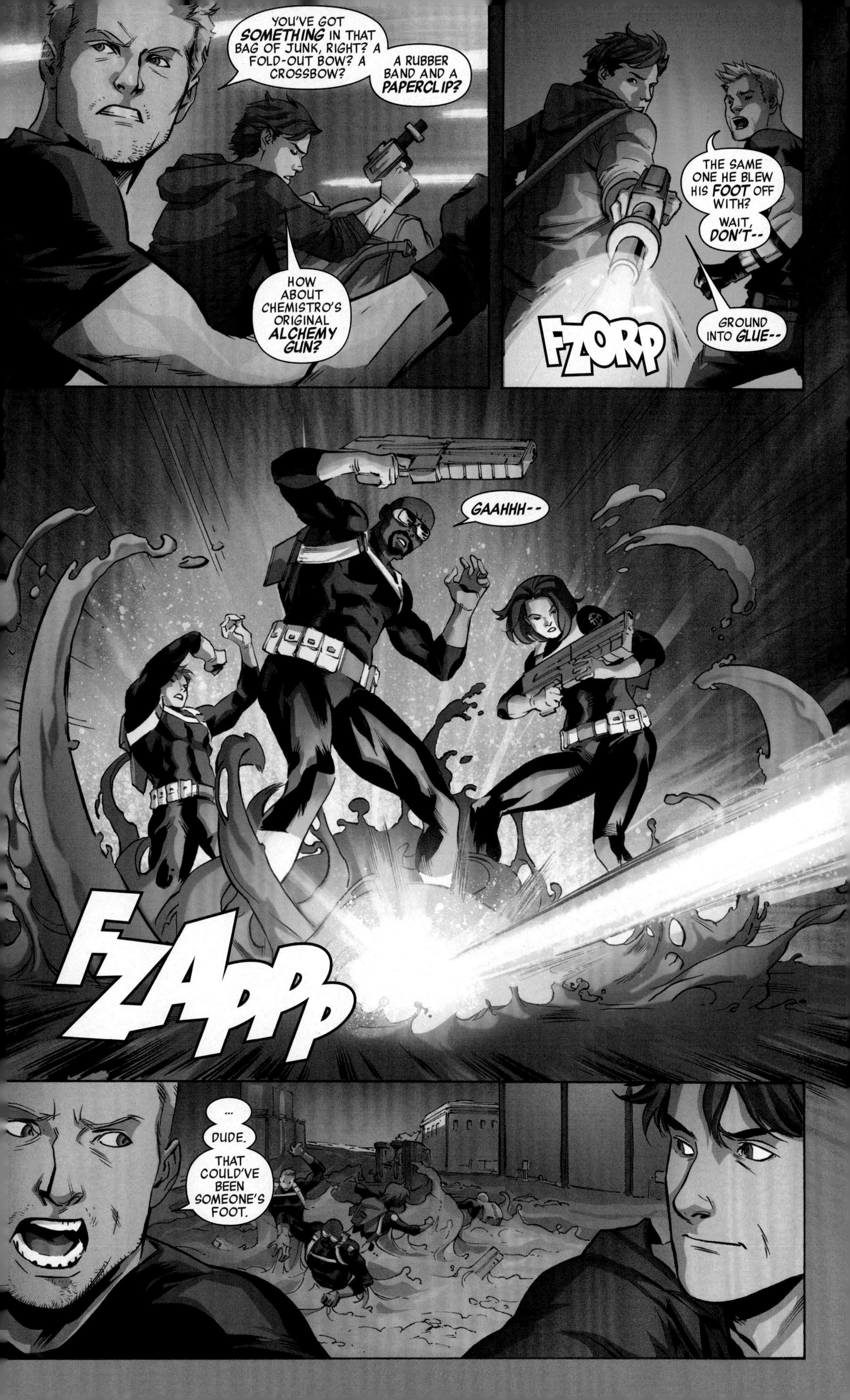
YOU'VE GOT SOMETHING IN THAT BAG OF JUNK, RIGHT? A FOLD-OUT BOW? A CROSSBOW?
A RUBBER BAND AND A PAPERCLIP?
HOW ABOUT CHEMISTRO'S ORIGINAL ALCHEMY GUN?
THE SAME ONE HE BLEW HIS FOOT OFF WITH?
WAIT, DON'T--
FZORP
GROUND INTO GLUE--
GAAHHH--
FZAPPP
...
DUDE.
THAT COULD'VE BEEN SOMEONE'S FOOT.

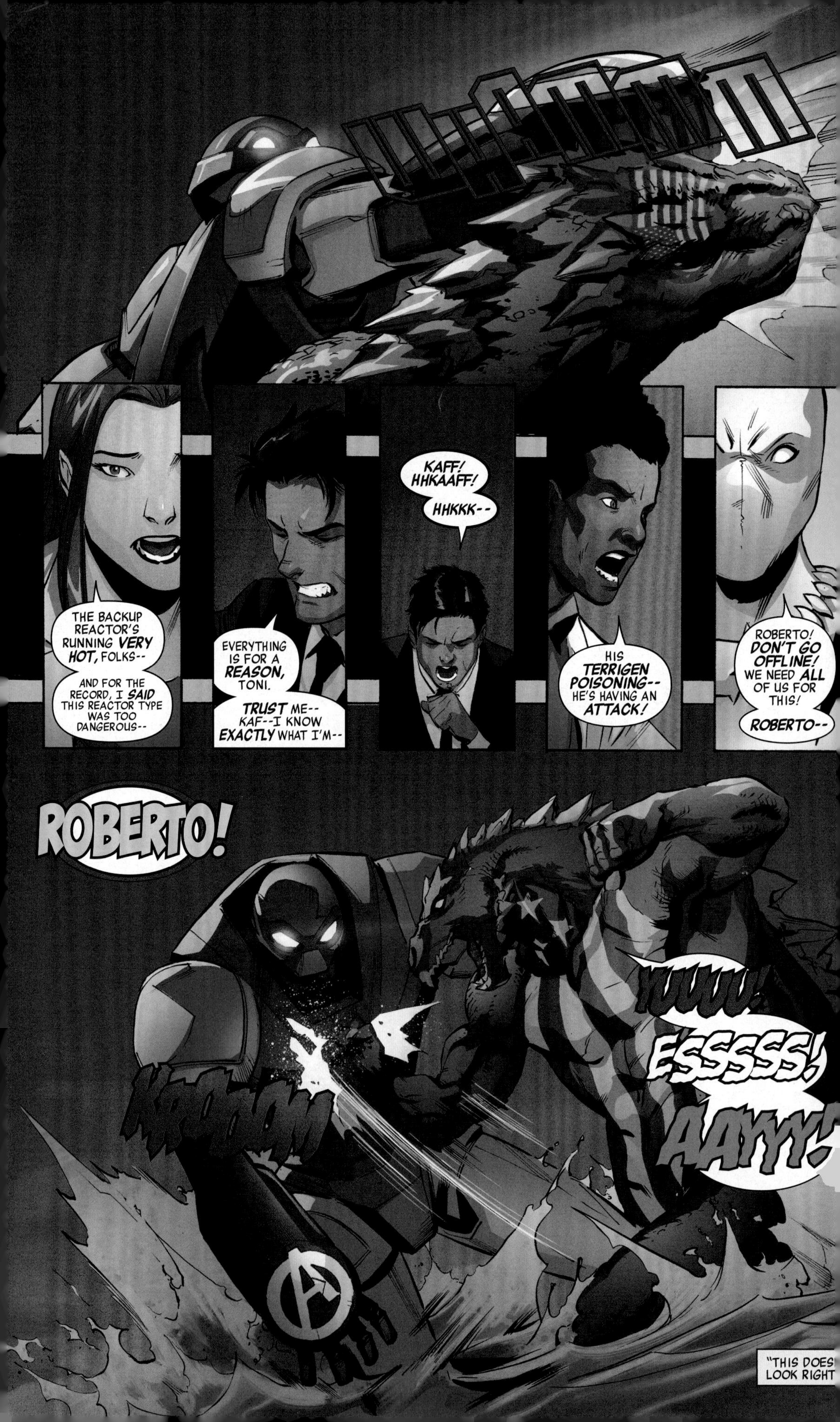

THE BACKUP REACTOR'S RUNNING VERY HOT, FOLKS--
AND FOR THE RECORD, I SAID THIS REACTOR TYPE WAS TOO DANGEROUS--
EVERYTHING IS FOR A REASON, TONI.
TRUST ME-- KAF--I KNOW EXACTLY WHAT I'M--
KAFF! HHKAAFF!
HHKKK--
HIS TERRIGEN POISONING-- HE'S HAVING AN ATTACK!
ROBERTO! DON'T GO OFFLINE! WE NEED ALL OF US FOR THIS!
ROBERTO--
ROBERTO!
ESSSSS!
AAYYY!
"THIS DOES
LOOK RIGHT

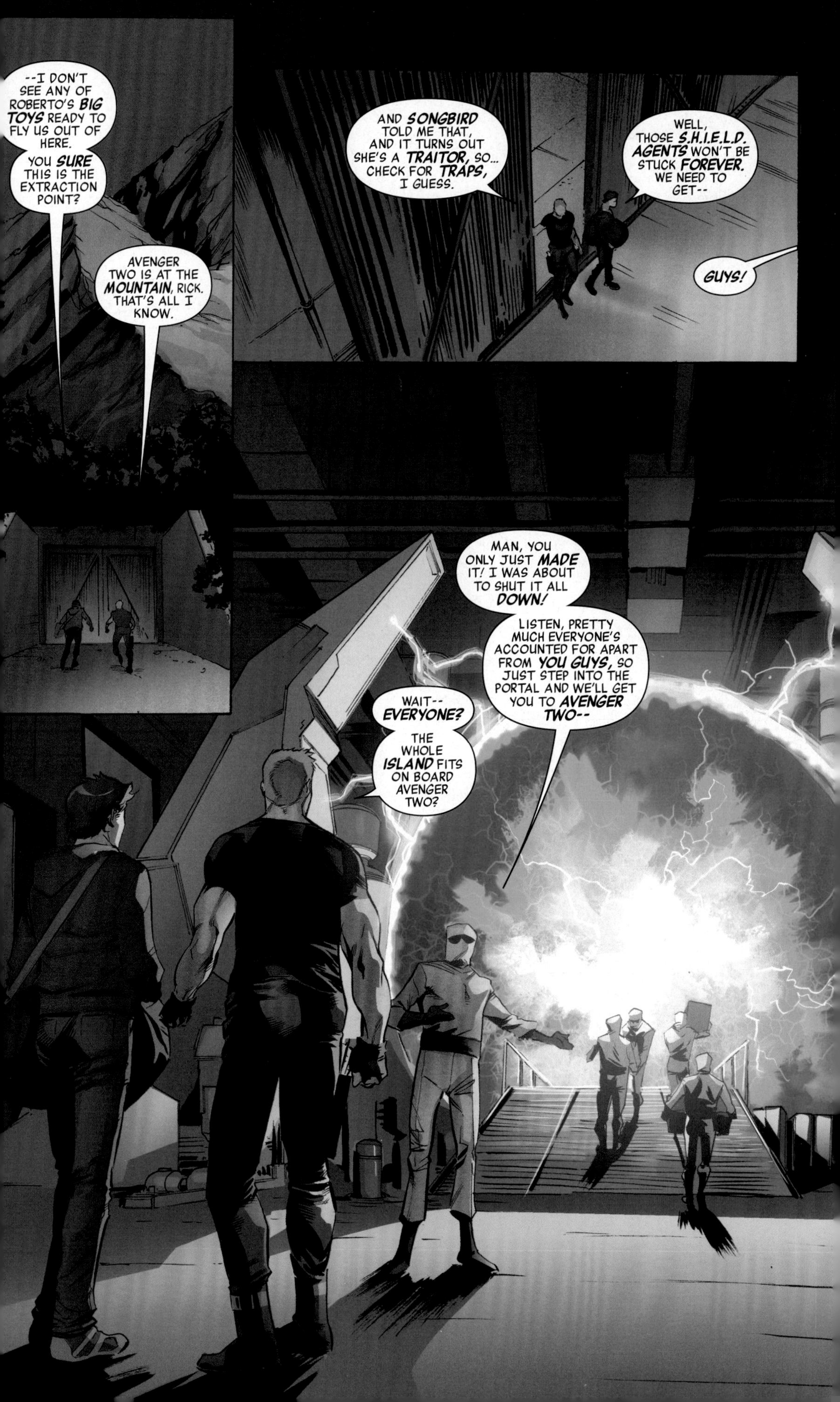
--I DON'T SEE ANY OF ROBERTO'S BIG TOYS READY TO FLY US OUT OF HERE.
YOU SURE THIS IS THE EXTRACTION POINT?
AVENGER TWO IS AT THE MOUNTAIN, RICK. THAT'S ALL I KNOW.
AND SONGBIRD TOLD ME THAT, AND IT TURNS OUT SHE'S A TRAITOR, SO... CHECK FOR TRAPS, I GUESS.
WELL, THOSE S.H.I.E.L.D. AGENTS WON'T BE STUCK FOREVER. WE NEED TO GET--
GUYS!
MAN, YOU ONLY JUST MADE IT! I WAS ABOUT TO SHUT IT ALL DOWN!
LISTEN, PRETTY MUCH EVERYONE'S ACCOUNTED FOR APART FROM YOU GUYS, SO JUST STEP INTO THE PORTAL AND WE'LL GET YOU TO AVENGER TWO--
WAIT-- EVERYONE?
THE WHOLE ISLAND FITS ON BOARD AVENGER TWO?

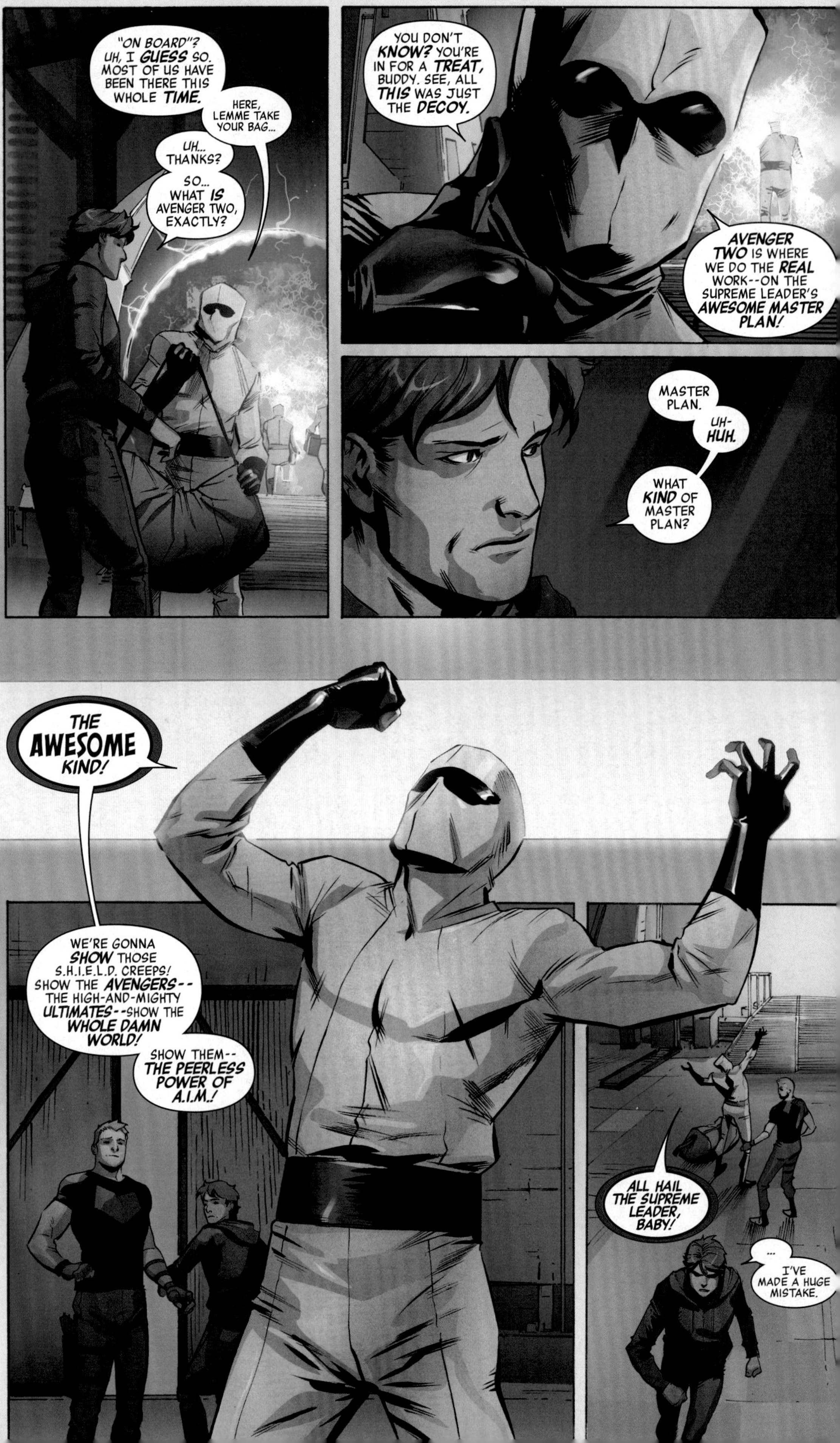
"ON BOARD"? UH, I GUESS SO. MOST OF US HAVE BEEN THERE THIS WHOLE TIME.
HERE, LEMME TAKE YOUR BAG...
UH... THANKS?
SO... WHAT IS AVENGER TWO, EXACTLY?
YOU DON'T KNOW? YOU'RE IN FOR A TREAT, BUDDY. SEE, ALL THIS WAS JUST THE DECOY.
AVENGER TWO IS WHERE WE DO THE REAL WORK--ON THE SUPREME LEADER'S AWESOME MASTER PLAN!
MASTER PLAN.
UH-HUH.
WHAT KIND OF MASTER PLAN?
THE AWESOME KIND!
WE'RE GONNA SHOW THOSE S.H.I.E.L.D. CREEPS! SHOW THE AVENGERS--THE HIGH-AND-MIGHTY ULTIMATES--SHOW THE WHOLE DAMN WORLD!
SHOW THEM--THE PEERLESS POWER OF A.I.M.!
ALL HAIL THE SUPREME LEADER, BABY!
...
I'VE MADE A HUGE MISTAKE.

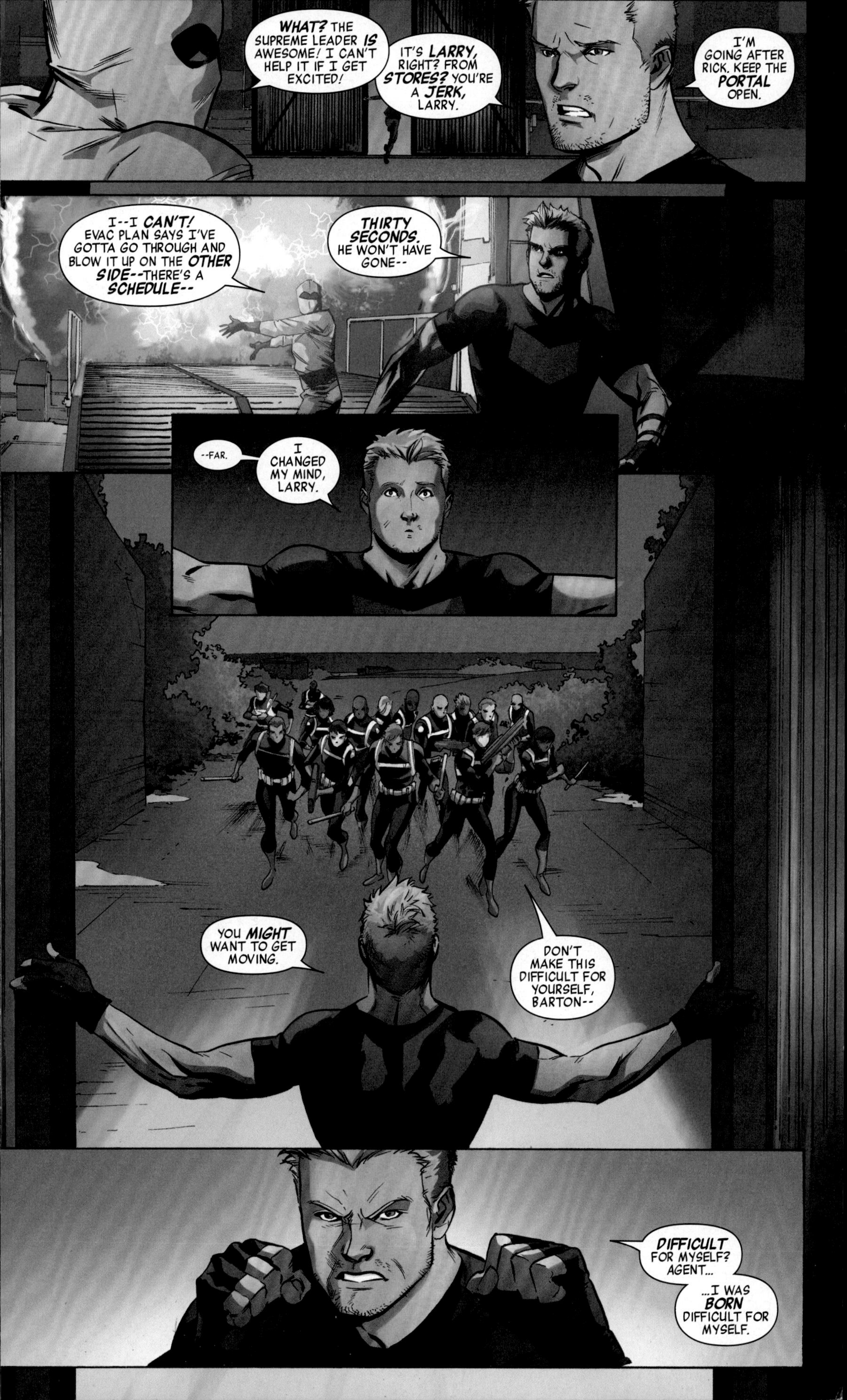

WHAT? THE SUPREME LEADER IS AWESOME! I CAN'T HELP IT IF I GET EXCITED!
IT'S LARRY, RIGHT? FROM STORES? YOU'RE A JERK, LARRY.
I'M GOING AFTER RICK. KEEP THE PORTAL OPEN.
I--I CAN'T! EVAC PLAN SAYS I'VE GOTTA GO THROUGH AND BLOW IT UP ON THE OTHER SIDE--THERE'S A SCHEDULE--
THIRTY SECONDS. HE WON'T HAVE GONE--
--FAR.
I CHANGED MY MIND, LARRY.
YOU MIGHT WANT TO GET MOVING.
DON'T MAKE THIS DIFFICULT FOR YOURSELF, BARTON--
DIFFICULT FOR MYSELF? AGENT...
...I WAS BORN DIFFICULT FOR MYSELF.

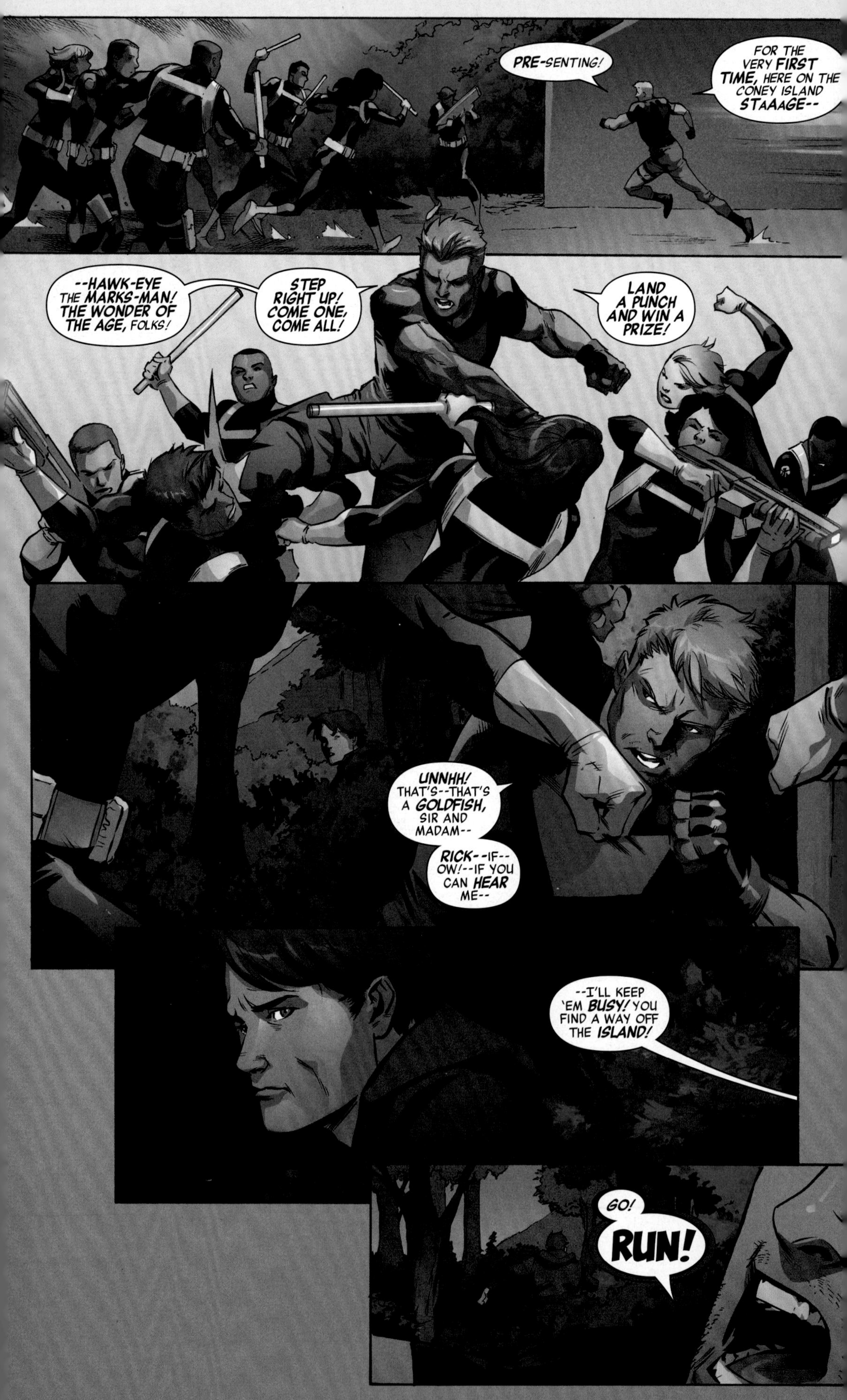
PRE-SENTING!
FOR THE VERY FIRST TIME, HERE ON THE CONEY ISLAND STAAAGE--
--HAWK-EYE THE MARKS-MAN! THE WONDER OF THE AGE, FOLKS!
STEP RIGHT UP! COME ONE, COME ALL!
LAND A PUNCH AND WIN A PRIZE!
UNNHH! THAT'S--THAT'S A GOLDFISH, SIR AND MADAM--
RICK--IF--OW!--IF YOU CAN HEAR ME--
--I'LL KEEP 'EM BUSY! YOU FIND A WAY OFF THE ISLAND!
GO!
RUN!

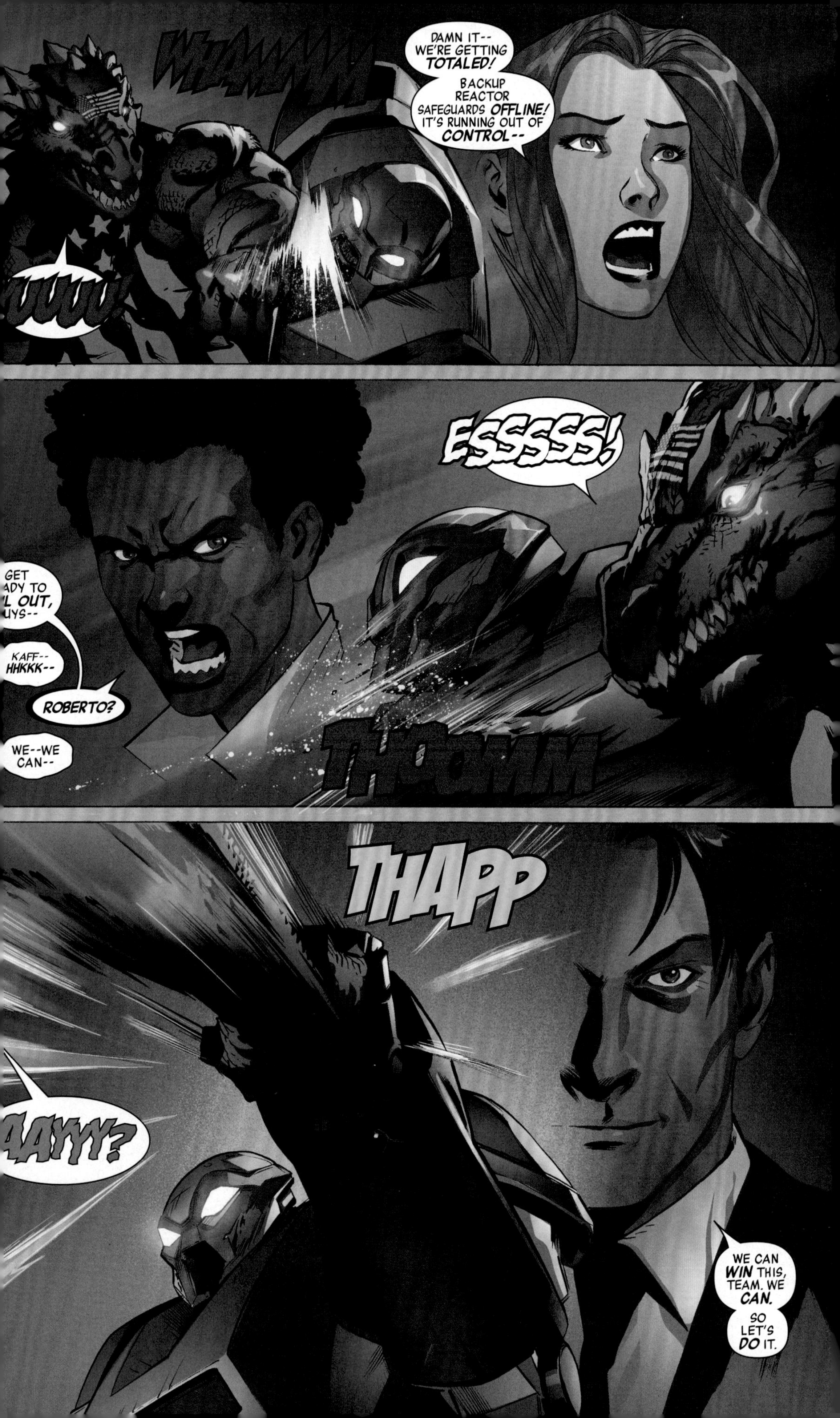
WHAMMMM
DAMN IT-- WE'RE GETTING TOTALED!
BACKUP REACTOR SAFEGUARDS OFFLINE! IT'S RUNNING OUT OF CONTROL--
UUUU!
ESSSSS!
GET ...ADY TO ...L OUT, ...UYS--
KAFF-- HHKKK--
ROBERTO?
WE--WE CAN--
THOOMM
THAPP
AAYYY?
WE CAN WIN THIS, TEAM. WE CAN.
SO LET'S DO IT.

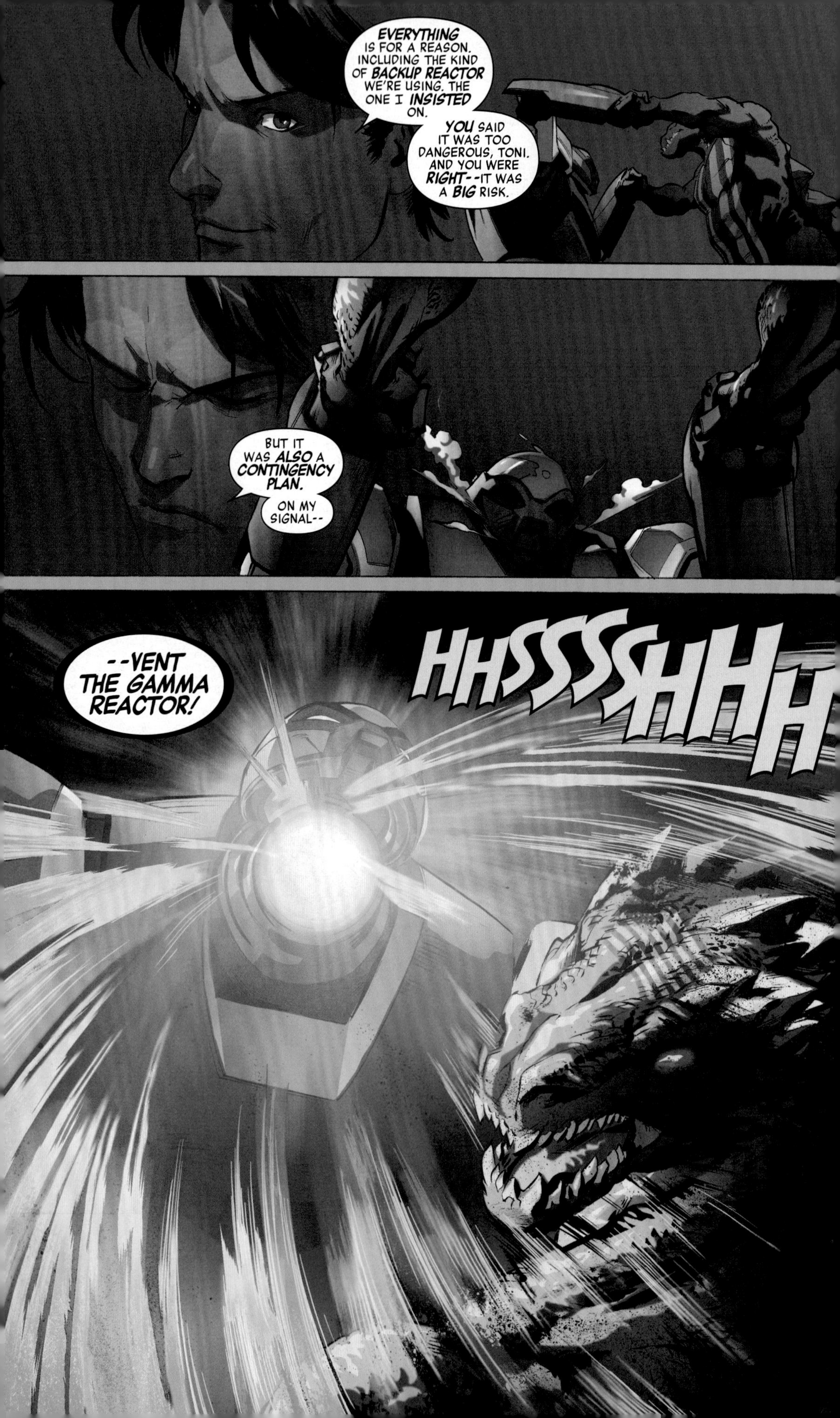
EVERYTHING IS FOR A REASON. INCLUDING THE KIND OF BACKUP REACTOR WE'RE USING. THE ONE I INSISTED ON.
YOU SAID IT WAS TOO DANGEROUS, TONI. AND YOU WERE RIGHT--IT WAS A BIG RISK.
BUT IT WAS ALSO A CONTINGENCY PLAN.
ON MY SIGNAL--
--VENT THE GAMMA REACTOR!
HHSSSSHHHH

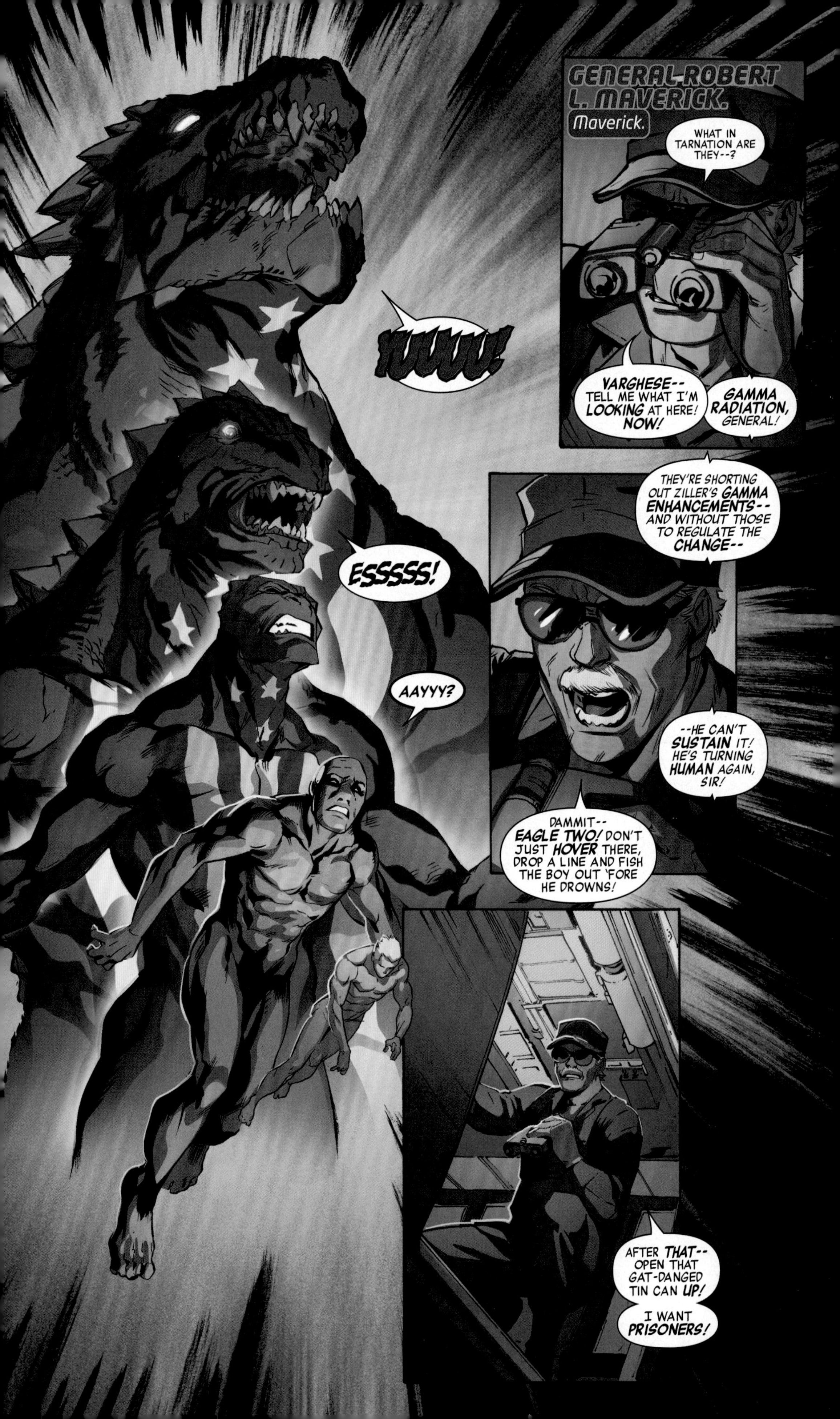

GENERAL ROBERT L. MAVERICK.
Maverick.
WHAT IN TARNATION ARE THEY--?
VARGHESE-- TELL ME WHAT I'M LOOKING AT HERE! NOW!
GAMMA RADIATION, GENERAL!
IIIIIII!
THEY'RE SHORTING OUT ZILLER'S GAMMA ENHANCEMENTS-- AND WITHOUT THOSE TO REGULATE THE CHANGE--
ESSSSS!
AAYYY?
--HE CAN'T SUSTAIN IT! HE'S TURNING HUMAN AGAIN, SIR!
DAMMIT-- EAGLE TWO! DON'T JUST HOVER THERE, DROP A LINE AND FISH THE BOY OUT 'FORE HE DROWNS!
AFTER THAT-- OPEN THAT GAT-DANGED TIN CAN UP!
I WANT PRISONERS!

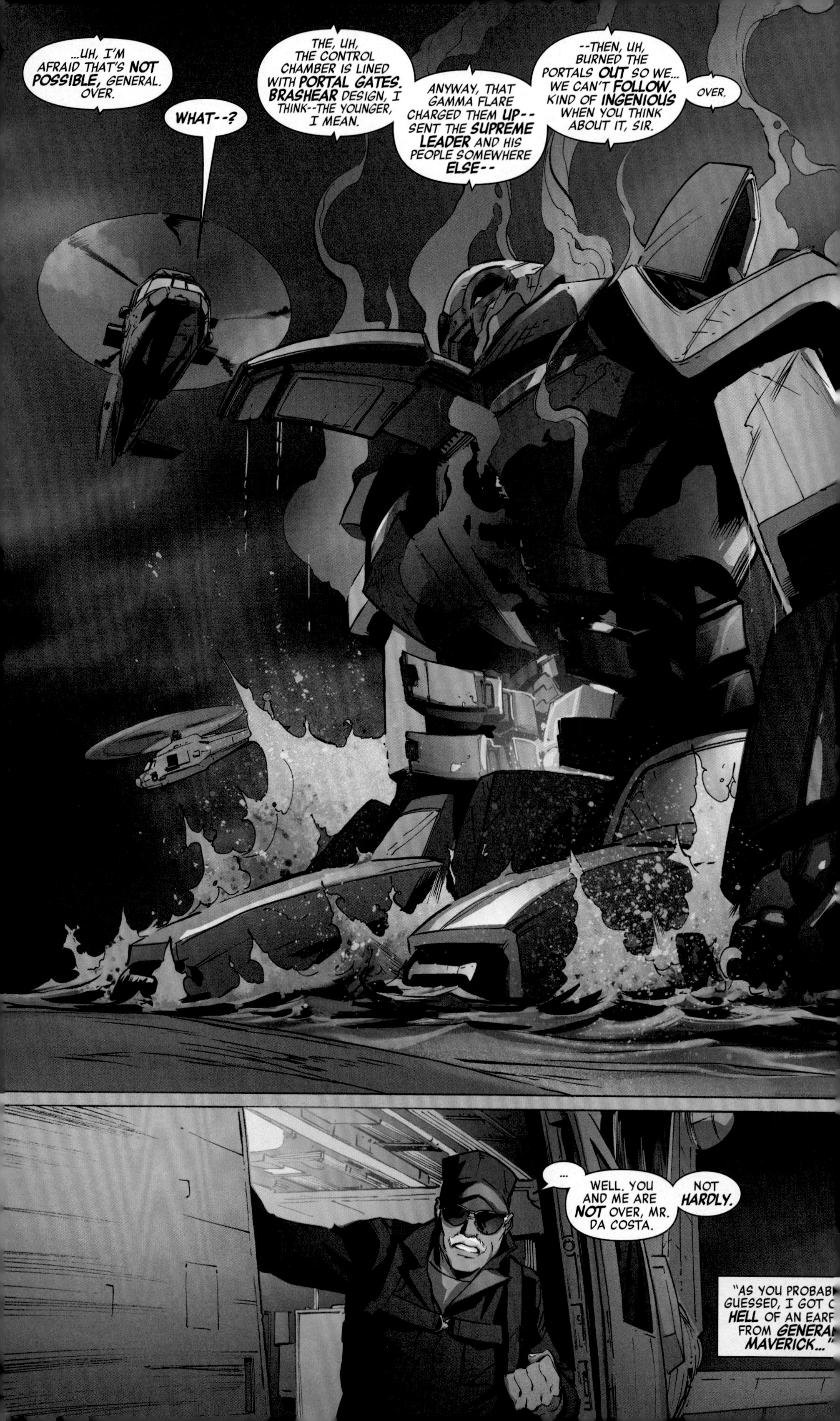
...UH, I'M AFRAID THAT'S NOT POSSIBLE, GENERAL. OVER.
WHAT--?
THE, UH, THE CONTROL CHAMBER IS LINED WITH PORTAL GATES. BRASHEAR DESIGN, I THINK--THE YOUNGER, I MEAN.
ANYWAY, THAT GAMMA FLARE CHARGED THEM UP--SENT THE SUPREME LEADER AND HIS PEOPLE SOMEWHERE ELSE--
--THEN, UH, BURNED THE PORTALS OUT SO WE... WE CAN'T FOLLOW. KIND OF INGENIOUS WHEN YOU THINK ABOUT IT, SIR.
OVER.
...
WELL. YOU AND ME ARE NOT OVER, MR. DA COSTA.
NOT HARDLY.
"AS YOU PROBAB GUESSED, I GOT HELL OF AN EAR FROM GENERA MAVERICK..."

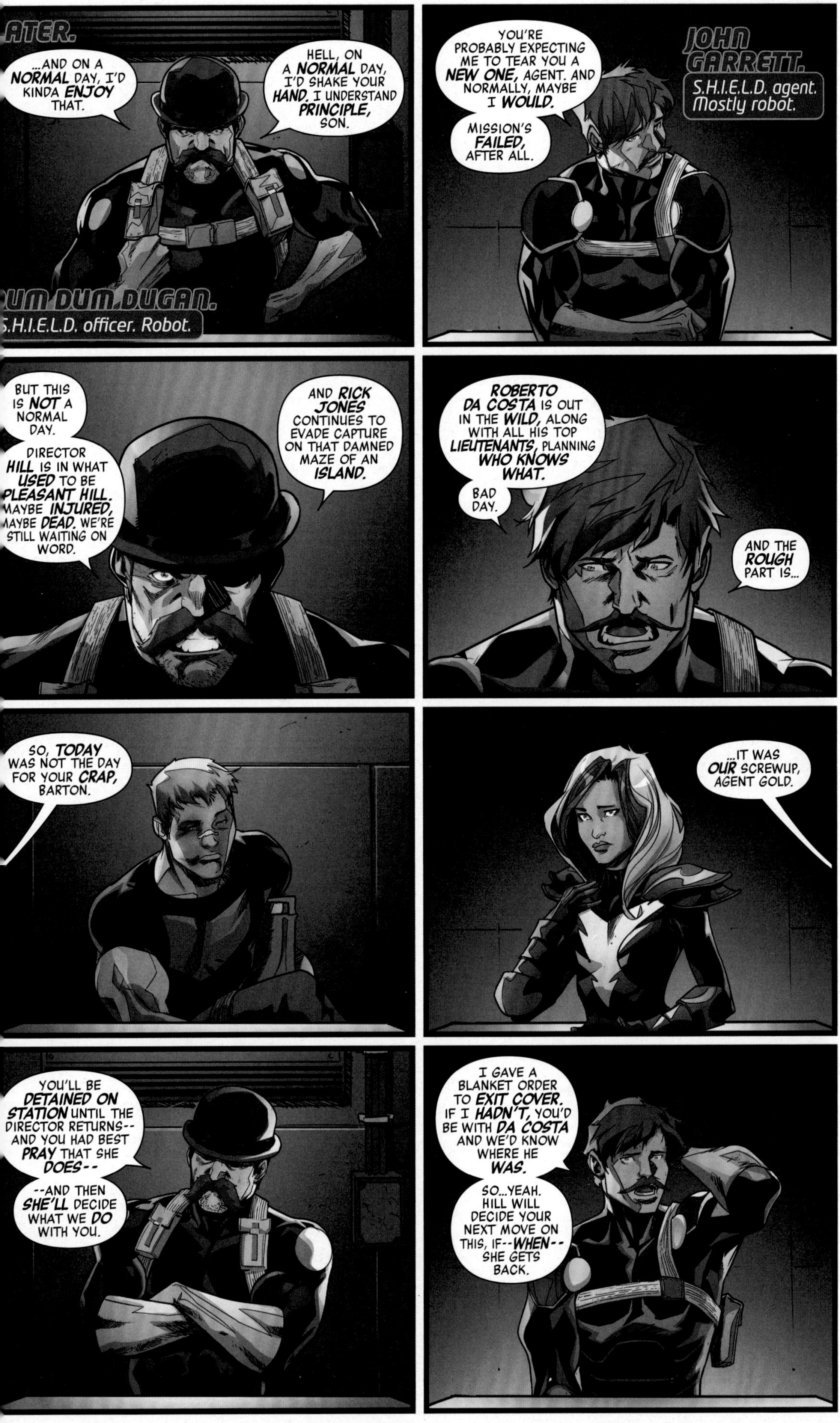

LATER.
...AND ON A NORMAL DAY, I'D KINDA ENJOY THAT.
HELL, ON A NORMAL DAY, I'D SHAKE YOUR HAND. I UNDERSTAND PRINCIPLE, SON.
DUM DUM DUGAN.
S.H.I.E.L.D. officer. Robot.
JOHN GARRETT.
S.H.I.E.L.D. agent. Mostly robot.
YOU'RE PROBABLY EXPECTING ME TO TEAR YOU A NEW ONE, AGENT. AND NORMALLY, MAYBE I WOULD.
MISSION'S FAILED, AFTER ALL.
BUT THIS IS NOT A NORMAL DAY.
DIRECTOR HILL IS IN WHAT USED TO BE PLEASANT HILL. MAYBE INJURED, MAYBE DEAD. WE'RE STILL WAITING ON WORD.
AND RICK JONES CONTINUES TO EVADE CAPTURE ON THAT DAMNED MAZE OF AN ISLAND.
ROBERTO DA COSTA IS OUT IN THE WILD, ALONG WITH ALL HIS TOP LIEUTENANTS, PLANNING WHO KNOWS WHAT.
BAD DAY.
AND THE ROUGH PART IS...
SO, TODAY WAS NOT THE DAY FOR YOUR CRAP, BARTON.
...IT WAS OUR SCREWUP, AGENT GOLD.
YOU'LL BE DETAINED ON STATION UNTIL THE DIRECTOR RETURNS-- AND YOU HAD BEST PRAY THAT SHE DOES--
--AND THEN SHE'LL DECIDE WHAT WE DO WITH YOU.
I GAVE A BLANKET ORDER TO EXIT COVER. IF I HADN'T, YOU'D BE WITH DA COSTA AND WE'D KNOW WHERE HE WAS.
SO...YEAH. HILL WILL DECIDE YOUR NEXT MOVE ON THIS, IF--WHEN-- SHE GETS BACK.

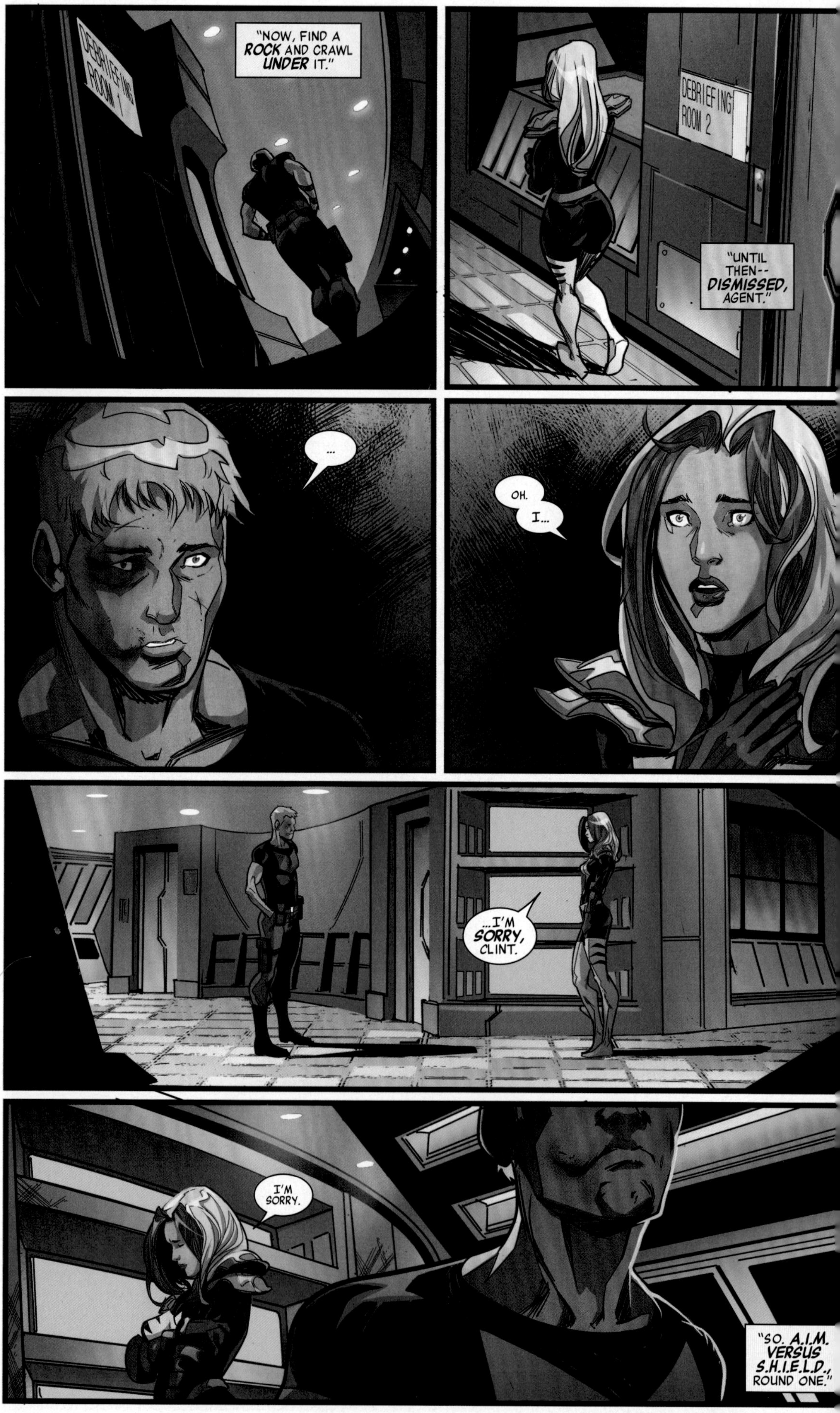
DEBRIEFING ROOM 1
"NOW, FIND A ROCK AND CRAWL UNDER IT."
DEBRIEFING ROOM 2
"UNTIL THEN--DISMISSED, AGENT."
...
OH.
I...
...I'M SORRY, CLINT.
I'M SORRY.
"SO. A.I.M. VERSUS S.H.I.E.L.D., ROUND ONE."

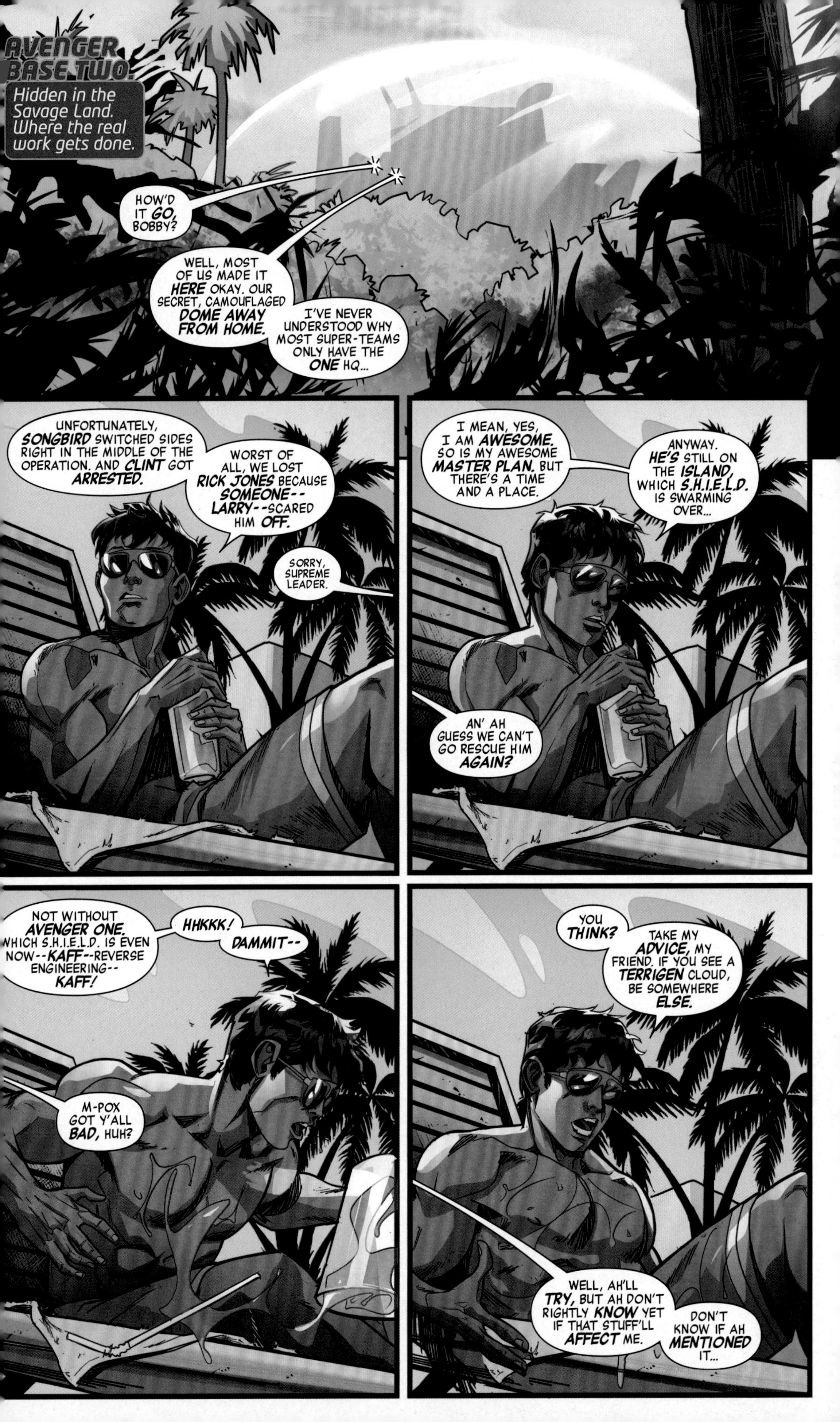
AVENGER BASE TWO.
Hidden in the Savage Land. Where the real work gets done.
HOW'D IT GO, BOBBY?
WELL, MOST OF US MADE IT HERE OKAY. OUR SECRET, CAMOUFLAGED DOME AWAY FROM HOME.
I'VE NEVER UNDERSTOOD WHY MOST SUPER-TEAMS ONLY HAVE THE ONE HQ...
UNFORTUNATELY, SONGBIRD SWITCHED SIDES RIGHT IN THE MIDDLE OF THE OPERATION. AND CLINT GOT ARRESTED.
WORST OF ALL, WE LOST RICK JONES BECAUSE SOMEONE--LARRY--SCARED HIM OFF.
SORRY, SUPREME LEADER.
I MEAN, YES, I AM AWESOME. SO IS MY AWESOME MASTER PLAN. BUT THERE'S A TIME AND A PLACE.
ANYWAY. HE'S STILL ON THE ISLAND, WHICH S.H.I.E.L.D. IS SWARMING OVER...
AN' AH GUESS WE CAN'T GO RESCUE HIM AGAIN?
NOT WITHOUT AVENGER ONE. WHICH S.H.I.E.L.D. IS EVEN NOW--KAFF--REVERSE ENGINEERING--KAFF!
HHKKK!
DAMMIT--
M-POX GOT Y'ALL BAD, HUH?
YOU THINK?
TAKE MY ADVICE, MY FRIEND. IF YOU SEE A TERRIGEN CLOUD, BE SOMEWHERE ELSE.
WELL, AH'LL TRY, BUT AH DON'T RIGHTLY KNOW YET IF THAT STUFF'LL AFFECT ME.
DON'T KNOW IF AH MENTIONED IT...

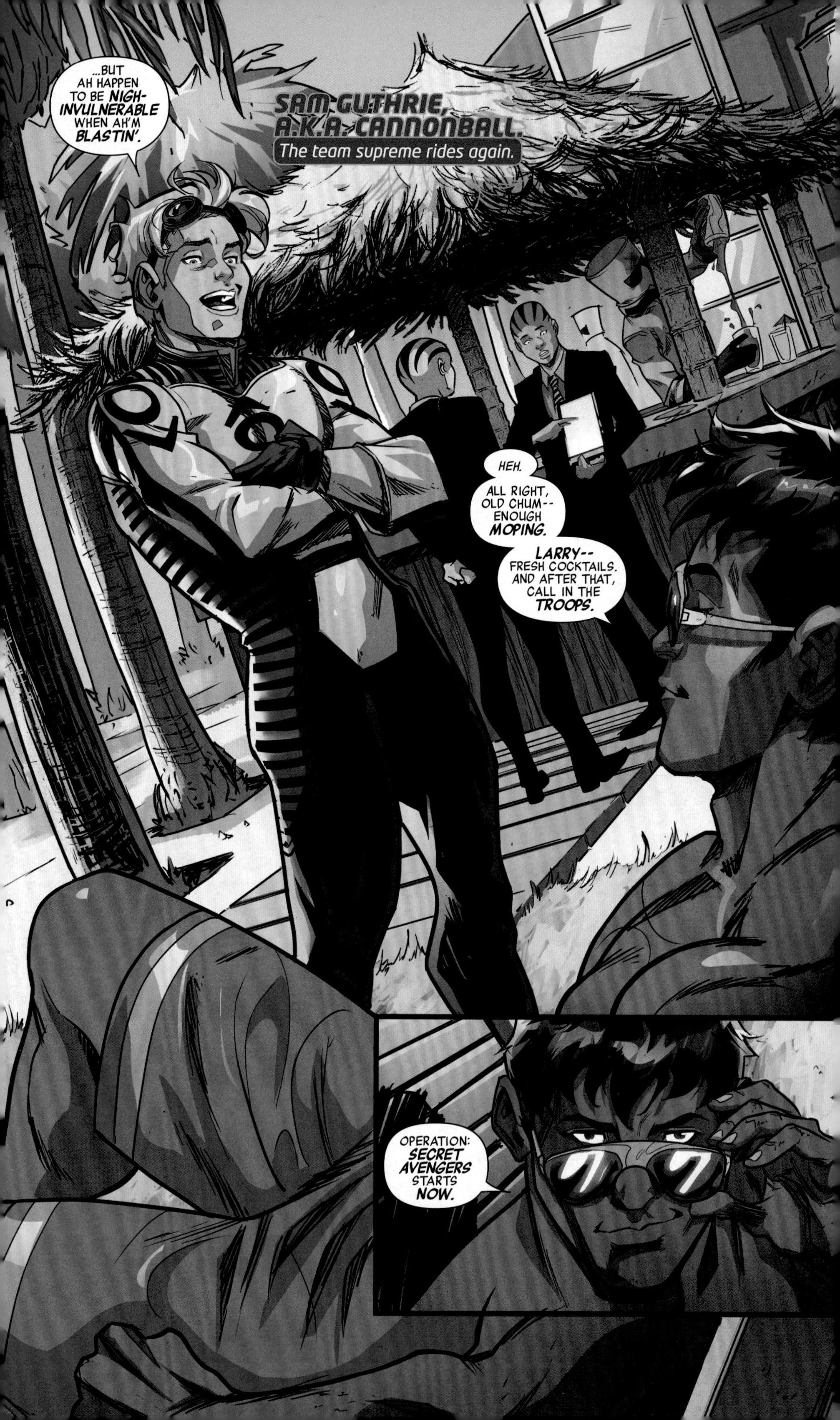
...BUT AH HAPPEN TO BE NIGH-INVULNERABLE WHEN AH'M BLASTIN'.
SAM GUTHRIE, A.K.A. CANNONBALL.
The team supreme rides again.
HEH.
ALL RIGHT, OLD CHUM-- ENOUGH MOPING.
LARRY-- FRESH COCKTAILS. AND AFTER THAT, CALL IN THE TROOPS.
OPERATION: SECRET AVENGERS STARTS NOW.

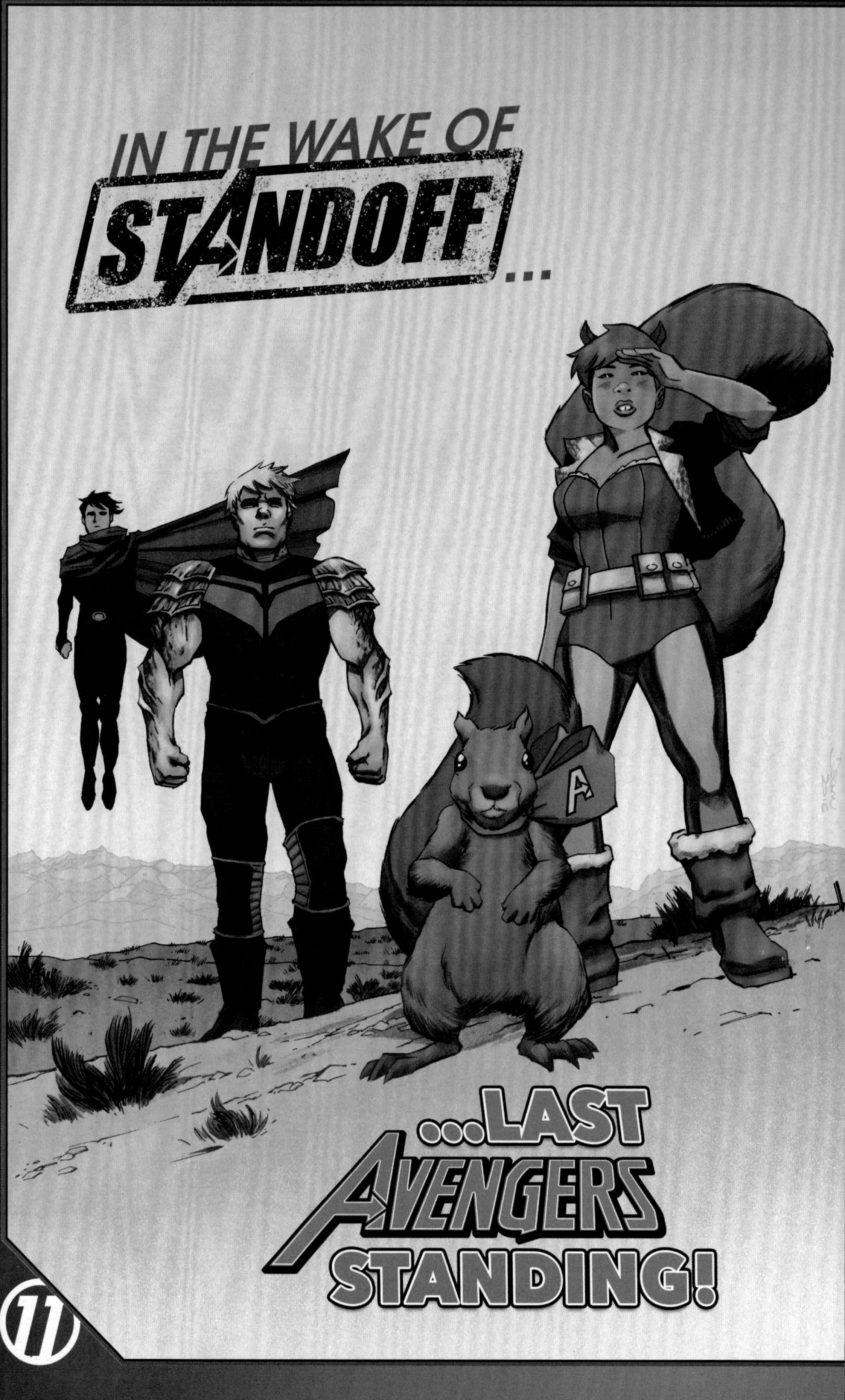
IN THE WAKE OF
STANDOFF...
...LAST
AVENGERS
STANDING!
11

"MEET THE PARENT"

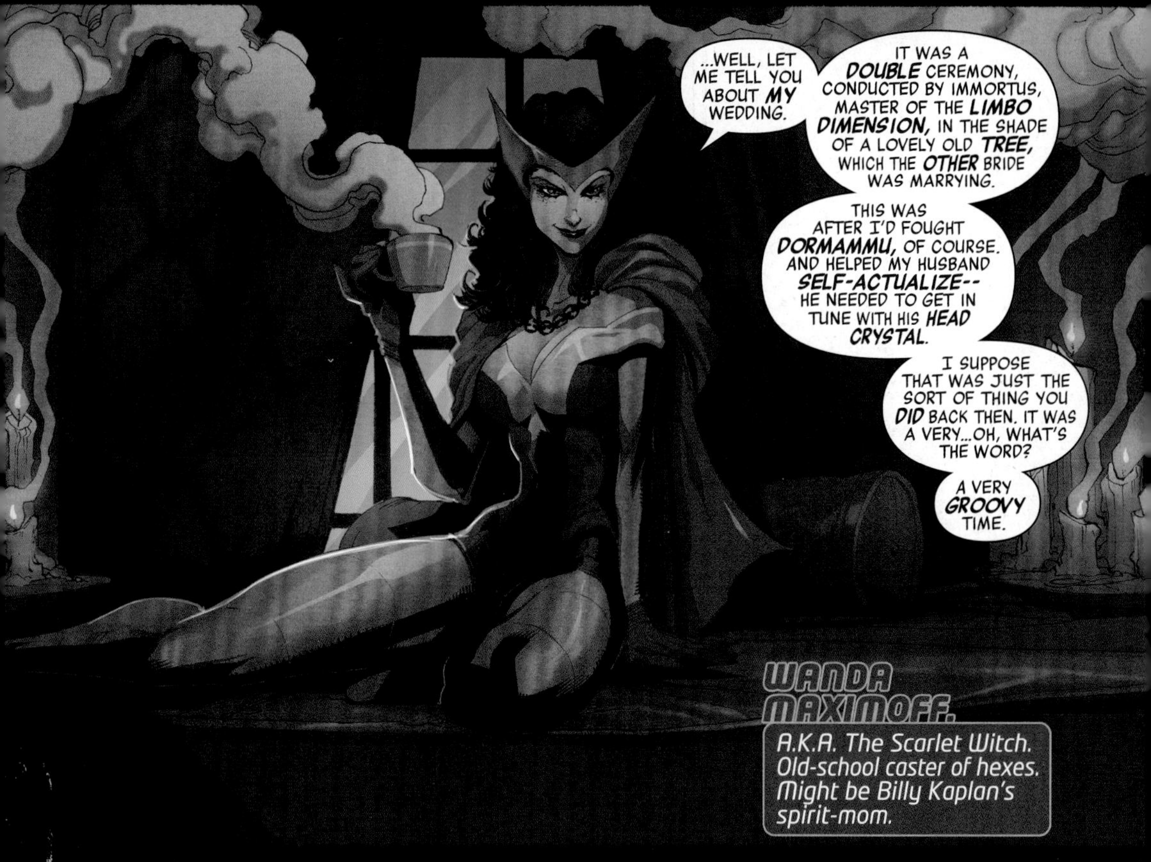

...WELL, LET ME TELL YOU ABOUT MY WEDDING.
IT WAS A DOUBLE CEREMONY, CONDUCTED BY IMMORTUS, MASTER OF THE LIMBO DIMENSION, IN THE SHADE OF A LOVELY OLD TREE, WHICH THE OTHER BRIDE WAS MARRYING.
THIS WAS AFTER I'D FOUGHT DORMAMMU, OF COURSE. AND HELPED MY HUSBAND SELF-ACTUALIZE-- HE NEEDED TO GET IN TUNE WITH HIS HEAD CRYSTAL.
I SUPPOSE THAT WAS JUST THE SORT OF THING YOU DID BACK THEN. IT WAS A VERY...OH, WHAT'S THE WORD?
A VERY GROOVY TIME.
WANDA MAXIMOFF.
A.K.A. The Scarlet Witch. Old-school caster of hexes. Might be Billy Kaplan's spirit-mom.

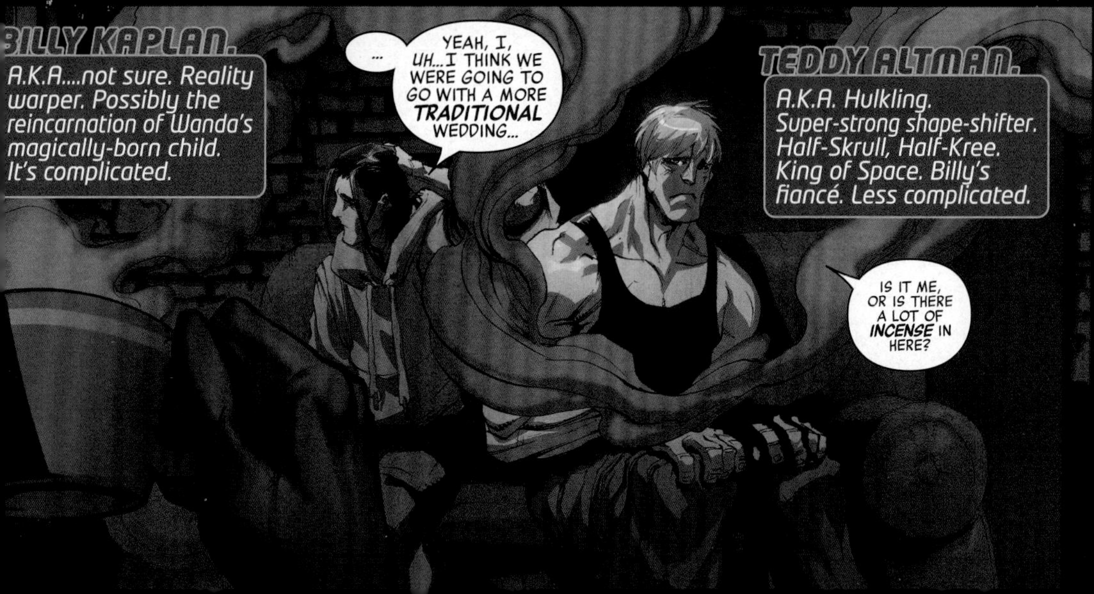

BILLY KAPLAN.
A.K.A....not sure. Reality warper. Possibly the reincarnation of Wanda's magically-born child. It's complicated.
...
YEAH, I, UH...I THINK WE WERE GOING TO GO WITH A MORE TRADITIONAL WEDDING...
TEDDY ALTMAN.
A.K.A. Hulkling. Super-strong shape-shifter. Half-Skrull, Half-Kree. King of Space. Billy's fiancé. Less complicated.
IS IT ME, OR IS THERE A LOT OF INCENSE IN HERE?

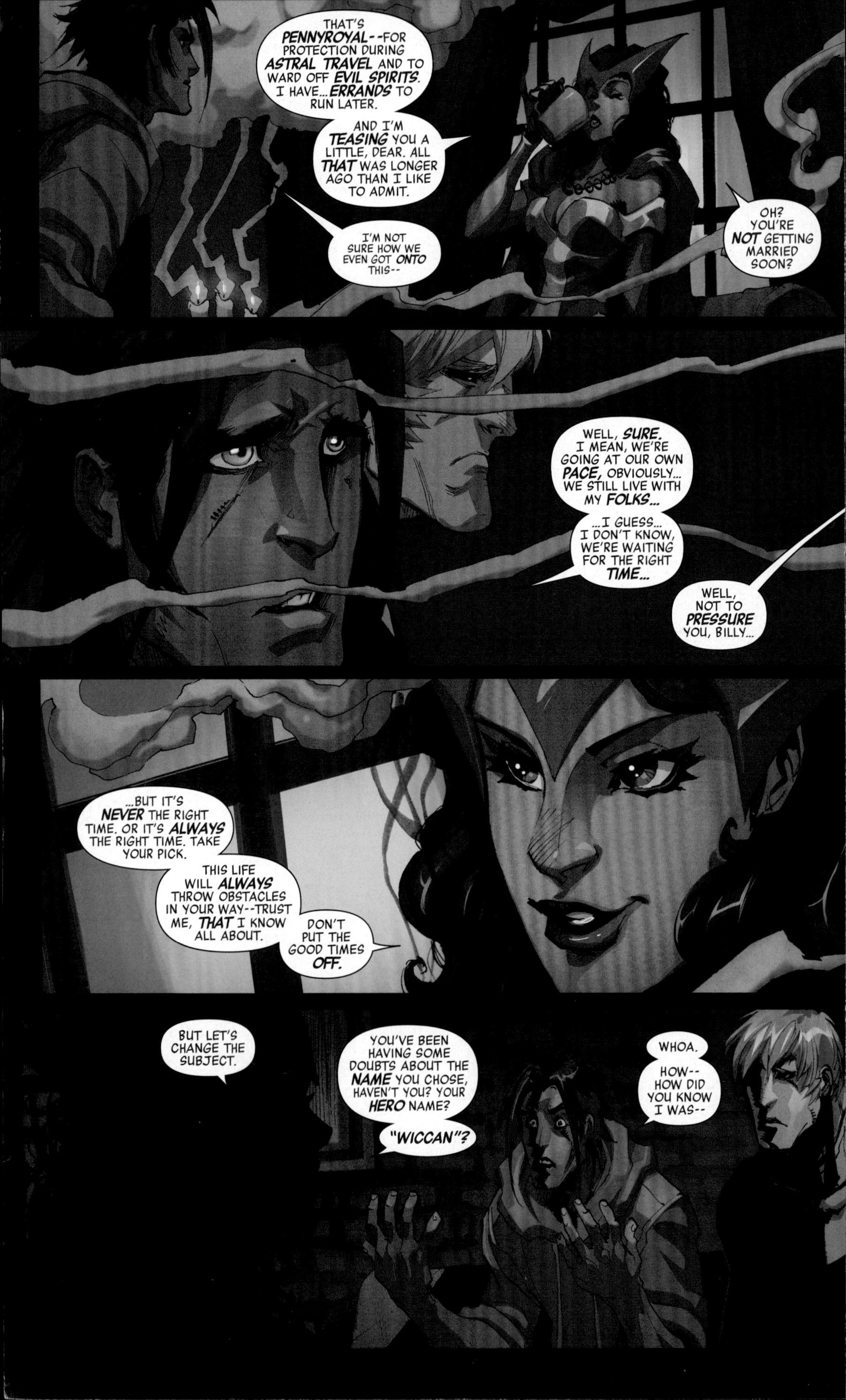
THAT'S PENNYROYAL--FOR PROTECTION DURING ASTRAL TRAVEL AND TO WARD OFF EVIL SPIRITS. I HAVE...ERRANDS TO RUN LATER.
AND I'M TEASING YOU A LITTLE, DEAR. ALL THAT WAS LONGER AGO THAN I LIKE TO ADMIT.
I'M NOT SURE HOW WE EVEN GOT ONTO THIS--
OH? YOU'RE NOT GETTING MARRIED SOON?
WELL, SURE. I MEAN, WE'RE GOING AT OUR OWN PACE, OBVIOUSLY... WE STILL LIVE WITH MY FOLKS...
...I GUESS... I DON'T KNOW, WE'RE WAITING FOR THE RIGHT TIME...
WELL, NOT TO PRESSURE YOU, BILLY...
...BUT IT'S NEVER THE RIGHT TIME. OR IT'S ALWAYS THE RIGHT TIME. TAKE YOUR PICK.
THIS LIFE WILL ALWAYS THROW OBSTACLES IN YOUR WAY--TRUST ME, THAT I KNOW ALL ABOUT.
DON'T PUT THE GOOD TIMES OFF.
BUT LET'S CHANGE THE SUBJECT.
YOU'VE BEEN HAVING SOME DOUBTS ABOUT THE NAME YOU CHOSE, HAVEN'T YOU? YOUR HERO NAME?
"WICCAN"?
WHOA.
HOW-- HOW DID YOU KNOW I WAS--

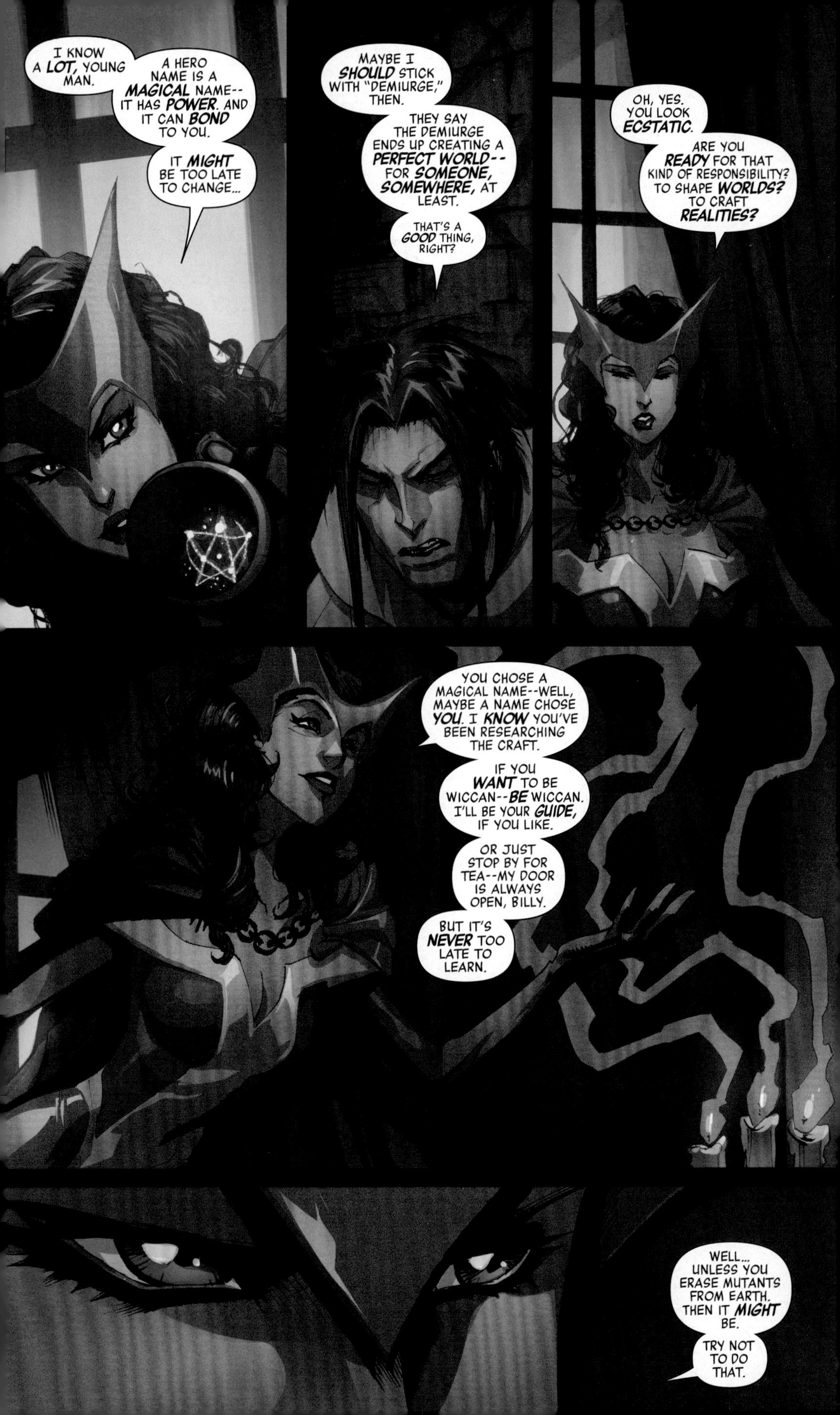

I KNOW A LOT, YOUNG MAN.
A HERO NAME IS A MAGICAL NAME-- IT HAS POWER. AND IT CAN BOND TO YOU.
IT MIGHT BE TOO LATE TO CHANGE...
MAYBE I SHOULD STICK WITH "DEMIURGE," THEN.
THEY SAY THE DEMIURGE ENDS UP CREATING A PERFECT WORLD-- FOR SOMEONE, SOMEWHERE, AT LEAST.
THAT'S A GOOD THING, RIGHT?
OH, YES. YOU LOOK ECSTATIC.
ARE YOU READY FOR THAT KIND OF RESPONSIBILITY? TO SHAPE WORLDS? TO CRAFT REALITIES?
YOU CHOSE A MAGICAL NAME--WELL, MAYBE A NAME CHOSE YOU. I KNOW YOU'VE BEEN RESEARCHING THE CRAFT.
IF YOU WANT TO BE WICCAN--BE WICCAN. I'LL BE YOUR GUIDE, IF YOU LIKE.
OR JUST STOP BY FOR TEA--MY DOOR IS ALWAYS OPEN, BILLY.
BUT IT'S NEVER TOO LATE TO LEARN.
WELL... UNLESS YOU ERASE MUTANTS FROM EARTH. THEN IT MIGHT BE.
TRY NOT TO DO THAT.

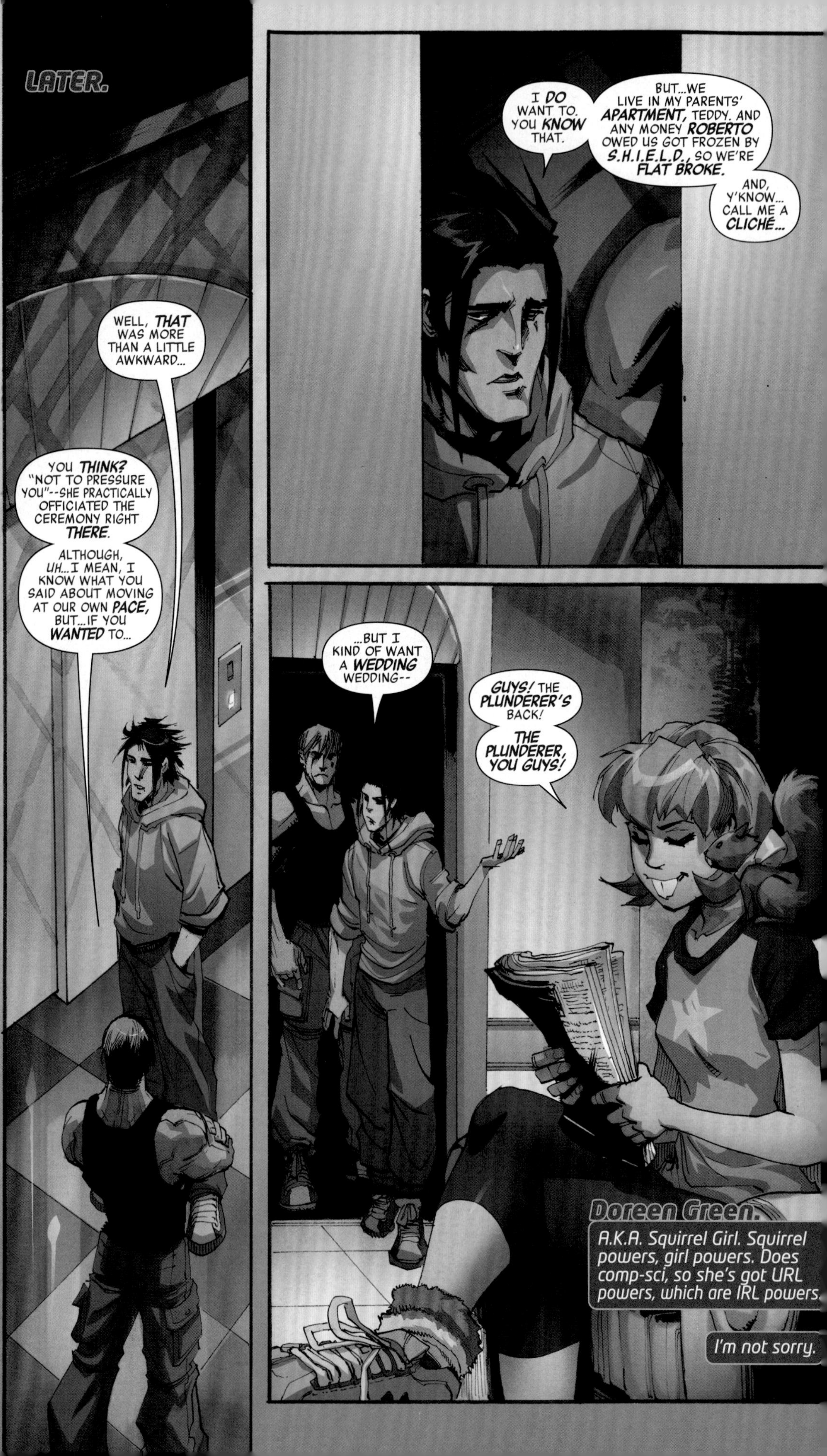
LATER.
WELL, THAT WAS MORE THAN A LITTLE AWKWARD...
YOU THINK? "NOT TO PRESSURE YOU"--SHE PRACTICALLY OFFICIATED THE CEREMONY RIGHT THERE.
ALTHOUGH, UH...I MEAN, I KNOW WHAT YOU SAID ABOUT MOVING AT OUR OWN PACE, BUT...IF YOU WANTED TO...
I DO WANT TO. YOU KNOW THAT.
BUT...WE LIVE IN MY PARENTS' APARTMENT, TEDDY. AND ANY MONEY ROBERTO OWED US GOT FROZEN BY S.H.I.E.L.D., SO WE'RE FLAT BROKE.
AND, Y'KNOW... CALL ME A CLICHÉ...
...BUT I KIND OF WANT A WEDDING WEDDING--
GUYS! THE PLUNDERER'S BACK!
THE PLUNDERER, YOU GUYS!
Doreen Green.
A.K.A. Squirrel Girl. Squirrel powers, girl powers. Does comp-sci, so she's got URL powers, which are IRL powers.
I'm not sorry.

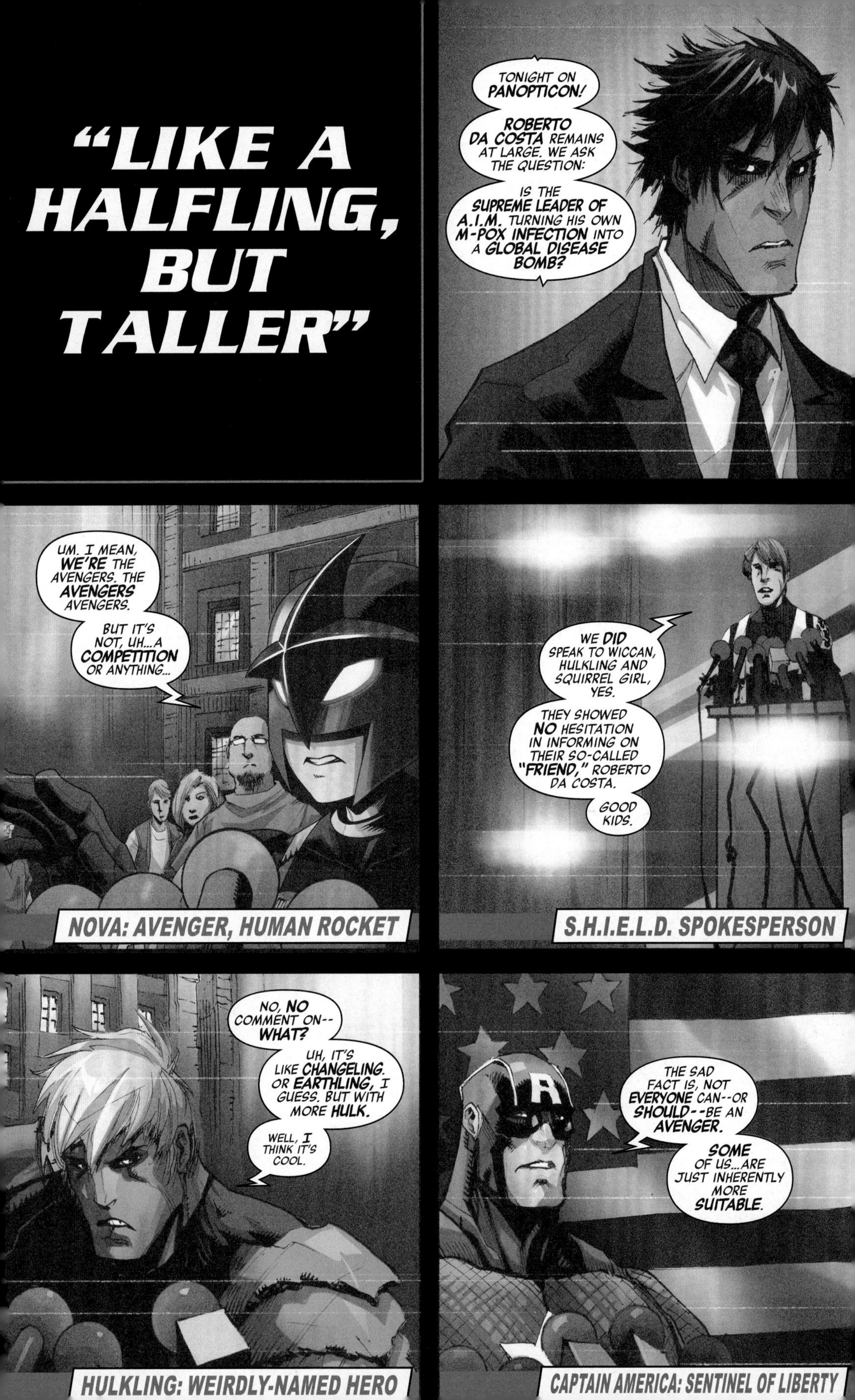
"LIKE A HALFLING, BUT TALLER"
TONIGHT ON PANOPTICON!
ROBERTO DA COSTA REMAINS AT LARGE. WE ASK THE QUESTION:
IS THE SUPREME LEADER OF A.I.M. TURNING HIS OWN M-POX INFECTION INTO A GLOBAL DISEASE BOMB?
UM. I MEAN, WE'RE THE AVENGERS. THE AVENGERS AVENGERS.
BUT IT'S NOT, UH...A COMPETITION OR ANYTHING...
NOVA: AVENGER, HUMAN ROCKET
WE DID SPEAK TO WICCAN, HULKLING AND SQUIRREL GIRL, YES.
THEY SHOWED NO HESITATION IN INFORMING ON THEIR SO-CALLED "FRIEND," ROBERTO DA COSTA.
GOOD KIDS.
S.H.I.E.L.D. SPOKESPERSON
NO, NO COMMENT ON--WHAT?
UH, IT'S LIKE CHANGELING. OR EARTHLING, I GUESS. BUT WITH MORE HULK.
WELL, I THINK IT'S COOL.
HULKLING: WEIRDLY-NAMED HERO
THE SAD FACT IS, NOT EVERYONE CAN--OR SHOULD--BE AN AVENGER.
SOME OF US...ARE JUST INHERENTLY MORE SUITABLE.
CAPTAIN AMERICA: SENTINEL OF LIBERTY

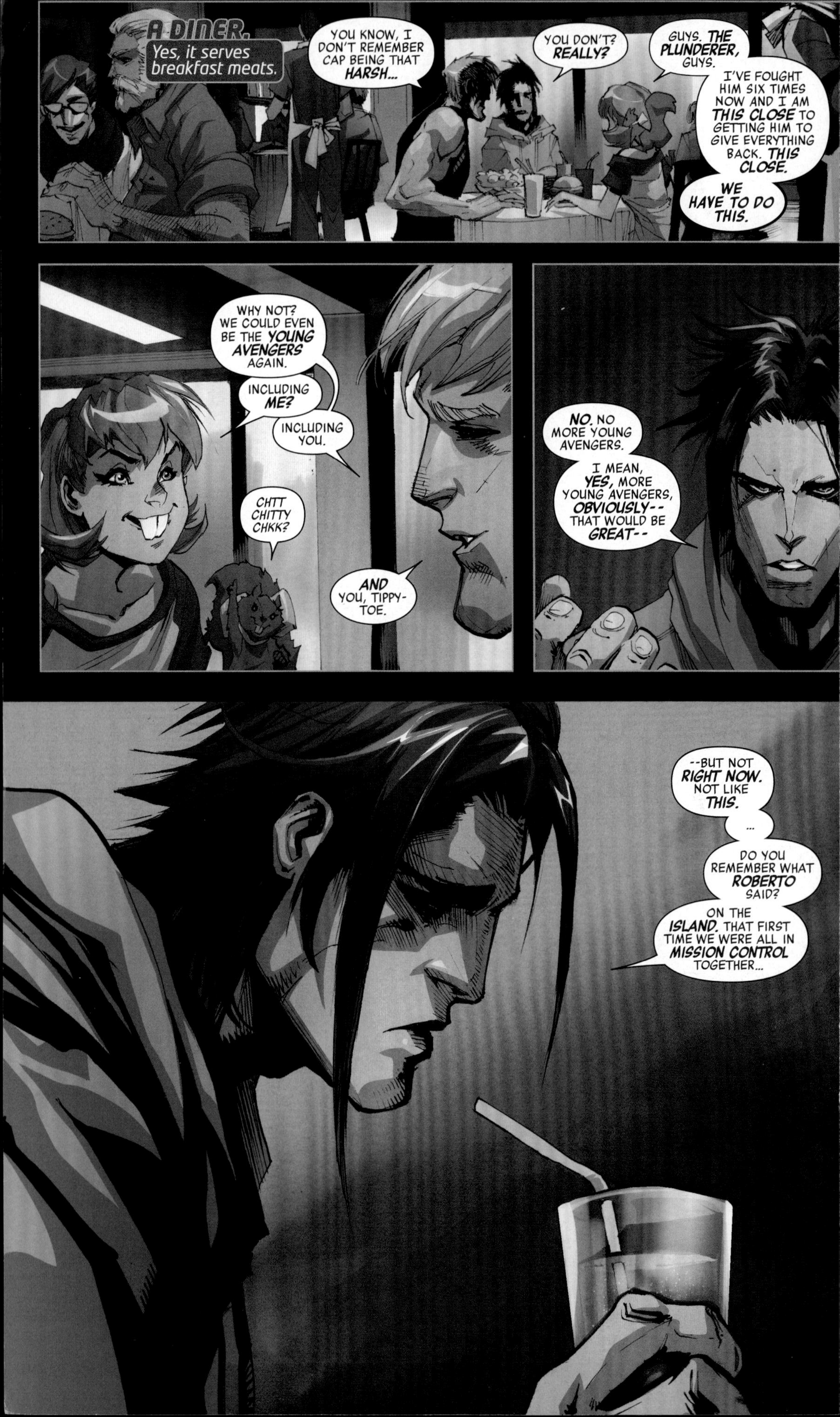
A DINER.
Yes, it serves breakfast meats.
YOU KNOW, I DON'T REMEMBER CAP BEING THAT HARSH...
YOU DON'T? REALLY?
GUYS. THE PLUNDERER, GUYS.
I'VE FOUGHT HIM SIX TIMES NOW AND I AM THIS CLOSE TO GETTING HIM TO GIVE EVERYTHING BACK. THIS CLOSE.
WE HAVE TO DO THIS.
WHY NOT? WE COULD EVEN BE THE YOUNG AVENGERS AGAIN.
INCLUDING ME?
INCLUDING YOU.
CHTT CHITTY CHKK?
AND YOU, TIPPY-TOE.
NO. NO MORE YOUNG AVENGERS.
I MEAN, YES, MORE YOUNG AVENGERS, OBVIOUSLY-- THAT WOULD BE GREAT--
--BUT NOT RIGHT NOW. NOT LIKE THIS.
...
DO YOU REMEMBER WHAT ROBERTO SAID?
ON THE ISLAND. THAT FIRST TIME WE WERE ALL IN MISSION CONTROL TOGETHER...

"WHAT ROBERTO SAID:"

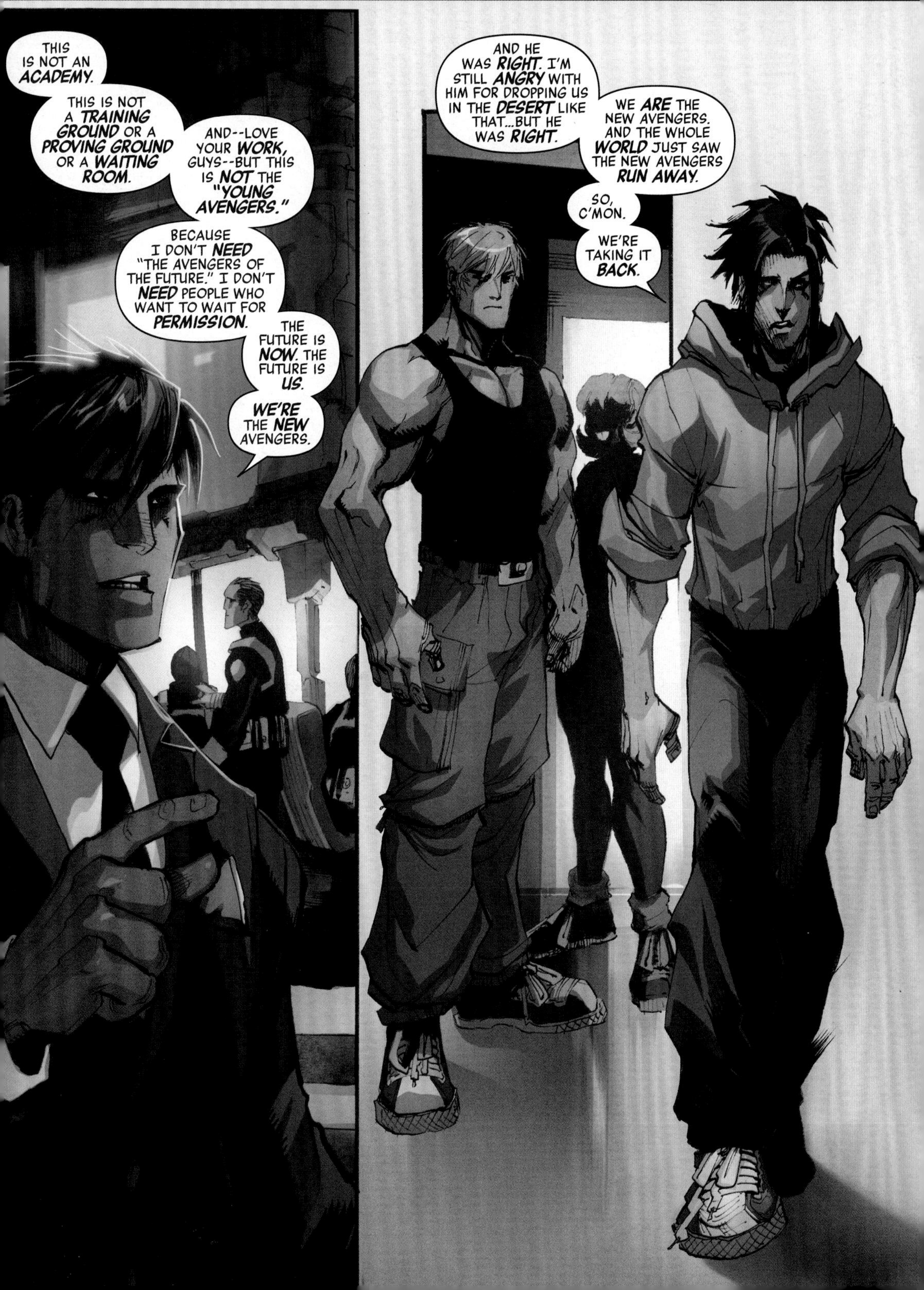
THIS IS NOT AN ACADEMY.
THIS IS NOT A TRAINING GROUND OR A PROVING GROUND OR A WAITING ROOM.
AND--LOVE YOUR WORK, GUYS--BUT THIS IS NOT THE "YOUNG AVENGERS."
BECAUSE I DON'T NEED "THE AVENGERS OF THE FUTURE." I DON'T NEED PEOPLE WHO WANT TO WAIT FOR PERMISSION.
THE FUTURE IS NOW. THE FUTURE IS US.
WE'RE THE NEW AVENGERS.
AND HE WAS RIGHT. I'M STILL ANGRY WITH HIM FOR DROPPING US IN THE DESERT LIKE THAT...BUT HE WAS RIGHT.
WE ARE THE NEW AVENGERS. AND THE WHOLE WORLD JUST SAW THE NEW AVENGERS RUN AWAY.
SO, C'MON.
WE'RE TAKING IT BACK.

"LIVE FROM THE SCENE OF THE DISASTER"

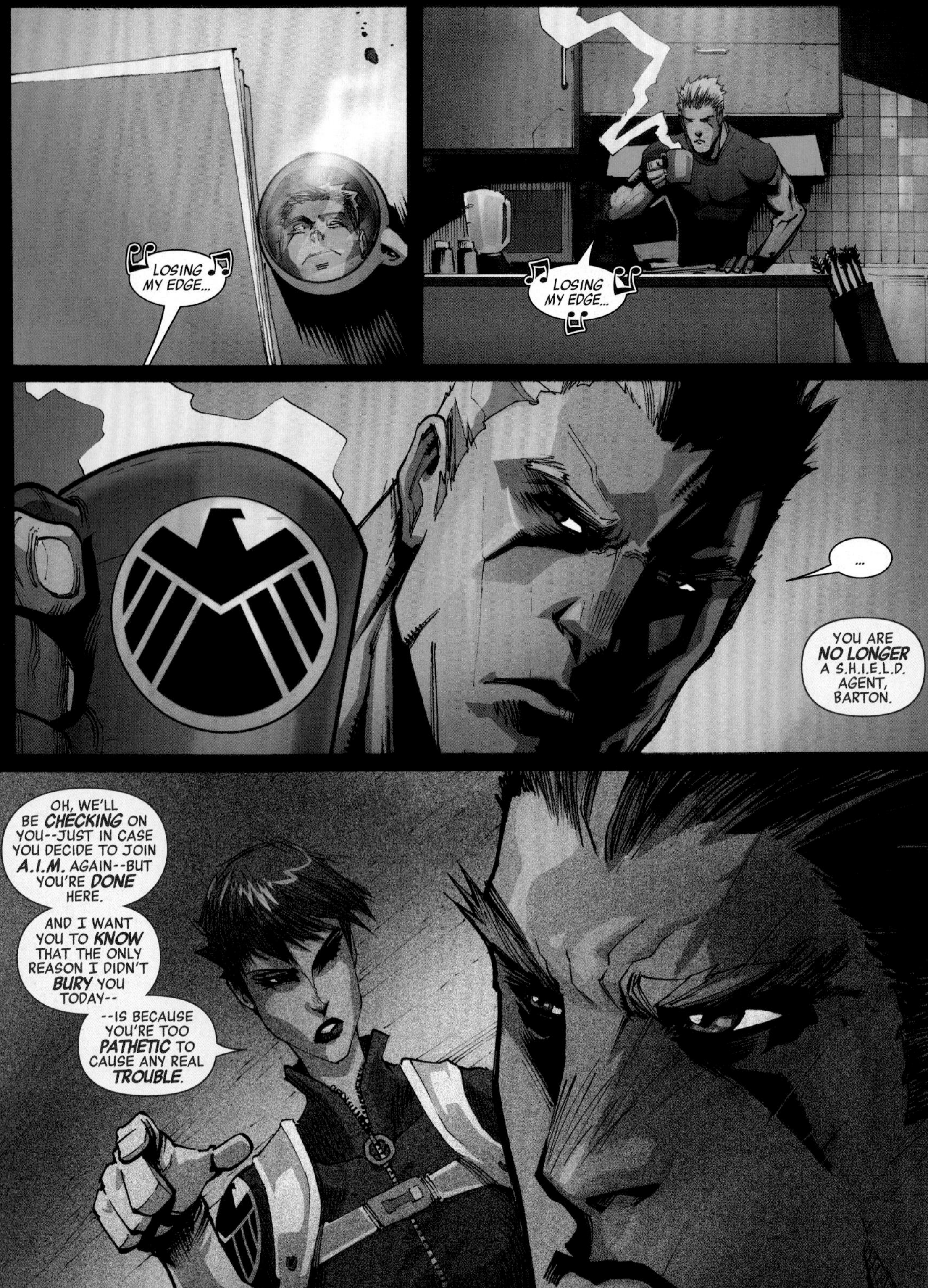

LOSING MY EDGE...
LOSING MY EDGE...
...
YOU ARE NO LONGER A S.H.I.E.L.D. AGENT, BARTON.
OH, WE'LL BE CHECKING ON YOU--JUST IN CASE YOU DECIDE TO JOIN A.I.M. AGAIN--BUT YOU'RE DONE HERE.
AND I WANT YOU TO KNOW THAT THE ONLY REASON I DIDN'T BURY YOU TODAY--
--IS BECAUSE YOU'RE TOO PATHETIC TO CAUSE ANY REAL TROUBLE.

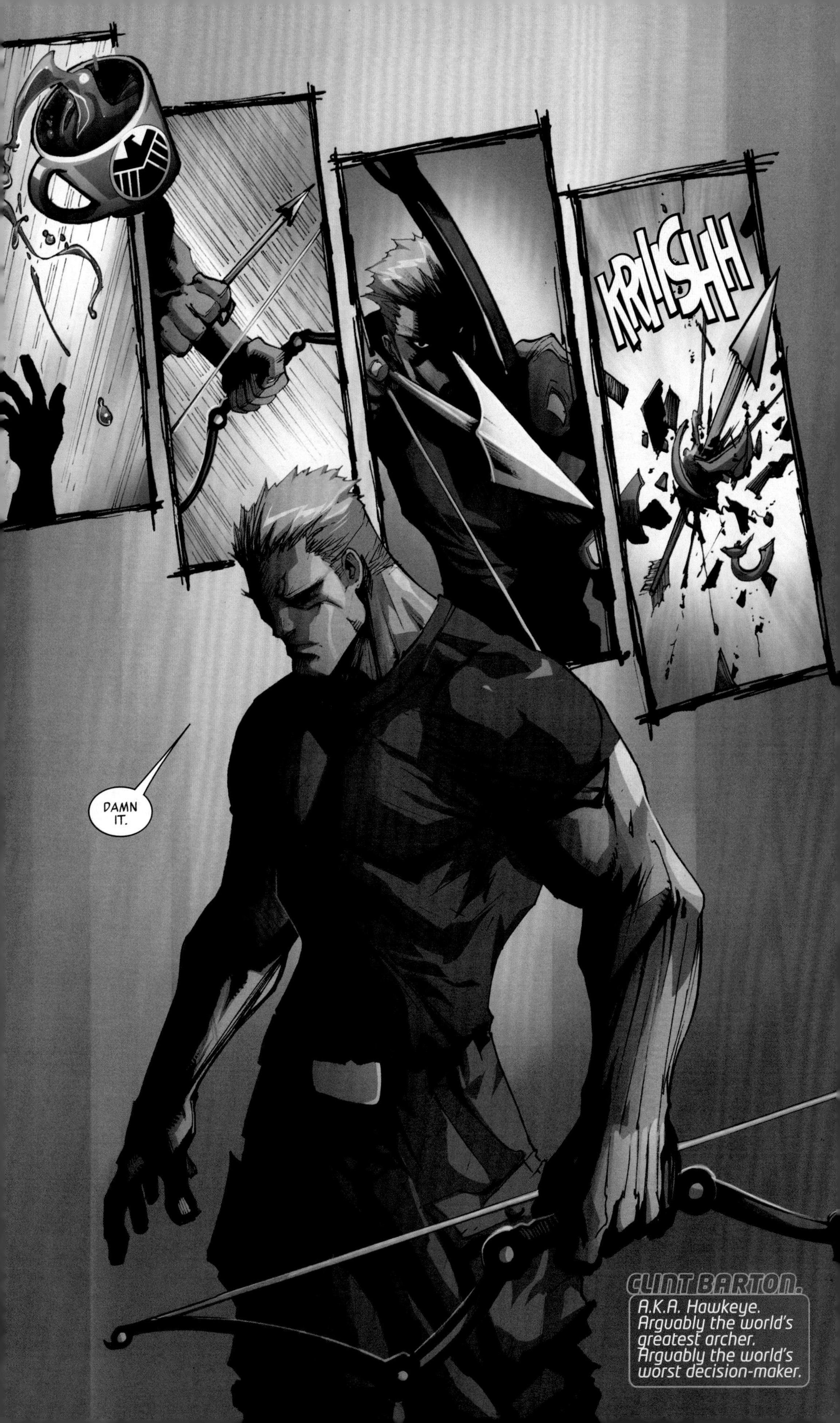
KRUSHH
DAMN IT.
CLINT BARTON.
A.K.A. Hawkeye. Arguably the world's greatest archer. Arguably the world's worst decision-maker.

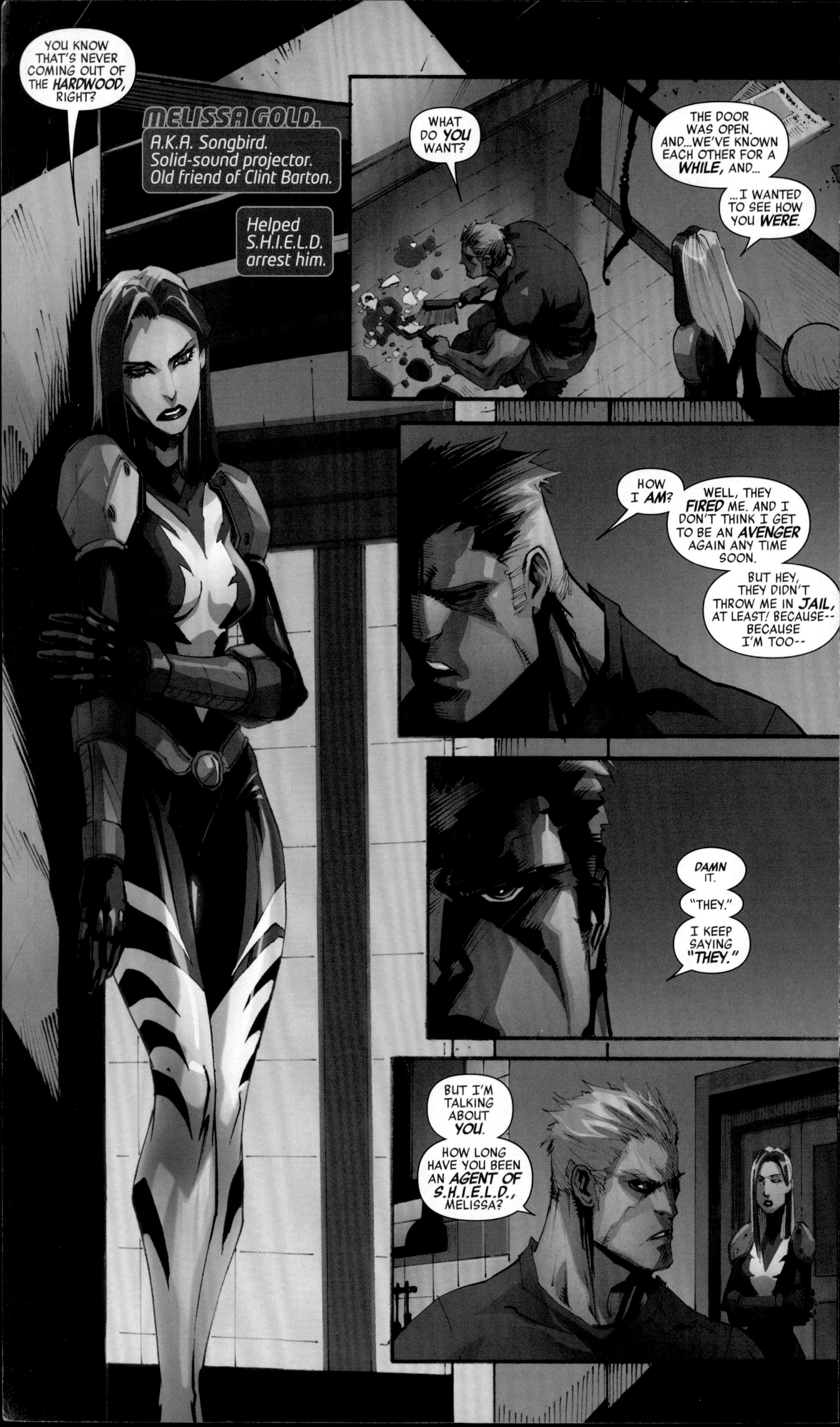
YOU KNOW THAT'S NEVER COMING OUT OF THE HARDWOOD, RIGHT?
MELISSA GOLD.
A.K.A. Songbird. Solid-sound projector. Old friend of Clint Barton.
Helped S.H.I.E.L.D. arrest him.
WHAT DO YOU WANT?
THE DOOR WAS OPEN. AND...WE'VE KNOWN EACH OTHER FOR A WHILE, AND...
...I WANTED TO SEE HOW YOU WERE.
HOW I AM?
WELL, THEY FIRED ME. AND I DON'T THINK I GET TO BE AN AVENGER AGAIN ANY TIME SOON.
BUT HEY, THEY DIDN'T THROW ME IN JAIL, AT LEAST! BECAUSE-- BECAUSE I'M TOO--
DAMN IT.
"THEY."
I KEEP SAYING "THEY."
BUT I'M TALKING ABOUT YOU.
HOW LONG HAVE YOU BEEN AN AGENT OF S.H.I.E.L.D., MELISSA?

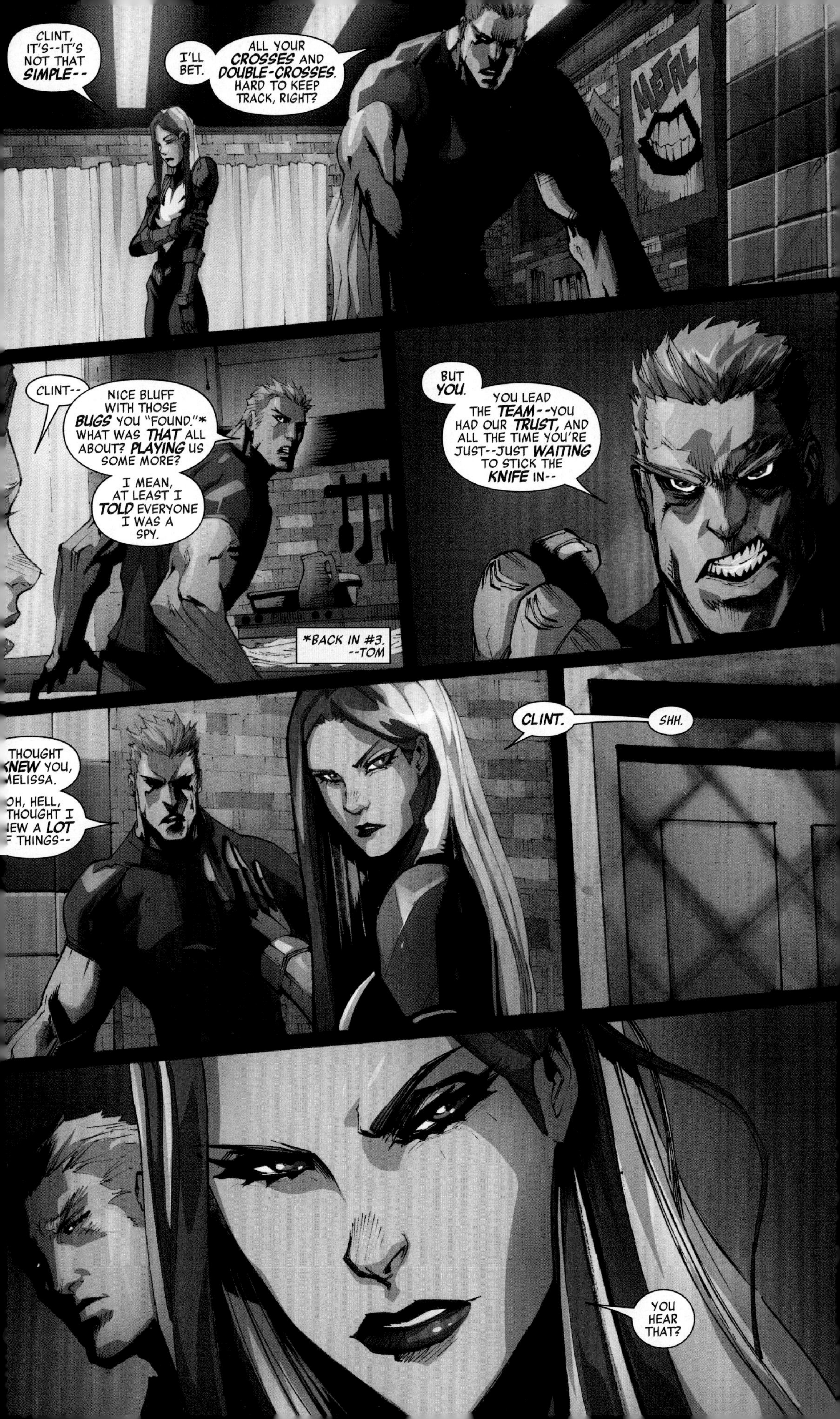
CLINT, IT'S--IT'S NOT THAT SIMPLE--
I'LL BET.
ALL YOUR CROSSES AND DOUBLE-CROSSES. HARD TO KEEP TRACK, RIGHT?
CLINT--
NICE BLUFF WITH THOSE BUGS YOU "FOUND."* WHAT WAS THAT ALL ABOUT? PLAYING US SOME MORE?
I MEAN, AT LEAST I TOLD EVERYONE I WAS A SPY.
*BACK IN #3. --TOM
BUT YOU.
YOU LEAD THE TEAM--YOU HAD OUR TRUST, AND ALL THE TIME YOU'RE JUST--JUST WAITING TO STICK THE KNIFE IN--
THOUGHT KNEW YOU, MELISSA.
OH, HELL, THOUGHT I IEW A LOT F THINGS--
CLINT.
SHH.
YOU HEAR THAT?

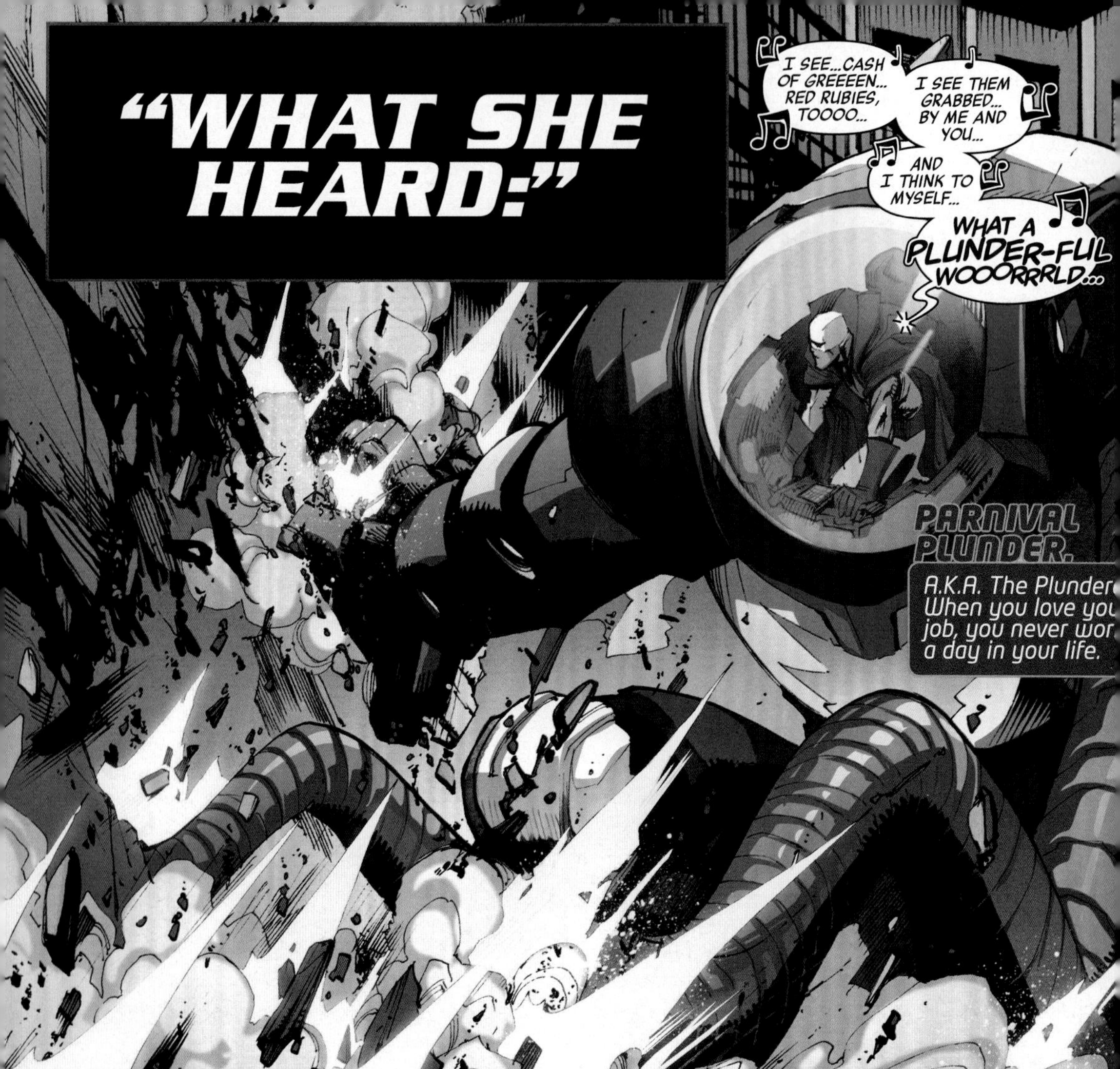
"WHAT SHE HEARD:"
I SEE...CASH OF GREEEEN... RED RUBIES, TOOOO...
I SEE THEM GRABBED... BY ME AND YOU...
AND I THINK TO MYSELF...
WHAT A PLUNDER-FUL WOOORRRLD...
PARNIVAL PLUNDER.
A.K.A. The Plunder
When you love you
job, you never wor
a day in your life.

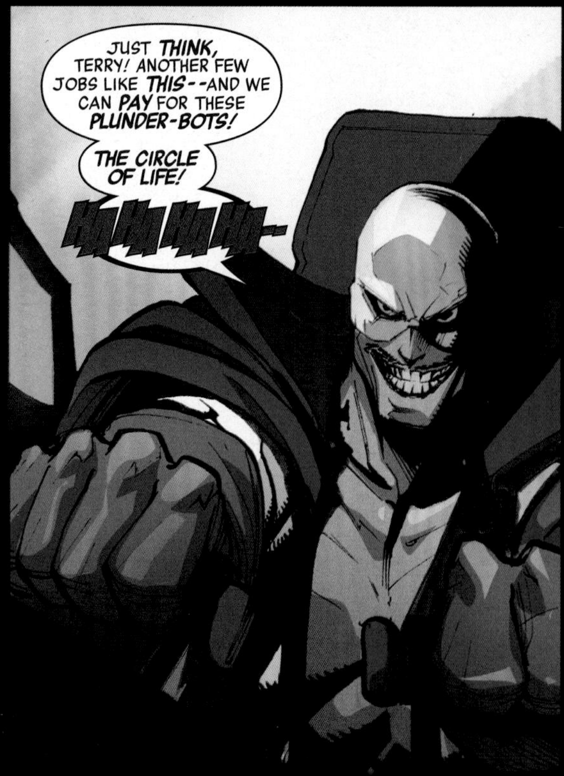
JUST THINK, TERRY! ANOTHER FEW JOBS LIKE THIS--AND WE CAN PAY FOR THESE PLUNDER-BOTS!
THE CIRCLE OF LIFE!

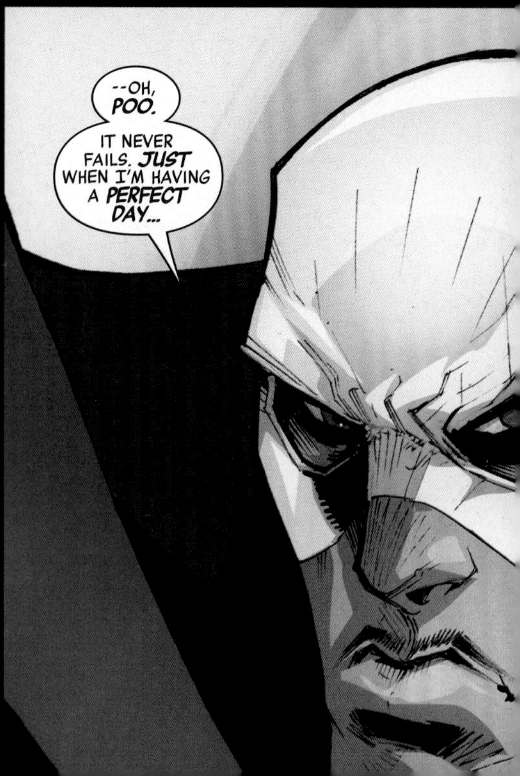
--OH, POO.
IT NEVER FAILS. JUST WHEN I'M HAVING A PERFECT DAY...

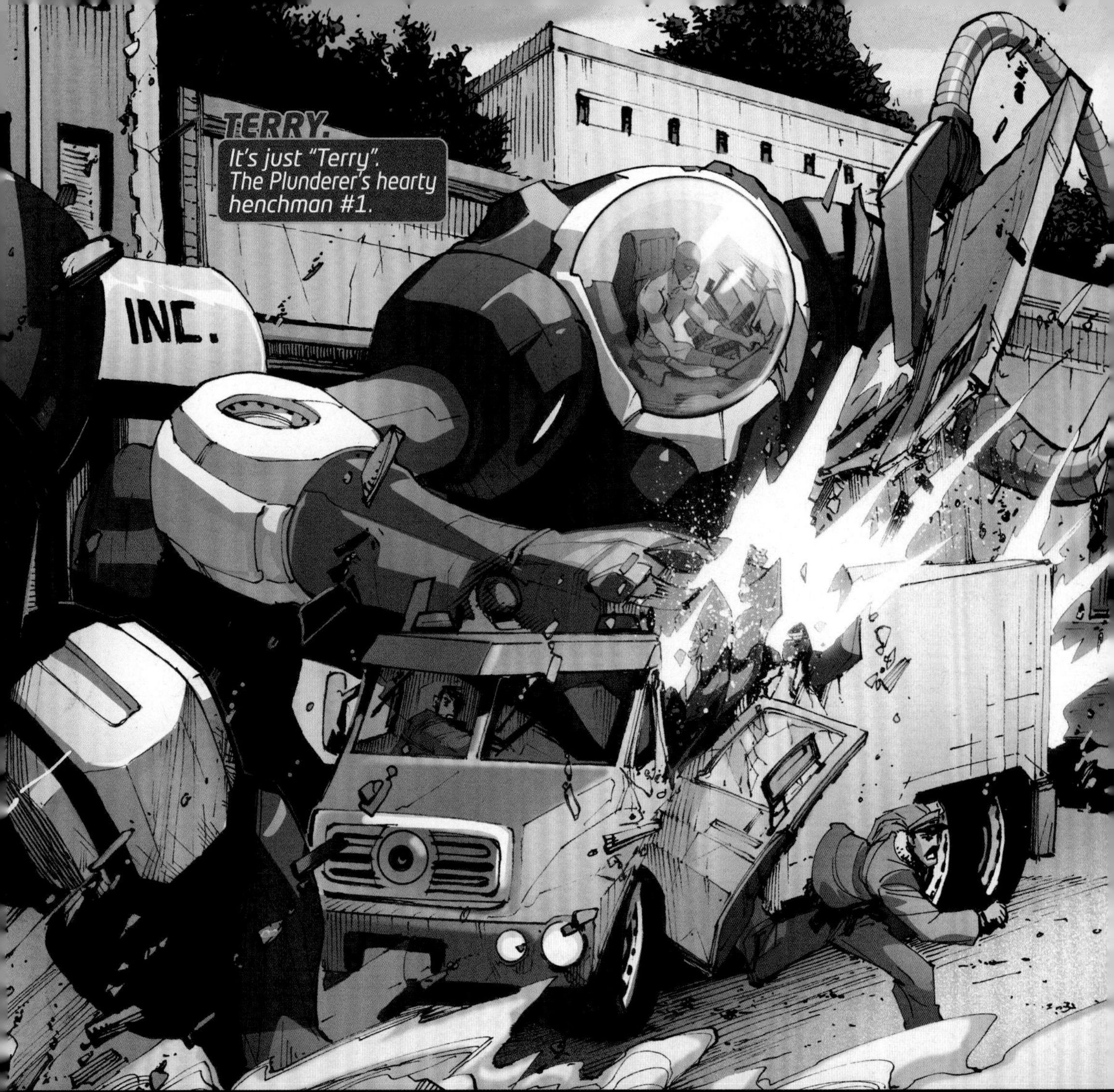
TERRY.
It's just "Terry". The Plunderer's hearty henchman #1.
INC.

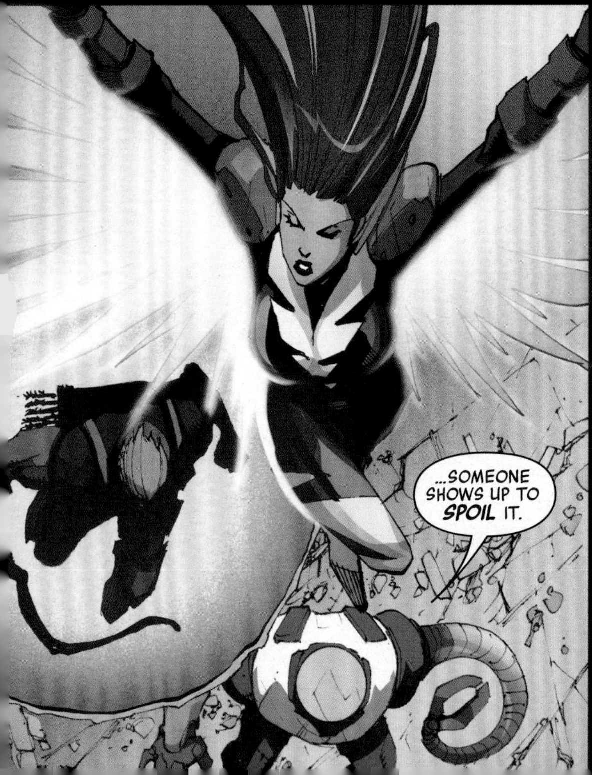
...SOMEONE SHOWS UP TO SPOIL IT.

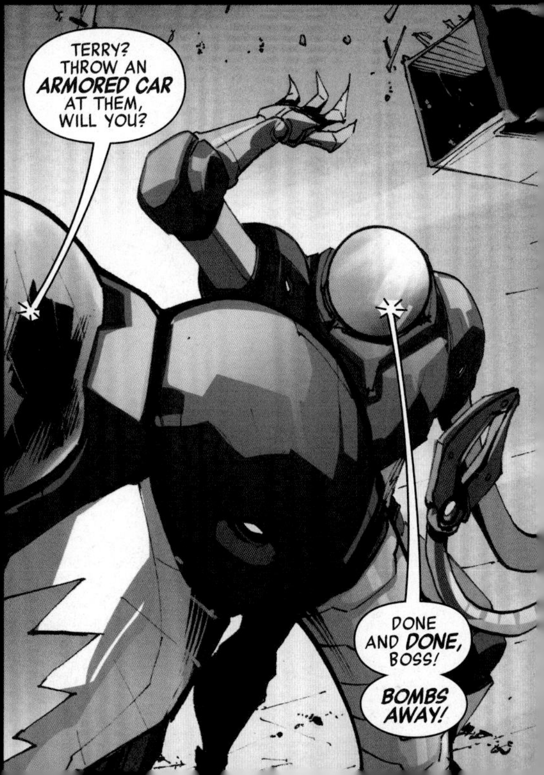
TERRY? THROW AN ARMORED CAR AT THEM, WILL YOU?
DONE AND DONE, BOSS!
BOMBS AWAY!

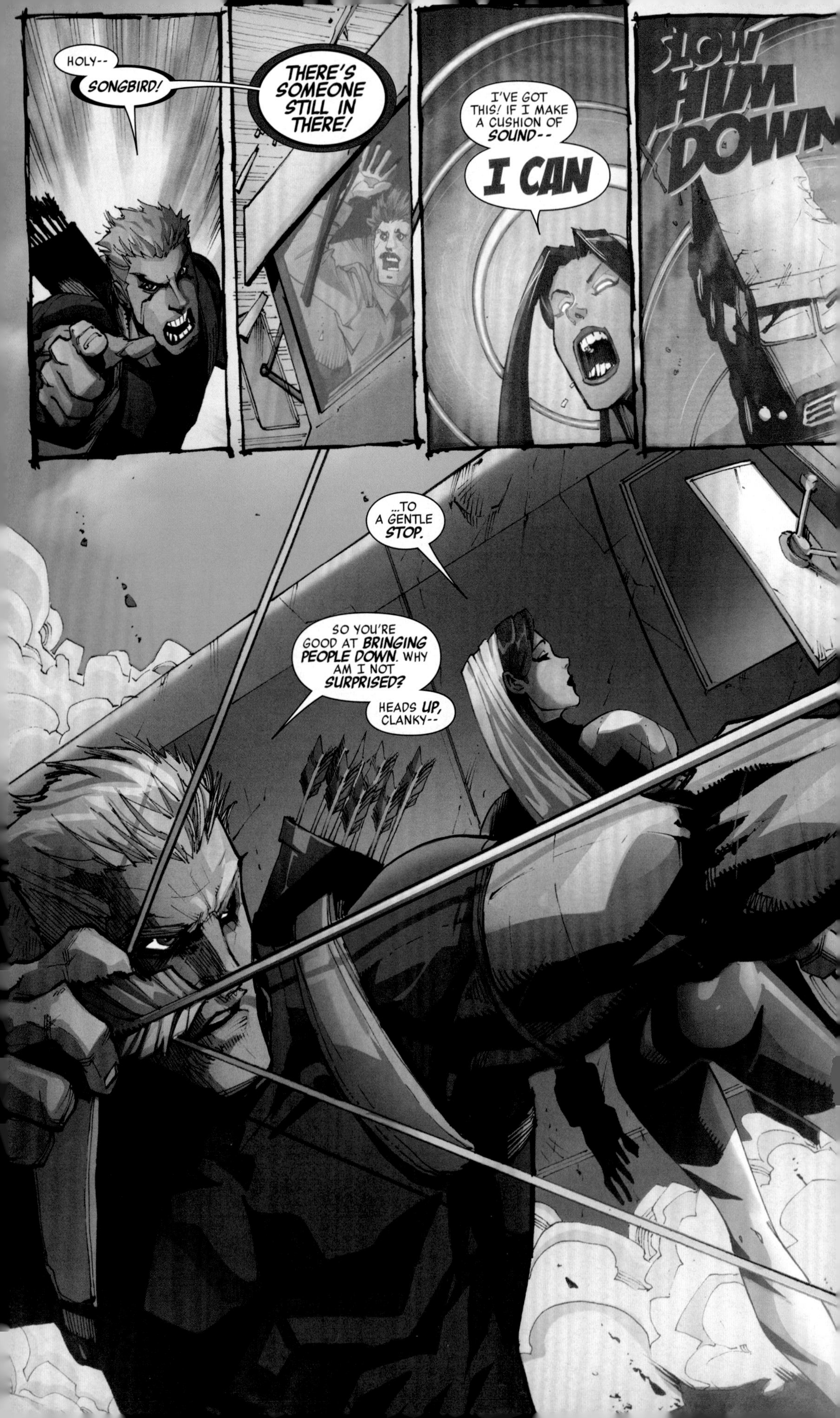
HOLY--
SONGBIRD!
THERE'S SOMEONE STILL IN THERE!
I'VE GOT THIS! IF I MAKE A CUSHION OF SOUND--
I CAN
SLOW HIM DOWN
...TO A GENTLE STOP.
SO YOU'RE GOOD AT BRINGING PEOPLE DOWN. WHY AM I NOT SURPRISED?
HEADS UP, CLANKY--

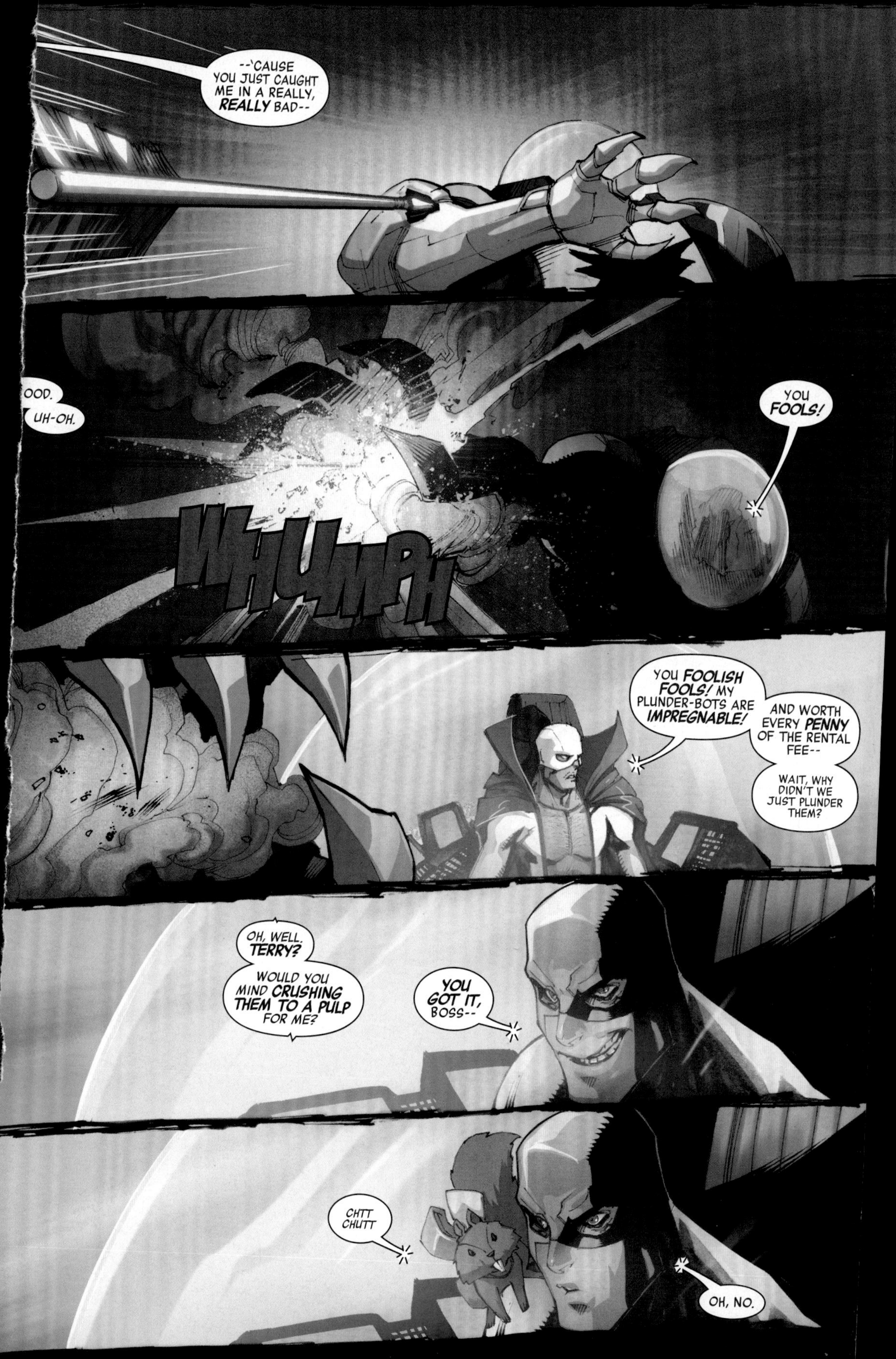
--'CAUSE YOU JUST CAUGHT ME IN A REALLY, REALLY BAD--
OOD.
UH-OH.
YOU FOOLS!
WHUMPH
YOU FOOLISH FOOLS! MY PLUNDER-BOTS ARE IMPREGNABLE!
AND WORTH EVERY PENNY OF THE RENTAL FEE--
WAIT, WHY DIDN'T WE JUST PLUNDER THEM?
OH, WELL. TERRY?
WOULD YOU MIND CRUSHING THEM TO A PULP FOR ME?
YOU GOT IT, BOSS--
CHTT CHUTT
OH, NO.

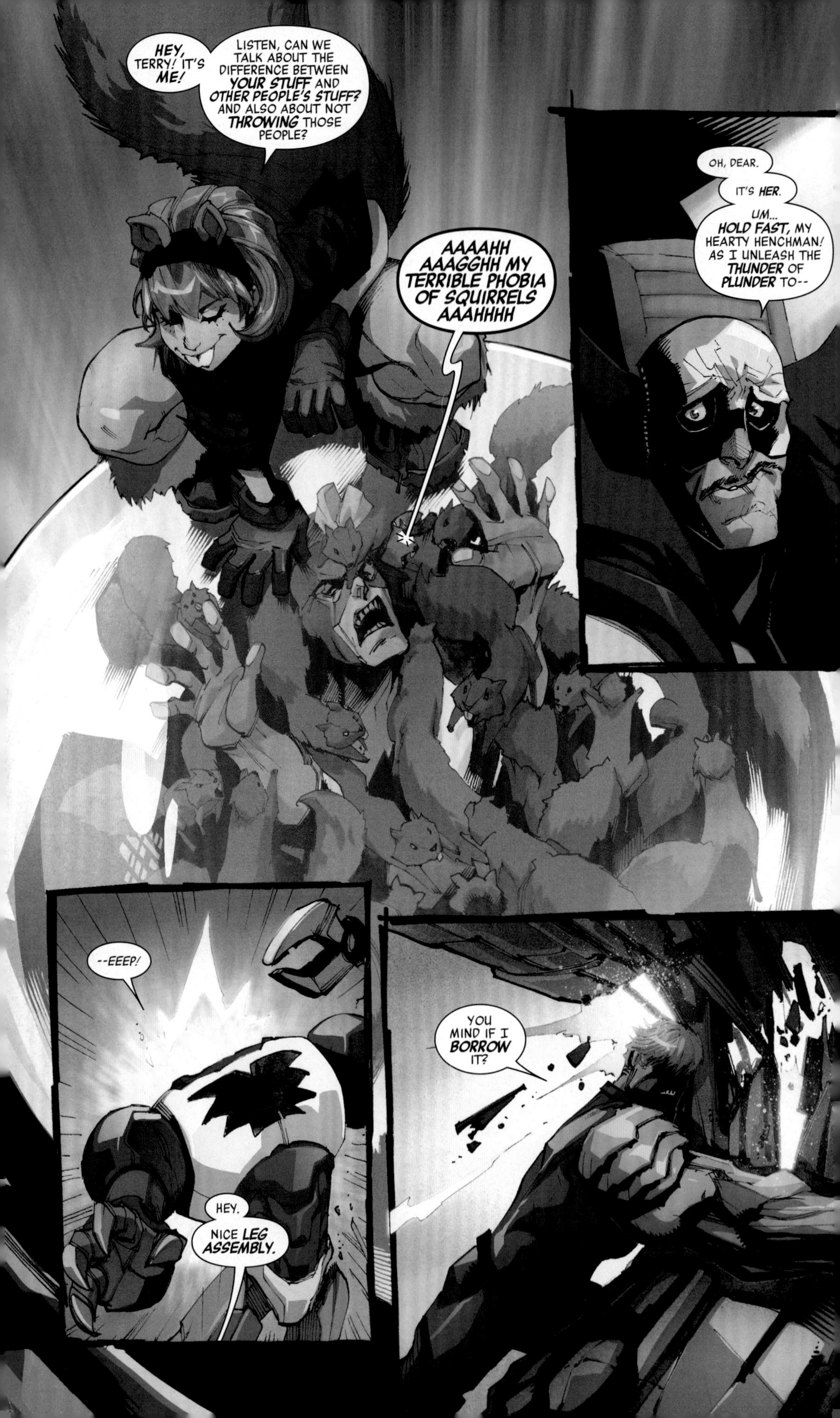
HEY, TERRY! IT'S ME!
LISTEN, CAN WE TALK ABOUT THE DIFFERENCE BETWEEN YOUR STUFF AND OTHER PEOPLE'S STUFF? AND ALSO ABOUT NOT THROWING THOSE PEOPLE?
AAAAHH AAAGGHH MY TERRIBLE PHOBIA OF SQUIRRELS AAAHHHH
OH, DEAR.
IT'S HER.
UM... HOLD FAST, MY HEARTY HENCHMAN! AS I UNLEASH THE THUNDER OF PLUNDER TO--
--EEEP!
HEY.
NICE LEG ASSEMBLY.
YOU MIND IF I BORROW IT?

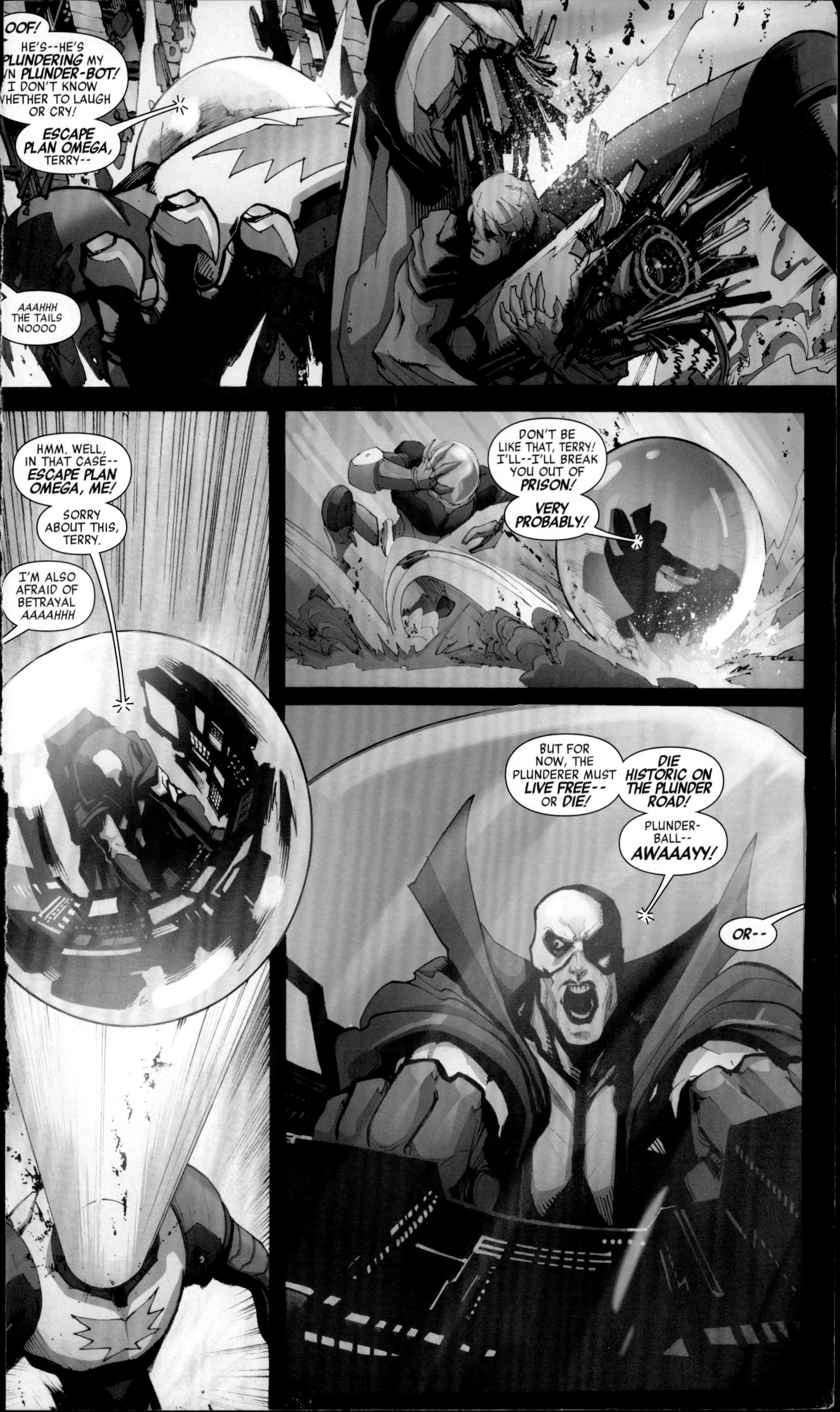

OOF!
HE'S--HE'S PLUNDERING MY OWN PLUNDER-BOT! I DON'T KNOW WHETHER TO LAUGH OR CRY!
ESCAPE PLAN OMEGA, TERRY--
AAAHHH THE TAILS NOOOO
HMM. WELL, IN THAT CASE-- ESCAPE PLAN OMEGA, ME!
SORRY ABOUT THIS, TERRY.
I'M ALSO AFRAID OF BETRAYAL AAAAHHH
DON'T BE LIKE THAT, TERRY! I'LL--I'LL BREAK YOU OUT OF PRISON!
VERY PROBABLY!
BUT FOR NOW, THE PLUNDERER MUST LIVE FREE-- OR DIE!
DIE HISTORIC ON THE PLUNDER ROAD!
PLUNDER-BALL-- AWAAAYY!
OR--

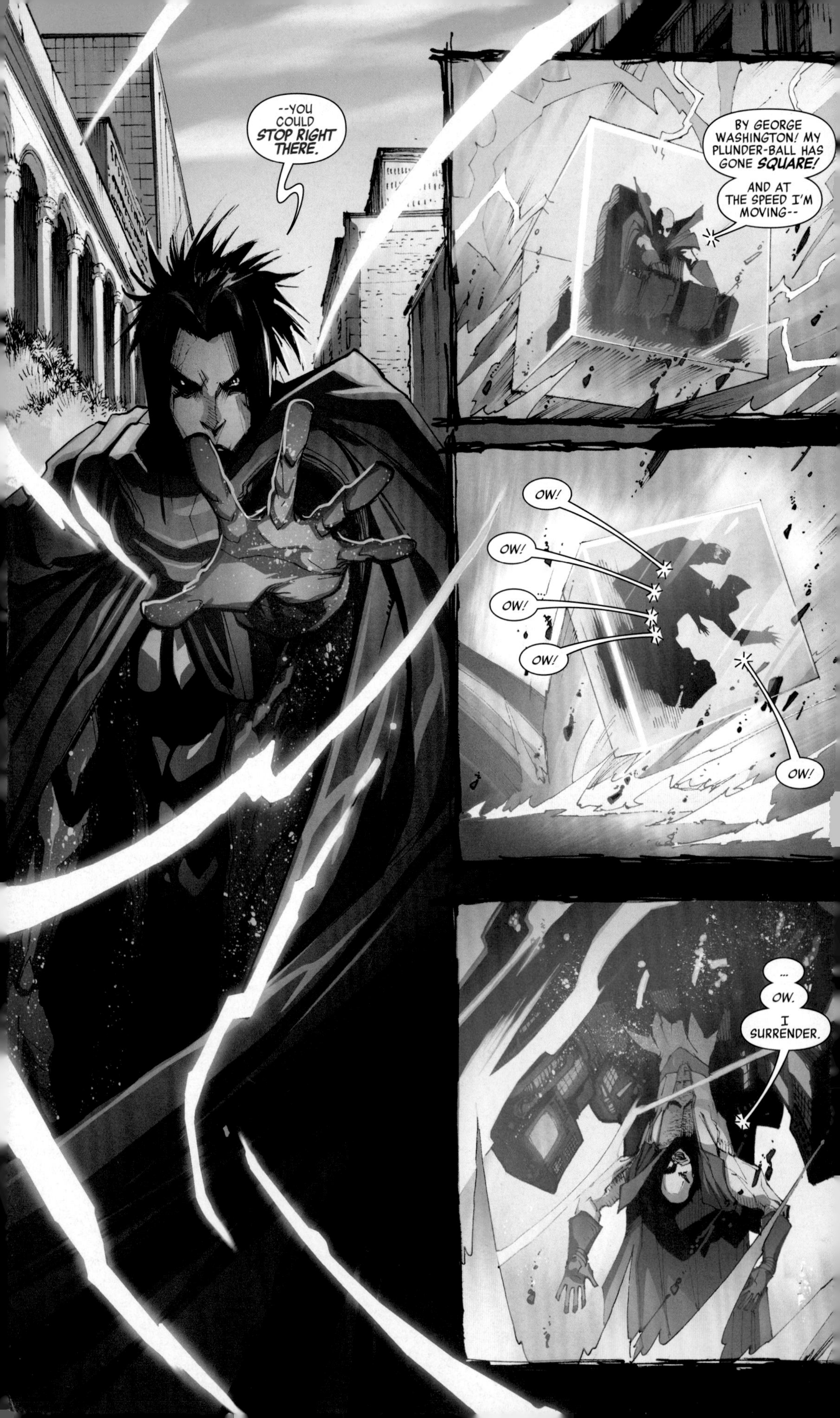
--YOU COULD STOP RIGHT THERE.
BY GEORGE WASHINGTON! MY PLUNDER-BALL HAS GONE SQUARE!
AND AT THE SPEED I'M MOVING--
OW!
OW!
OW!
OW!
OW!
...
OW.
I SURRENDER.

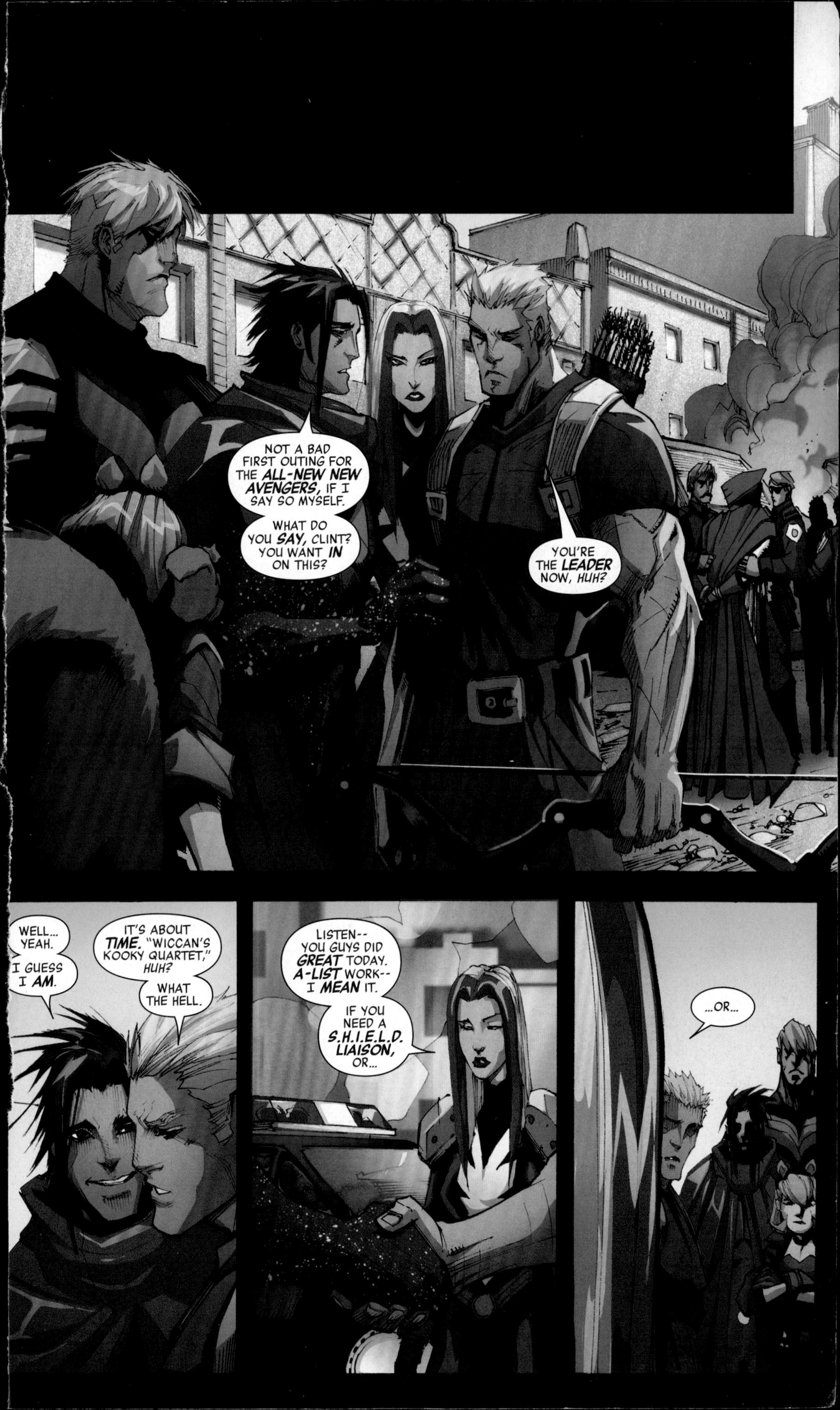
NOT A BAD FIRST OUTING FOR THE ALL-NEW NEW AVENGERS, IF I SAY SO MYSELF.
WHAT DO YOU SAY, CLINT? YOU WANT IN ON THIS?
YOU'RE THE LEADER NOW, HUH?
WELL... YEAH.
I GUESS I AM.
IT'S ABOUT TIME. "WICCAN'S KOOKY QUARTET," HUH?
WHAT THE HELL.
LISTEN-- YOU GUYS DID GREAT TODAY. A-LIST WORK-- I MEAN IT.
IF YOU NEED A S.H.I.E.L.D. LIAISON, OR...
...OR...

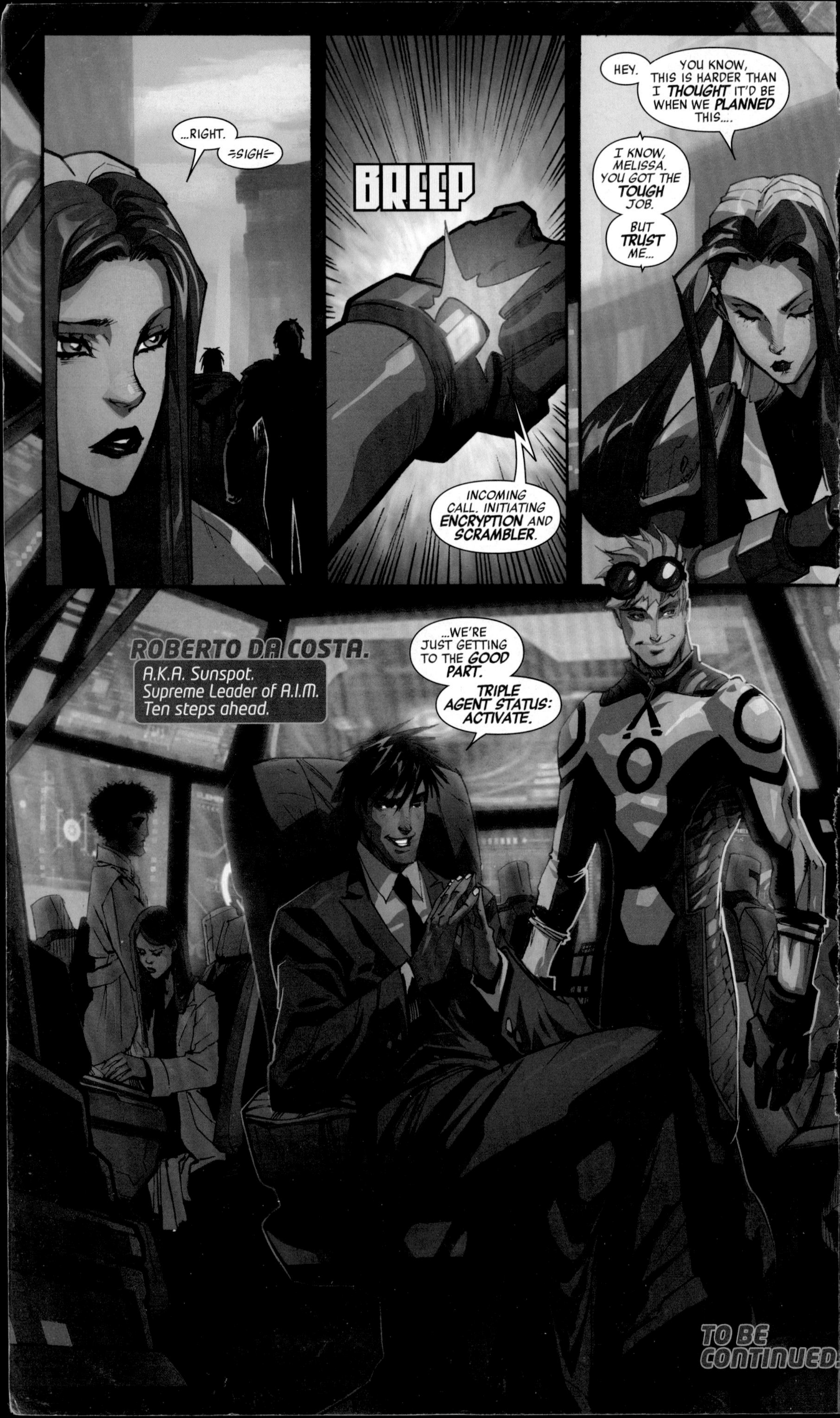
...RIGHT.
=SIGH=
BREEP
INCOMING CALL. INITIATING ENCRYPTION AND SCRAMBLER.
HEY.
YOU KNOW, THIS IS HARDER THAN I THOUGHT IT'D BE WHEN WE PLANNED THIS....
I KNOW, MELISSA. YOU GOT THE TOUGH JOB.
BUT TRUST ME...
ROBERTO DA COSTA.
A.K.A. Sunspot. Supreme Leader of A.I.M. Ten steps ahead.
...WE'RE JUST GETTING TO THE GOOD PART.
TRIPLE AGENT STATUS: ACTIVATE.
TO BE CONTINUED.